WILLIAMS-SONOMA

Savoring

Desserts

Best Recipes from the Award-Winning International Cookbooks

GENERAL EDITOR

Chuck Williams

AUTHORS

Georgeanne Brennan · Kerri Conan · Lori de Mori · Abigail Johnson Dodge

Janet Fletcher · Joyce Goldstein · Diane Holuigue

Joyce Jue · Cynthia Nims · Ray Overton · Jacki Passmore

Julie Sahni · Michele Scicolone · Marilyn Tausend

Oxmoor House®

CONTENTS

Esse, 6.60 frs

Top: A farmer in China carries fresh fruits to a village market. **Above:** Sweet, fresh, French pastries are carefully displayed in pâtisseries each day to tempt passers-by with their glistening toppings of sugar or honey-dipped nuts. **Right:** An extravagant bouquet of cones irresistibly draws the eye to the billows of the Italian favorite, creamy gelati.

*C*hocolate mousse. Candied apples. Cherry pie. Cannoli. Rice pudding. Flan. By their very nature, sweets are festive, and the arrival of dessert is guaranteed to bring a smile to every face around the table. A piece of perfectly ripe fresh fruit, both healthful and delicious, is one of the most common ways to end a meal in many cultures. But strew juicy apricot slices over ice cream, turn that banana into a fritter or a handful of berries into a cobbler, and a simple refreshment becomes an enticing event. The professional pastry chef and the home baker alike answer our need to celebrate milestones and help us enrich every day with a bit of indulgence, whether it's with a lavishly frosted birthday cake brought home in a string-tied bakery box or a batch of homemade cookies set out for an after-school treat.

Typically, recipes for desserts celebrate what is available in joyful profusion—hence the abundance of apple pies in New England and coconut-milk puddings in the Philippines—as well as what is rare and worth saving for a very special occasion. Even when there's little to be had, inventive cooks have found ways to add sweetness to scarcity and make a virtue of thrift. Carefully handwritten on index cards or demonstrated by patient aunts and grandmothers, dessert recipes pass along not just the tastes of a family but also the traditions of a culture and a country.

A buffet displaying favorite desserts from around the world would be an irresistible sight. Pie, of course, would hold pride of place on the American table. There would be the traditional Yankee pies first made by English settlers forced into ingenuity by the abundance of unfamiliar native ingredients like pumpkin and cranberries. A crumb-topped Michigan cherry pie and its simpler, but no less delicious, springtime cousin, strawberry-rhubarb crisp, would be nearby. Caramel-dark fig and pecan pie oozes with the sweet, humid warmth of a Georgia summer afternoon, while Florida key lime pie tempts with tropical flavor. Santa Rosa plums glow in a rustic, European-inspired fruit tart, a symbol of the contemporary West Coast emphasis on fresh ingredients.

al gusto di   al gusto di

A sweet whiff of vanilla bean would herald the Mexican table, laden with golden custards, festive Spanish-inspired cakes, and flaky pineapple turnovers. Figs, mangos, papayas, and plantains glisten on platters, baked with thick *crema,* flambéed with tequila, or chilled with a squeeze of lime.

In Asia, we would discover bite-sized Chinese dumplings rolled in sesame seeds and stuffed with spoonfuls of sweet lotus-seed paste. An array of tropical fruits would alternate with Indian cashew-nut ice cream, crisp pastries soaked in saffron syrup, and creamy puddings thickened with sago or tapioca and splashed with coconut milk.

In Europe, we find both elaborate creations and humble homemade desserts, from glossy, jewel-bright French fruit tarts to simple bread puddings. Rich, eggy sweets—the source of Mexico's fondness for flans and custards—and dense fruit jams to serve alongside salty sheep's and goat's milk cheeses come courtesy of Spain. Plump, Proustian madeleines nestle up against crunchy Italian biscotti perfect for dunking in a shot of espresso or glass of sweet vin santo. Inspired by religious festivals, holiday treats abound, from the Venetian carnival fritters that stave off the austerity of the coming Lenten fast to Christmas fruit cakes packed with candied fruit and nuts from Sicily's famed citrus and almond trees.

In the following pages, we discover the unique elements of these diverse culinary contributions, as well as their similarities. The saffron sesame crunch of India's Gujarat region shares the same appeal as Tuscany's hazelnut cake. Peaches layered with Italian mascarpone or silky panna cotta with berries are inspired by the same pairing of sweet-tart fruits with rich cream as American blueberry shortcakes.

Differences can be as much geographic as cultural. Desserts are influenced by how they are prepared and how they are sweetened. Without ovens, Chinese cooks developed a repertoire of steamed and fried pastries along with hot and cold sweet soups, often with medicinal properties that go along with the Chinese tradition of balancing foods between yin and yang. Early American settlers learned how to tap the maple trees of their new homeland and boil the thin sap into a thick syrup and then a grainy maple sugar. In Southeast Asia, the sap of various palm trees was treated to make palm sugar. Even sugarcane, whose cultivation and processing is a worldwide business, is still used in culturally specific forms—just try finding the moist, molasses-laced brown sugar common to American supermarkets in Italy, or the strongly flavored dark sugar known as jaggery outside an Indian market.

In this collection, you'll find recipes from around the world for every occasion—the perfect way to commemorate a holiday, celebrate a birthday, or just sweeten the enjoyment of a wonderful day.

Left: A camel cart winds its way through the streets of Bikaner, Rajasthan, with the city's Jain temple visible in the background. **Above, left:** The awning of the Pasticceria San Lorenzo in Alassio, Italy, reads, *"I veri baci di Allasio,"* announcing the celebrated chocolate-and-hazelnut cookie of the seaside Ligurian town. **Above, right:** On a warm day in Turin, Italy, a waitress carries a tray of cold drinks to a trio of waiting customers.

NORTH AMERICA

*A*pple pie may be all-American, but ice cream is definitely one of America's most popular and beloved desserts. On any given warm summer afternoon, the tinny musical jingle of an ice-cream truck prompts every youngster within earshot to race out to the street and jostle for a creamy treat. Summer visits to the ice cream parlor for the perfect sundae or double-scoop cone are cherished childhood memories for many. Bright green pistachio, refreshing strawberry, lemon custard, toasted almond, chocolate chip, and rocky road studded with marshmallows and nuts—the seemingly endless rows of canisters filled with tantalizing tastes are emblematic of a country whose people revel in choice.

Almost equal to the passion for ice cream is a weakness for baked goods, from the simplest sugar cookie to the richest chocolate cake. In an age when many say they don't have time to cook, a surprising number of people still find time to bake. The deep-seated pleasure Americans derive from sharing something sweet underlies the continued popularity of such traditions as the holiday cookie swap and the bake sale.

Open a recipe box in any home and chances are that the dessert section will be the thickest, with handwritten recipes for a grandmother's fruitcake or a great aunt's cherry pie. America's desserts, more than any other part of the cuisine, are homegrown, inspired by native abundance and hardscrabble ingenuity. Working with indigenous ingredients like pecans, squash, and cranberries, and with local butter and cream and other ingredients unknown in their original homelands such as maple syrup, molasses, and cornmeal, the nation's early cooks produced many desserts, like pumpkin pie, that are uniquely American.

America's pies, if nothing else, guarantee it a place in food history. Starting with the savory meat pies of their English forebears, Americans moved pie in a sweet direction and have never stopped inventing. Across the country, pie is the preferred vehicle for showing off the seasonal harvest: tart cherries in Michigan, blueberries in Maine, key limes in Florida, and pecans in Georgia.

Not all of the local harvest ends up in pies. Old-fashioned shortcake, made with light baking powder biscuits layered with whipped cream and sweetened fresh berries, is as popular around Independence Day as pumpkin pie is on Thanksgiving. Crunchy-topped crisps and cobblers got their start among the first colonists and remain an essential part of the American repertoire.

Although dessert recipes are easy to share and Americans move often, regional differences persist. Just as New Yorkers love their creamy slices of cheesecake, so do Southerners crave their peach cobbler. The berries of the Pacific Northwest inspire West Coast cooks to make every conceivable jam, jelly, and berry-centered dessert. In California, top-quality produce available year-round is celebrated in seasonally inspired artisanal baked goods like fruit galettes or rustic tarts, filled with peaches and raspberries in summer, heirloom apples and quinces in fall, and strawberries in spring. The ice cream selection mirrors local favorites, with vibrant flavors like nectarine, Meyer lemon, blood orange, or apricot. In the Southwest, the Spanish had 225 years to leave their mark with flan, the silky caramel custard, and *cajeta,* a caramel goat's milk sauce that southwestern chefs use with everything from baked apples to ice cream.

A fondness for eggy, caramel-based sweets still defines the Mexican dessert menu. Throughout the villages and cities of Mexico, local *panaderías* (bakeries) as well as *dulcerías* (candy stores) are filled with a steady stream of regular customers. Puebla has a whole street of small *dulcerías,* and in Morelia, the capital of Michoacán, the Mercado de Dulces has some thirty shops displaying sweet, sticky delights. Nuns of early religious orders perfected the many recipes for sweets and confections that have been handed down from one generation of Mexican cooks to the next. Every region has its specialties, presented in orderly confusion among countless nut brittles, coconut-stuffed limes, and crystallized fruits.

With the exception of several classic cakes—including the three kings ring cake always served on Epiphany—pies and cakes are seldom served in Mexico. Cheesecakes, flans, and rice and bread puddings end most meals, often combined with fresh fruits like mango, papaya, pineapple, and the black-skinned ripe plantains that can be made to resemble extra-sweet, extra-sticky bananas.

Both children and adults in Mexico are particularly fond of hot chocolate, a tasty legacy of the country's Aztec heritage. Hot chocolate in Mexico is made from flat cakes of rough-textured chocolate, sweetened with coarse sugar and flavored with cinnamon and almond, that is melted into hot milk and then frothed with a special chocolate-mixing tool (or, more commonly, a blender) to make a comforting, warming drink at any hour.

Left: America's first apple trees were planted in Massachusetts in the early 1600s. Today, apple lovers all over the country eagerly await the fall harvest, with its promise of pies, crisps, cobblers, and cider. **Above, left:** A baker slides a sheet full of treats into the wood-fired oven at the Santa María *panadería* in Valle de Bravo, Mexico. **Above, right:** A juicy-fleshed mango, cut in the shape of a spiky flower, beckons from a street vendor's stand.

Cherry Pie with Vanilla Crumb Topping

The Midwest • America

Tart, or sour, cherries make the best pies. This recipe uses frozen cherries; canned cherries packed in water are an acceptable substitute, but they must first be drained thoroughly. If using fresh cherries, be aware that they release more juice during baking. Regardless of the type of cherries you use, increase the tapioca if you prefer a firmer pie. Serve a scoop of vanilla ice cream alongside each slice for a classic American treat.

PIE PASTRY FOR SINGLE-CRUST PIE

1¼ cups (6¼ oz/390 g) all-purpose (plain) flour

1 tablespoon granulated sugar

½ teaspoon salt

¼ cup (2 oz/60 g) chilled, unsalted butter, cut into ¾-inch (2-cm) pieces

3 tablespoons (1½ oz/45 g) chilled solid vegetable shortening, cut into ¾-inch (2-cm) pieces

3 tablespoons (1½ fl oz/45 mg) cold water

CRUMB TOPPING

6 tablespoons (3 oz/90 g) unsalted butter, at room temperature

¼ cup (2 oz/60 g) firmly packed light brown sugar

1 egg white, lightly beaten

½ teaspoon vanilla extract (essence)

¾ cup (4 oz/125 g) all-purpose (plain) flour

⅛ teaspoon kosher salt or coarse sea salt

FILLING

5 cups (25 oz/780 g) frozen tart pitted cherries (see note)

1 cup (8 oz/250 g) granulated sugar

3–4 tablespoons instant tapioca

Serves 8

1 To make the pastry in a food processor, combine the flour, granulated sugar, and salt and pulse to blend. Add the butter and shortening and pulse until the fats are in ½-inch (12-mm) pieces. Add the water and pulse until the dough just begins to come together in a rough mass. Alternatively, to make the pastry by hand, stir together the flour, granulated sugar, and salt in a bowl. Add the butter and shortening pieces and toss to coat with flour. Using a pastry blender or 2 knives, cut the fats into the flour mixture until the pieces are no larger than small peas. Drizzle with the water and toss with a fork until the dough is evenly moist and begins to come together in a rough mass.

2 Turn the dough out onto a lightly floured work surface and shape into a 5-inch (13-cm) disk. Wrap the disk in plastic wrap and refrigerate until well chilled, at least 2 hours.

3 On a lightly floured work surface, roll out the pastry disk into a 14-inch (35-cm) round, dusting the rolling pin with flour as needed to prevent sticking. Drape the pastry around the pin and carefully ease it into a 9-inch (23-cm) pie dish, pressing it into the bottom and sides. Trim the overhang so that it extends ¾ inch (2 cm) beyond the edge of the dish. Roll this overhang under to shape a high edge that rests on top of the dish rim. Crimp attractively around the rim and refrigerate the pie shell.

4 Preheat the oven to 425°F (220°C). To make the topping, combine the butter and brown sugar in a small bowl and, using a fork, blend until creamy. Mix in the egg white and vanilla until thoroughly incorporated. Sift the flour and salt into the butter mixture and stir until combined. Cover and refrigerate while preparing the filling.

5 To make the filling, in a large bowl, toss the cherries with the granulated sugar and the tapioca (use the smaller amount for a juicier pie), trying to break apart the fruit as it begins to thaw. Let stand for 20 minutes, stirring occasionally. The fruit should still be at least partially frozen.

6 Turn the filling into the pie shell, making sure to include all the sugar, syrup, and tapioca from the bottom of the bowl. Mound the cherries slightly in the middle. Crumble the topping over the cherries, keeping the topping at the center of the pie relatively thin. There should be fruit showing here and there so steam can escape from the filling while the pie bakes.

7 Bake for 10 minutes, then reduce the oven temperature to 400°F (200°C) and continue to bake, checking every 20 minutes or so to make sure the crust is browning evenly, until the edges of the crust and the topping are nicely browned and the cherries are bubbling, about 1 hour longer. If the edges darken before the pie is done, cover them with strips of aluminum foil for the final minutes of baking. Transfer to a wire rack and let cool completely before serving.

Brown Sugar and Molasses Peach Cobbler

The South • America

A true cobbler is a fruit-based dessert with a dense cake or biscuit topping that is either baked over the fruit or, as is the case here, baked around the fruit. This latter style is a direct descendant of the French *clafouti* and is not at all similar to the deep-dish pie that many diners expect when a cobbler is on the menu. Peaches, a big commercial crop in Georgia and South Carolina, are used here, but any ripe stone fruit or berries can be substituted.

¾ cup (6 oz/185 g) unsalted butter

1½ cups (7½ oz/235 g) all-purpose (plain) flour

1 cup (7 oz/220 g) firmly packed brown sugar

1 tablespoon baking powder

½ teaspoon salt

¼ teaspoon ground cinnamon

1½ cups (12 fl oz/375 ml) milk

⅓ cup (4 oz/125 g) dark molasses

2 eggs, beaten

2 teaspoons vanilla extract (essence)

1 cup (4 oz/125 g) chopped pecans

6–8 ripe peaches, peeled (page 224) and sliced (about 4 cups/1½ lb/750 g)

Serves 8

1 Preheat the oven to 350°F (180°C). Put the butter in an 8-by-12-inch (20-by-30-cm) baking dish and place in the oven to melt.

2 In a large bowl, stir together the flour, brown sugar, baking powder, salt, and cinnamon. In a bowl, whisk together the milk, molasses, eggs, and vanilla. Stir the milk mixture into the flour mixture until well blended. Stir in the pecans. Remove the hot baking dish containing the melted butter from the oven and pour the batter into it. Evenly spoon the sliced peaches with any juices over the batter.

3 Return the dish to the oven and bake until the batter is browned and has risen around the fruit, 40–45 minutes. Transfer to a rack to cool for 30 minutes, then serve warm directly from the dish.

Corn Cake

Pan de Elote • Veracruz • Mexico

When a rich, fancy dessert is just not right, this rustic, moist, sweet corn cake is usually perfect with an after-dinner coffee. There are many versions of this simple cake, but some of the most popular are from Veracruz or nearby Puebla.

½ cup (4 oz/125 g) unsalted butter, at room temperature, plus 2 tablespoons

½ cup (4 oz/125 g) sugar, plus extra for garnish (optional)

1 cup (6 oz/185 g) fresh corn kernels

4 eggs

1 tablespoon all-purpose (plain) flour

1 teaspoon baking powder

1 teaspoon salt

1 tablespoon corn oil

Serves 8

1 Preheat the oven to 350°F (180°C).

2 In a bowl, using an electric mixer, beat together the ½ cup butter and the ½ cup sugar until creamy. Put the corn kernels in a food processor and process until ground, with some texture remaining. Add the ground corn to the butter mixture and beat until well mixed. Beat in the eggs one at a time, beating well after each addition. Add the flour, baking powder, and salt and beat until just combined.

3 Put the 2 tablespoons butter and the oil in a 9-inch (23-cm) ovenproof frying pan and heat in the oven until the butter is melted. Add the creamed corn mixture and bake until set and a toothpick inserted into the middle comes out clean, about 20 minutes. There should be no liquid visible when the pan is shaken or tilted. Remove from the oven and sprinkle with sugar, if desired.

4 Cut the cake into wedges and serve warm, directly from the pan.

Chunky Apple Cake

The Midwest • America

For this fluffy, spicy apple cake, call on your favorite pie apples, such as Granny Smith or McIntosh. In the Midwest, the Mutsu apple, a Japanese hybrid, is a also good choice.

2½ cups (12½ oz/390 g) all-purpose (plain) flour

1½ teaspoons baking powder

½ teaspoon *each* baking soda (bicarbonate of soda), kosher salt, and ground cinnamon

¼ teaspoon *each* ground cloves, ground allspice, and freshly grated nutmeg

About 2 lb (1 kg) baking apples (see note)

½ cup (4 oz/125 g) unsalted butter, at room temperature

1 cup (8 oz/250 g) granulated sugar

1 cup (7 oz/220 g) firmly packed brown sugar

2 eggs

¾ cup (6 fl oz/180 ml) buttermilk

¼ cup (1 oz/30 g) confectioners' (icing) sugar

Serves 12

1 Preheat the oven to 350°F (180°C). Butter a 10-inch (25-cm) tube pan.

2 In a bowl, sift together the flour, baking powder, baking soda, salt, cinnamon, cloves, allspice, and nutmeg. Peel and core the apples. Chop into coarse ½-inch (12-mm) dice. You should have 4 heaping cups (about 1¼ lb/625 g) diced apples.

3 In a bowl, using an electric mixer on medium speed, beat the butter and granulated and brown sugars until soft and fluffy, about 3 minutes. Add the eggs one at time, beating well after each addition. Beat 1 minute longer until the batter is creamy. Reduce the speed to low and add the flour mixture in 3 batches alternately with the buttermilk, beginning and ending with the flour mixture. Gently fold in the apples, making sure all the pieces are coated with batter and are evenly distributed. Pour into the prepared pan.

4 Bake the cake until a toothpick inserted into the center comes out clean, 50–60 minutes. Transfer to a wire rack to cool. Invert the cake onto a cake plate and lift off the pan. If desired, reposition the cake upright. Using a fine-mesh sieve, dust the top with the confectioners' sugar.

AMERICA'S BREAD BASKET

As America expanded westward in the early 1800s, its hardworking pioneers discovered that the dry, harsh climate of the Great Plains was ideal for growing wheat, especially the hard-kerneled varieties from Russia. Small family plots quickly merged to form oceans of supple grass that turned first green, then gold, as the stalks dried before harvest. Within a hundred years, this undulating landscape grew to feed the entire nation and much of the world. As the wheat fields were established, large flour mills and commercial bakeries sprouted up alongside them.

Today, central and western Kansas specialize in hard red winter wheat, a type grown through-out the Great Plains that is planted in fall and harvested in early summer. Containing a relatively high protein level, this workhorse wheat is valued for its versatility and is milled into sturdy flours for making breads, rolls, buns, and a range of other baked foods, and for export. Hard white winter wheat, a related class grown in the same areas, has a slightly sweeter flavor and lighter color and is gaining favor among makers of artisanal breads and Asian noodles.

In North Dakota, most wheat farmers grow durum, a hard, high-protein class that is the source of the semolina used for making the best dried pasta. This state and others in the north also grow hard red spring varieties, which contain the most protein. Like durum, these wheat fields are harvested in the fall. Less versatile than hard red winter wheat, the flours milled from these grains go into making bread and rolls. A small part of the upper Midwest is also planted with soft white wheat, used for crackers, snack items, and pastries.

Wheat is typically brought to market as flour through a commodity-supply chain that involves a series of grain elevators, mills, and railroad cars. Harvests from many farms are weighed, graded, paid for, and then combined at the elevator. But a movement toward "identity preservation," which would keep organic and specialty grains out of this mixed-wheat basket, has gained momentum. In much the same way that chefs have become involved with their ingredient producers, bakers are working to identify and isolate the grains and blends that they prefer, and to establish relationships with the farmers who grow them.

Pecan Cheesecake with Caramel

Pay de Queso y Nuez con Cajeta • Guanajuato • Mexico

Many restaurants in Mexico offer cheesecake on their dessert menu as an alternative to the more familiar flan and rice pudding. This version is embellished with a topping of pecans, which are native to Mexico, and *cajeta*. The latter, a thick goat's milk caramel syrup, is a specialty of Celaya, a small town in Guanajuato where many households make and sell the confection. The name *cajeta* refers to the little wooden boxes in which it is traditionally sold.

CAJETA

4 cups (32 fl oz/1 l) goat's milk

1 cup (8 oz/250 g) sugar

½ cup (4 fl oz/125 ml) cow's milk

¼ teaspoon baking soda (bicarbonate of soda)

1 tablespoon vanilla extract (essence), rum, or brandy

½ cup (2 oz/60 g) pecans, toasted (page 224) and finely chopped, plus chopped pecans for garnish

Pinch of sea salt

CRUST

1½ cups (4½ oz/140 g) finely crushed vanilla wafers

¼ cup (2 oz/60 g) unsalted butter, melted

FILLING

1½ lb (750 g) cream cheese, at room temperature

¾ cup (6 oz/185 g) sugar

1 teaspoon vanilla extract (essence)

3 eggs

TOPPING

2 cups (16 fl oz/500 ml) sour cream

¼ cup (2 oz/60 g) sugar

2 teaspoons vanilla extract (essence)

25–30 pecan halves

Serves 12

1 To make the *cajeta,* in a large, heavy saucepan, bring the goat's milk to a simmer over medium heat. Add the sugar and stir until completely dissolved. In a small bowl, stir together the cow's milk and baking soda. Ladle in a small amount of the hot goat's milk, stirring constantly. Remove the pan from the heat and whisk the soda mixture into the hot goat's milk. Return the pan to the stove, stir well with a wooden spoon, and continue to simmer over medium heat, stirring frequently, until the mixture begins to thicken, about 30 minutes. As the mixture darkens, reduce the heat to low and stir constantly until the *cajeta* becomes a dark caramel color and coats the back of the spoon, another 20 minutes or so. Pour the *cajeta* into a bowl and let cool, then stir in the vanilla or liquor. Pour half of the *cajeta* into another bowl, stir in the ½ cup (2 oz/60 g) chopped nuts and salt, and set aside. Refrigerate the remaining *cajeta*.

2 Preheat the oven to 350°F (180°C).

3 To make the crust, in a bowl, mix together the crushed vanilla wafers and butter until the crumbs are evenly moistened. Transfer to a 9-inch (23-cm) springform pan. Pat the crumb mixture evenly onto the bottom and 1 inch (2.5 cm) up the sides of the pan. Refrigerate for 30 minutes.

4 To make the filling, in a bowl, using an electric mixer, beat the cream cheese until creamy. Add the sugar and vanilla and beat until blended. Add the eggs one at a time and beat just until smooth, scraping down the sides and along the bottom of the bowl so the ingredients are thoroughly mixed.

5 Drizzle the *cajeta* that contains the pecans evenly over the prepared crust. Pour the cheese filling over the *cajeta*.

6 Bake until the cheesecake is firm, 50–60 minutes. Remove from the oven and immediately place in the refrigerator on a kitchen towel. Chill for 15 minutes. Raise the oven temperature to 450°F (230°C).

7 To make the topping, mix the sour cream, sugar, and vanilla together in a bowl. Pour over the top of the cheesecake and bake for 10 minutes. Transfer to a wire rack to cool.

8 Place a circle of pecan halves around the entire outer edge of the cheesecake. Cover and refrigerate until well chilled, for at least 24 hours or up to 3 days.

9 To serve, release the sides of the springform pan, leaving the cake in the bottom, and place the cake on a serving plate. Heat the remaining *cajeta* to lukewarm. Drizzle some of it around the plate. Slice the cake, place the slices on individual plates, drizzle each serving with more *cajeta,* and garnish with the remaining chopped pecans.

Gingerbread Squares with Jeweled Lemon Sauce

The South • America

English colonists are credited with putting gingerbread on the southern table. This dense, dark cake, flavored with molasses and sweet spices, gets its appealing "warmth" from the addition of three types of ginger—ground, fresh, and crystallized—in addition to freshly ground black pepper. It has a long shelf life, which makes it an ideal "snacking" cake to have on hand when neighbors show up unexpectedly. Store tightly wrapped in the refrigerator for up to a week and bring to room temperature before serving.

1 Preheat the oven to 375°F (190°C). Butter an 8-by-12-inch (20-by-30-cm) baking dish. Dust with flour, tapping out the excess.

2 In a large saucepan over medium heat, combine the molasses, brown sugar, and butter. Cook, stirring, until the butter is melted and the mixture is bubbly, about 5 minutes. Stir in the orange juice, orange zest, crystallized ginger, and fresh ginger. Remove from the heat and let cool for 15 minutes.

3 In a large bowl, stir together the flour, baking soda, ground ginger, cinnamon, nutmeg, cloves, salt, and pepper. When the molasses mixture is lukewarm, beat in the eggs and the vanilla. Pour into the bowl of flour and stir until well combined. Pour the batter into the prepared pan.

4 Bake the cake until the top is springy and a toothpick inserted into the center of the cake comes out clean, 40–45 minutes. Let cool on a wire rack for 20 minutes.

5 To make the sauce, in a saucepan, stir together the granulated sugar and cornstarch. Place over medium-high heat and pour in the water, whisking until the mixture just boils and is smooth and thickened, about 5 minutes. Remove from the heat and stir in the lemon zest and juice and the Grand Marnier, if using. Add the butter 1 tablespoon at a time, stirring until it melts and is well incorporated and the sauce is glossy. (The sauce can be cooled, covered, and refrigerated for up to 3 days. To serve, reheat gently over low heat, stirring to prevent scorching.)

6 Cut the cake into squares. Serve it warm, drizzled with the warm sauce.

1 cup (11 oz/345 g) dark molasses

½ cup (3½ oz/105 g) firmly packed dark brown sugar

½ cup (4 oz/125 g) unsalted butter

1 cup (8 fl oz/250 ml) fresh orange juice

Finely grated zest of 2 oranges

2 tablespoons chopped crystallized ginger

1 tablespoon peeled and grated fresh ginger

2½ cups (12½ oz/390 g) all-purpose (plain) flour

2 teaspoons baking soda (bicarbonate of soda)

2 teaspoons *each* ground ginger and ground cinnamon

¼ teaspoon *each* freshly grated nutmeg and ground cloves

¼ teaspoon *each* salt and pepper

2 eggs, lightly beaten

1 tablespoon vanilla extract (essence)

SAUCE

⅔ cup (5 oz/155 g) granulated sugar

2 tablespoons cornstarch (cornflour)

1½ cups (12 fl oz/375 ml) water

Finely grated zest and juice of 3 lemons

1 tablespoon Grand Marnier (optional)

2 tablespoons unsalted butter

Serves 8–10

Coffee Pots de Crème

The Pacific Northwest • America

Many coffee-flavored desserts use instant espresso powder, but the very best flavor comes from infusing coffee beans, as in this recipe. Northwest coffee drinkers like their coffee darkly roasted and with character, so choose whole French or espresso-roast beans.

3 cups (24 fl oz/750 ml) half-and-half (half cream)

½ cup (2 oz/60 g) dark roast coffee beans, crushed

5 egg yolks

½ cup (4 oz/125 g) sugar

Boiling water as needed

½ cup (4 fl oz/125 ml) heavy (double) cream

2 tablespoons coffee liqueur

6 chocolate-covered coffee beans (optional)

Serves 6

1 Preheat the oven to 300°F (150°C). Set six ½-cup (4–fl oz/125-ml) pot de crème pots in a baking dish. In a saucepan over medium-high heat, combine the half-and-half and the coffee beans and bring just to a boil. Cover. Set aside for no more than 15 minutes.

2 In a bowl, whisk together the egg yolks and the sugar. Line a sieve with dampened cheesecloth (muslin) and strain the coffee-infused half-and-half into a measuring pitcher. Slowly whisk the coffee mixture into the yolk mixture just until blended; do not allow it to become frothy. Pour back into the pitcher, then divide among the pot de crème pots.

3 Add boiling water to the baking dish to reach halfway up the sides of the pots. Cover the baking dish loosely with aluminum foil. Bake until the custard is set, 30–40 minutes. Carefully transfer the pots to a rack to cool completely. Cover and refrigerate if not serving right away. Just before serving, whip the cream until soft peaks begin to form, then whip in the coffee liqueur. Top each pot de crème with a dollop of the cream and finish with a chocolate-covered coffee bean, if desired.

Three Kings Ring Cake

Rosca de Reyes • Veracruz • Mexico

A tiny doll symbolizing the Christ child is hidden within this decorated ring-shaped cake, traditionally served for Three Kings' Day on January 6 in Mexico. The person who receives the doll in his or her slice is obligated to organize a tamale party on February 2, Candlemas Day. *Acitrón* is the candied fruit of the biznaga cactus and is sold in Hispanic markets.

DOUGH

½ cup (4 fl oz/125 ml) warm water (110°F/43°C)

5 teaspoons (2 packages) active dry yeast

½ cup (4 oz/125 g) unsalted butter, melted and cooled

½ cup (4 oz/125 g) sugar

4 egg yolks, lightly beaten with 2 tablespoons water, plus 2 whole eggs, well beaten

1 tablespoon finely grated orange zest

1 tablespoon finely grated lime zest

½ teaspoon orange flower water (page 224) (optional)

1 teaspoon sea salt

4–5 cups (20–25 oz/625–780 g) all-purpose (plain) flour, preferably unbleached

1 cup (6 oz/185 g) crystallized fruits, chopped

½ cup finely chopped pecans

2 tiny porcelain or ovenproof plastic dolls

TOPPING

2 whole eggs

1 tablespoon heavy (double) cream

⅓ cup (3 oz/90 g) sugar

6 crystallized or sun-dried figs, cut into strips (optional)

1 candied orange, cut into strips (optional)

1 crystallized *acitrón* (see note), cut into strips (optional)

Strips of other crystallized fruits (optional)

Makes 2 large ring cakes; serves 16

1 To make the dough, pour the warm water into a large bowl, sprinkle on the yeast, and let stand until foamy, about 5 minutes. Stir in the butter, sugar, diluted egg yolks, whole eggs, grated orange and lime zests, orange flower water (if using), and salt.

2 Add 3 cups (15 oz/470 g) of the flour and beat vigorously for 3 minutes with a wooden spoon or on low speed with an electric stand mixer fitted with the dough hook. Gradually add more of the remaining flour, ¼ cup (1½ oz/45 g) at a time, and beat until the dough forms a slightly sticky ball and begins to pull away from the sides of the bowl.

3 Turn the dough out onto a floured work surface and knead, adding more flour as needed, until smooth and elastic, about 10 minutes. You will know it has had enough kneading when blisters start to form on the surface. Shape the dough into a ball.

4 Oil or butter a large bowl. Roll the dough in the bowl so the surface is coated. Cover with a damp, tightly woven kitchen towel and let the dough rest in a warm place until doubled in bulk, about 1½ hours.

5 Grease 2 baking sheets with oil or butter. Turn the dough out onto a lightly floured surface and divide into 2 equal portions. Sprinkle each piece with half of the crystallized fruits and pecans, then knead them in until they are evenly distributed throughout the dough. Push a doll into each piece of dough. One at a time, using your palms, roll each piece into a log about 24 inches (60 cm) long and 2 inches (5 cm) in diameter. Form each log into a ring, pinching the ends together, and place a ring on each baking sheet. To keep each ring's shape, place a well-oiled ovenproof bowl or soufflé dish in the center. Cover lightly with a kitchen towel and let rise until almost doubled in size, 45–60 minutes.

6 Preheat the oven to 375°F (190°C).

7 To make the topping, in a bowl, whisk together the eggs and cream. Brush the tops of the rings with the egg mixture. Decorate with bands of sprinkled sugar, interspersed with strips of crystallized and candied fruits, if using. Bake until the surface is golden, about 25 minutes. Do not overbake. Transfer the cakes to racks to cool completely.

Meyer Lemon Ice Cream

California • America

Specialty citrus is a thriving niche in California agriculture. Meyer lemons, which are lower in acid than more common lemons and have an orange-blossom fragrance, are one of the unusual varieties that growers have planted in California. Pair this ice cream with Blood Orange Sorbet (right) and serve with tuiles or other crisp cookies.

¾ cup (6 oz/185 g) sugar

2 tablespoons finely grated Meyer lemon zest

6 egg yolks

1½ cups (12 fl oz/375 ml) half-and-half (half cream)

1½ cups (12 fl oz/375 ml) heavy (double) cream

Pinch of salt

3 tablespoons fresh Meyer lemon juice, or to taste

Makes about 1½ qt (1.5 l) ice cream

1 In a food processor, combine the sugar and the lemon zest and process until the sugar becomes very moist and the grated zest becomes even finer. In a bowl, whisk together the egg yolks and the processed sugar until the mixture is pale and thick and forms a ribbon when the whisk is lifted.

2 In a saucepan over medium heat, combine the half-and-half and ½ cup (4 fl oz/125 ml) of the cream. Bring to a simmer. Pour the hot liquid into the beaten eggs, whisking constantly, then return the mixture to the saucepan. Add the salt and cook over medium-low heat, stirring with a wooden spoon, until the mixture thickens and coats the spoon, about 3 minutes. Do not allow it to simmer, or it will curdle. Remove from the heat and let cool for 15 minutes, stirring occasionally. Then stir in the remaining 1 cup (8 fl oz/250 ml) cream. Add the 3 tablespoons Meyer lemon juice, or enough to give the custard a tart edge.

3 Pour the mixture through a fine-mesh sieve placed over a bowl, then cover the bowl and refrigerate to chill thoroughly. Transfer to an ice-cream maker and freeze according to the manufacturer's instructions.

4 Serve the ice cream in a bowl or a parfait glass.

CALIFORNIA CITRUS

The Santa Barbara farmers' market shines year-round, but in winter it glows with citrus. Platters of sliced oranges for sampling and mounds of lemons and limes beckon shoppers with their freshness and tangy promise. California citrus is shipped world-wide, but it's never more alluring than in its own sunny backyard. In addition to lemons and seedless navel oranges, the Golden State grows significant quantities of Valencia oranges, grapefruits, mandarin oranges, and pomelos. More adventurous farmers are planting blood oranges, Oroblancos (a pomelo-grapefruit hybrid), Meyer lemons, and kumquats. And thanks to California's trendsetting chefs, a growing demand exists for such exotic citrus as the Buddha's hand, limequat, citron, and Cara Cara orange, a pink-fleshed navel.

Citrus cultivation in the state can be traced to the 1840s, when William Wolfskill planted the first lemon and orange seedlings in what is now Los Angeles. Today, the San Joaquin Valley in Central California harbors most of the state's citrus groves. The orchards line the highway around Fresno, scenting the air at bloom time and providing a splendid sight when the fruit is mature. Home gardeners love tending citrus, and lemon and orange trees beautify many backyard gardens.

Blood Orange Sorbet

California · America

Blood oranges are among the formerly exotic citrus fruits that have become more plentiful in California farmers' markets and produce stores. Some blood orange varieties develop a blush on the rind; others look no different from navel oranges. The fruit's striking juice is sweet and tart, with hints of raspberry, and its deep burgundy color yields dramatic-looking juice for this sorbet, a perfect complement to Meyer Lemon Ice Cream (left).

1½ cups (12 oz/375 g) sugar

½ cup (4 fl oz/125 ml) water

6 lb (3 kg) blood oranges

Makes about 1½ qt (1.5 l) sorbet

1 In a saucepan over medium heat, combine the sugar and the water and bring to a simmer, swirling the pan to dissolve the sugar. Simmer the syrup for a few seconds, just until it becomes clear. Remove from the heat, then cover and refrigerate until cold.

2 Halve and juice the blood oranges, then strain the juice. You should have about 5 cups (40 fl oz/1.25 l). Place in a bowl.

3 Add just enough of the syrup to the blood orange juice to sweeten it to your taste. Cover the bowl and refrigerate the sweetened juice to chill thoroughly.

4 Transfer the chilled blood orange juice to an ice-cream maker and freeze according to the manufacturer's instructions.

5 Serve the sorbet in a bowl or a parfait glass.

Chilled Papaya with Lime

Papaya Fría con Lima • Colima • Mexico

Along southern Mexico's dusty roads grow hundreds of skinny, stalklike plants, 15–20 feet (5–6.5 m) tall, crowned with a cluster of giant leaves. Sheltered under the leaves are sublimely sweet papayas in muted shades of sunset yellow, orange, and pink. The flesh is so delicious that it needs nothing more than a squirt of tart lime juice to transform it into a simple, satisfying dessert.

1 firm but ripe papaya, about 2 lb (1 kg)

1 lime, cut into 8 wedges

Serves 4

1 When the papaya is completely ripe, refrigerate it for at least 4–6 hours, but no longer than 2 days. Cut the fruit in half vertically and scrape the glistening gray-black seeds into a small bowl. Cut the fruit into slices ½ inch (12 mm) thick and remove the skin with a small, sharp knife.

2 Arrange the papaya slices overlapping on individual dessert plates or a decorative platter. Serve with the lime wedges and a sprinkling of the peppery papaya seeds.

Bittersweet Chocolate Cake with Raspberry Sauce

California • America

This intense flourless cake is pure chocolate bliss. San Franciscans have a love affair with chocolate, thanks to Ghirardelli and Guittard, two local top-quality manufacturers. The newest producer, Berkeley-based Scharffen Berger Chocolate Maker, promises to keep the Bay Area at the forefront of chocolate obsession. A raspberry sauce flavored with framboise (raspberry brandy) or kirsch makes the ideal complement for this dense, moist cake.

1 Preheat the oven to 350°F (180°C). Butter the bottom and sides of a 9-inch (23-cm) springform pan. Dust with flour, tapping out the excess.

2 In a food processor, combine the hazelnuts and 1 tablespoon of the granulated sugar. Pulse until the nuts are very finely ground; do not grind to a paste.

3 In a stand mixer fitted with the whip attachment, combine the egg yolks, the ¾ cup granulated sugar, and the vanilla and beat on high speed until pale and thick, 4–5 minutes, stopping to scrape down the sides of the bowl once or twice.

4 In a small saucepan over low heat, melt the butter. Remove from the heat, add the chocolate, and let stand until the chocolate melts, 2–3 minutes. Stir until smooth. In a bowl, using a whisk or a handheld electric mixer on medium-high speed, whip the egg whites until soft peaks form, then gradually add the remaining 2 tablespoons granulated sugar. Whip until the whites are firm and glossy.

5 With the stand mixer on low speed, add the chocolate mixture to the egg yolks. Beat until blended, stopping to scrape down the sides of the bowl once or twice. Add the ground nuts and beat just until incorporated; the batter will be stiff.

6 Transfer the batter to a large bowl. Stir in one-third of the egg whites to lighten the batter, then gently fold in the remaining whites in 2 batches. Pour the batter into the prepared pan. Bake until the center is firm to the touch and the surface begins to crack, about 50 minutes. Transfer to a rack and let cool completely. Unclasp and remove the pan sides, then carefully slide the cake onto a flat serving plate.

7 To make the sauce, in a food processor, purée the raspberries until smooth. Add the 3 tablespoons superfine sugar and process until fully incorporated. Taste and add more sugar if desired. When sweetened to taste, pass the purée through a fine-mesh sieve placed over a bowl to eliminate the seeds. Stir in the framboise or kirsch.

8 To serve, cut the cake into 12 wedges. Accompany each wedge with 1 tablespoon raspberry sauce.

1 cup (5 oz/155 g) plus 2 tablespoons hazelnuts (filberts)

3 tablespoons plus ¾ cup (6 oz/185 g) granulated sugar

6 eggs, separated

1 teaspoon vanilla extract (essence)

¾ cup (6 oz/185 g) unsalted butter

6 oz (185 g) bittersweet chocolate, coarsely chopped

SAUCE

1½ cups (6 oz/185 g) raspberries

3 tablespoons superfine (caster) sugar, or more to taste

1 teaspoon framboise or kirsch

Serves 12

Almond Ring

Rosca de Almendra · Mexico, D.F. · Mexico

This light, crumbly cake is a fixture on the Mexico City table of María Dolores Torres Yzábal. One or two spoonfuls of homemade raspberry sauce add a kick of bright color as well as a sweet-tart complement to the simple flavor of the cake.

CAKE

5 egg whites, at room temperature

Pinch of sea salt

¾ cup (6 oz/185 g) granulated sugar

3 cups (16½ oz/515 g) blanched almonds, finely ground

3 tablespoons unsalted butter, melted and cooled

¼ teaspoon almond extract (essence)

SAUCE

2 cups fresh or thawed frozen raspberries

½ cup (3½ oz/105 g) superfine (caster) sugar

1 tablespoon fresh lemon juice

¼ cup (2 fl oz/60 ml) amaretto liqueur

Serves 8–10

1 Preheat the oven to 350°F (180°C). Lightly butter a 4-cup (32–fl oz/1-l) ring mold.

2 To make the cake, in a bowl, using an electric mixer, beat together the egg whites and salt until soft peaks form. Gradually add the granulated sugar and continue to beat until stiff peaks form. Fold in the ground almonds, melted butter, and almond extract. Gently pour the mixture into the prepared mold.

3 Bake the cake until it is golden and a toothpick inserted into the middle comes out clean, about 30 minutes. Let cool in the mold on a wire rack for 10 minutes, then run a knife blade around the edges to loosen the cake and turn it out onto a serving plate. Let cool completely.

4 To make the sauce, set aside some whole berries. In a blender or food processor, purée the remaining berries until broken up. Add the superfine sugar, lemon juice, and amaretto and continue to process until smooth. Strain through a fine-mesh sieve.

5 Slice the ring and place the slices on individual plates. Top with the sauce, garnish with the reserved whole berries, and serve.

Yankee Pumpkin Pie

New England · America

When most Americans think of pumpkins, it is the big Connecticut field pumpkin that comes to mind. These jack-o'-lantern pumpkins have thin walls that are perfect for carving scary faces at Halloween, but they make lousy pies, as their flesh is watery, stringy, and bland. Sugar and New England pie pumpkins are small enough to handle easily and have creamy, flavorful flesh, making them the perfect base for this beloved national pie.

1 pumpkin (see note), about 1 lb (500 g)

Pastry for a single-crust 9-inch (23-cm) pie (page 17)

½ cup (3½ oz/105 g) firmly packed light brown sugar

4 teaspoons all-purpose (plain) flour

¼ teaspoon ground cinnamon

¼ teaspoon freshly grated nutmeg

Pinch of ground cloves

Pinch of salt

1 cup (8 fl oz/250 ml) heavy (double) cream

¼ cup (3 oz/90 g) maple syrup

3 eggs, at room temperature, lightly beaten

¾ teaspoon vanilla extract (essence)

MAPLE WHIPPED CREAM (OPTIONAL)

1 cup (8 fl oz/250 ml) heavy (double) cream

3 tablespoons maple syrup

Serves 10

1 Preheat the oven to 400°F (200°C). Line a jelly-roll pan or a baking sheet with aluminum foil and lightly grease. Cut the pumpkin in half through the stem end. Using a spoon, scrape out the seeds and fibers and discard. Place each half, cut side down, on the prepared pan. Bake until tender when pierced with a knife, about 1 hour. Set the pan on a wire rack to cool. When the pumpkin is cool enough to handle, scrape the flesh into a food processor and purée until smooth, about 3 minutes. Alternatively, scoop the flesh into a sieve set over a large bowl and, using a rubber spatula, press the pumpkin through the sieve. You will need 1¾ cups (12 oz/375 g) purée for the filling.

2 Meanwhile, on a lightly floured work surface, roll out the pastry disk into a 14-inch (35-cm) round, dusting the rolling pin with flour as needed to prevent sticking. Drape the pastry around the pin and carefully ease it into a 9-inch (23-cm) pie dish, pressing it into the bottom and sides. Trim the overhang so that it extends ¾ inch (2 cm) beyond the edge of the pie dish rim. Roll the overhang under to shape a high edge that rests on top of the rim. Crimp attractively around the rim and freeze the pie shell for at least 30 minutes.

3 Raise the oven temperature to 425°F (220°C). Line the frozen pie shell with a large piece of aluminum foil, fill with pie weights or a combination of uncooked rice and dried beans, and bake until set to the touch, about 15 minutes. Remove the weights and foil and continue to bake the shell until golden, 4–5 minutes longer. Transfer to a rack and let cool. Reduce the oven temperature to 325°F (165°C).

4 In a large bowl, combine the reserved pumpkin purée, brown sugar, flour, cinnamon, nutmeg, cloves, and salt and whisk until smooth. Add the cream, maple syrup, eggs, and vanilla and whisk until just smooth. Pour into the cooled pie shell.

5 Bake until the center jiggles slightly when the dish is nudged, about 50 minutes. Transfer to a rack and let cool. Cover and refrigerate until chilled.

6 To make the whipped cream, in a chilled bowl, using an electric mixer set on medium-high speed, beat until soft peaks form, about 2 minutes. Add the maple syrup and continue to beat until well blended and the cream forms soft peaks, about 30 seconds longer. When you lift the beaters, the tips of the peaks should flop over gently.

7 To serve, cut the pie into wedges and top each serving with a spoonful of maple whipped cream, if desired.

Classic Custard

Jericalla · Puebla · Mexico

This rich custard, named after the small city of Jerico in Colombia, is also popular in Mexico, where it can be found in markets, restaurants, and many home kitchens.

3 cups (24 fl oz/750 ml) milk

¾ cup (6 oz/185 g) sugar

2-inch (5-cm) piece true cinnamon bark

½ vanilla bean, split lengthwise

3 egg yolks

Serves 6–8

1 In a saucepan over medium heat, stir together the milk, sugar, and cinnamon. Using the tip of a small knife, scrape the seeds from the vanilla bean into the milk. Bring to a slow boil, stirring until the sugar is dissolved, then reduce the heat to low and simmer gently until the mixture is just thick enough to coat the back of a spoon, about 20 minutes. Strain the milk mixture and let cool slightly.

2 Preheat the oven to 325°F (165°C).

3 In a bowl, beat the egg yolks until blended. Add ⅓ cup (3 fl oz/80 ml) of the hot milk, stirring constantly, then pour the egg mixture into the rest of the milk mixture, continuing to stir constantly. Divide the mixture evenly among 6–8 flameproof dishes or ramekins. Place the custard dishes on a rack in a baking pan, making sure they do not touch, and pour hot water into the pan to a depth of 1 inch (2.5 cm). Bake until a toothpick inserted in the middle of a custard comes out clean, about 1 hour.

4 Remove the custard dishes from the water bath, arrange on a baking sheet, turn the oven to broil (grill), and slip under the broiler (grill) until the tops are golden brown. Let the custards cool, then cover and refrigerate for several hours until chilled.

5 Serve cold in the dishes, or run a knife blade around the edge of each dish to loosen the custard and then unmold onto dessert plates.

VANILLA

In the distant past, before Mexico's recorded history, the native vine of the vanilla orchid rambled through the tropical trees of the humid rain forests of southeastern Mexico. The region, now Veracruz, was home to the Totonacs, who learned to cultivate the long, ripe pods of the plant and to cure them to develop their aroma. In later years, these *vainilla* "beans" were especially prized as a tribute paid to the ruling Aztec nobles and used to flavor a chocolate beverage drunk exclusively by them.

According to Totonac legend, a time existed when there was no vanilla. The ruler of the ancient city of El Tajín commanded that his beautiful daughter, "Light of the Morning Star," serve the goddess of agriculture. Every day the princess brought offerings to the temple of the goddess, which had been built by her father. One day, a neighboring young prince caught sight of the young maiden performing her duty and immediately fell in love. As she passed by, he leapt from behind a tree, took her in his arms, and ran with her up the slope of a mountain. Although she was startled at first, the princess soon returned his ardor and willingly joined him in flight.

The couple grew tired and was captured by pursuing priests who had been guarding the temple. They were instantly beheaded. From the spot where their blood spilled, an emerald-green vine sprang up and, with clinging tendrils, began to intertwine the branches of the nearby trees. Delicate yellow flowers bloomed, then before the priests' eyes, the orchids turned into slender green vanilla beans from which later came such a splendid aroma that the Totonacs made the beans a divine offering to their gods and to the world.

Although vanilla is now grown in other tropical countries, Mexican vanilla is among the most deeply flavored and richly scented. The plant can reach 45 feet (15 meters) or more in height as it climbs trees or other convenient supports. Along with the pods, or beans, which are cured before use, the robust vines bear beautiful orchids. Today, the main commercial use for vanilla in Mexico is as one of the ingredients in Coca-Cola™. Only a small amount is bottled as vanilla extract for flavoring.

Pineapple Turnovers

Empanadas con Piña • Yucatán • Mexico

These turnovers, filled with pecans, coconut, and raisins in a pineapple glaze, are similar to those sold on the streets of Mérida. They are baked or fried before they are served hot.

1 If baking the turnovers, preheat the oven to 375°F (190°C) and grease a baking sheet.

2 To make the dough, in a bowl, mix together the cream cheese and butter until well blended, using a spoon, an electric mixer, or your hands. Add the flour and salt and mix well. Turn the dough out onto a lightly floured work surface and gently knead for about 1 minute, then form into a ball. Wrap the dough with plastic wrap and refrigerate for at least 15 minutes.

3 To make the filling, whisk the pineapple juice and cornstarch together in a saucepan. Heat over medium heat, stirring until the cornstarch is dissolved. Add the sugar and bring the mixture to a boil, continuing to stir. Reduce the heat to low and simmer, stirring occasionally, until the mixture is quite thick, 3–5 minutes. Remove from the heat and stir in the pecans, coconut, and raisins. Let cool.

4 On a lightly floured surface, roll out the dough until slightly less than ¼ inch (6 mm) thick. Divide the dough in half and roll again to no more than ⅛ inch (3 mm) thick. Depending on whether you are making regular turnovers or bite-sized turnovers, cut out rounds 3 inches (7.5 cm) in diameter or 1½–2 inches (4–5 cm) in diameter. Gather up any scraps of dough, reroll, and cut into more rounds.

5 Place about 1 teaspoon filling, or less for the bite-sized turnovers, in the center of each round. Fold one side over the filling, seal tightly with your fingers, and then crimp the edges with the tines of a fork.

6 If baking, brush the tops with the beaten egg, sprinkle with sugar and cinnamon, and place on the baking sheet. Bake for 12 minutes. Check to see if the turnovers are browning evenly; if they are not, rotate the pan 180 degrees. Continue to bake until golden brown, 4–5 minutes more. Serve immediately.

7 Alternatively, to fry the turnovers, omit the egg wash. Pour oil to a depth of ½ inch (12 mm) into a frying pan and place over medium-high heat until very hot but not smoking. Add the turnovers a few at a time and fry until they turn a crusty golden brown, 2–3 minutes per side. Transfer to absorbent paper to drain. Keep warm in a low oven. Sprinkle with sugar and cinnamon while still hot and serve.

DOUGH

6 oz (185 g) low-fat cream cheese, at room temperature

1 cup (8 oz/250 g) unsalted butter, at room temperature

2 cups (10 oz/315 g) unbleached all-purpose (plain) flour

½ teaspoon sea salt

FILLING

½ cup (4 fl oz/125 ml) pineapple juice

2 tablespoons cornstarch (cornflour)

3 tablespoons sugar

½ cup (2 oz/60 g) chopped pecans

½ cup (2 oz/60 g) unsweetened shredded fresh or dried coconut

¼ cup (1½ oz/45 g) raisins

1 egg, lightly beaten with 1 teaspoon water, if baking

Sugar and ground cinnamon

Safflower or canola oil, if frying

Makes 15–20 regular turnovers or 30 bite-sized turnovers

Crème Fraîche Ice Cream with Apricots

California · America

This luscious ice cream has the flavor of cheesecake. Try substituting peeled (page 224) and sliced peaches or 2 cups (8 oz/250 g) mixed berries for the apricots.

1 cup (8 fl oz/250 ml) half-and-half (half cream)

1 cup (8 fl oz/250 ml) heavy (double) cream

½ vanilla bean, split lengthwise

6 egg yolks

¾ cup (6 oz/185 g) sugar

1 cup (8 fl oz/250 ml) crème fraîche

6 apricots, halved, pitted, and sliced

1 tablespoon sugar, or to taste

2 teaspoons fresh lemon juice

Serves 6

1 In a saucepan, combine the half-and-half and the cream. Using the tip of a small knife, scrape the vanilla bean seeds into the cream mixture, then add the pod. Bring to a simmer over medium heat. Cover and let stand for 15 minutes. In a bowl, whisk together the egg yolks and the ¾ cup sugar until a ribbon forms when the whisk is lifted, about 1 minute. Whisk in the warm cream mixture, then return to the saucepan. Cook over medium-low heat, stirring constantly with a wooden spoon, until the mixture coats the spoon, about 2 minutes. Do not allow it to simmer, or it will curdle.

2 Remove from the heat and let cool, stirring occasionally, for 15 minutes, then whisk in the crème fraîche. Pour through a sieve placed over a bowl to remove the vanilla pod. Cover and chill thoroughly. Transfer to an ice-cream maker and freeze according to the manufacturer's instructions. You should have about 1 qt (1 l).

3 About 30 minutes before serving, place the apricot slices in a bowl. Add 1 tablespoon sugar, or more if the fruit is underripe, and the lemon juice. Stir gently and set aside.

4 Scoop the ice cream into dessert goblets or compote dishes. Arrange the apricot slices alongside and drizzle with some of the accumulated juices.

Santa Rosa Plum Galette

California • America

California's magnificent summer fruits, either alone or in combination, make ravishing galettes. This version showcases the tangy Santa Rosa plum, the creation of renowned California plant breeder Luther Burbank, who named the plum for the town north of San Francisco where he pursued his horticultural research. A galette is easy to make because the crust does not require crimping or fitting into a tart shell or pie pan.

DOUGH

2 cups (10 oz/315 g) unbleached all-purpose (plain) flour

¾ teaspoon salt

½ cup (4 oz/125 g) chilled unsalted butter, cut into small pieces

7 tablespoons (3½ oz/105 g) chilled solid vegetable shortening, cut into small pieces

About ¼ cup (2 fl oz/60 ml) ice water

2 lb (1 kg) ripe but firm Santa Rosa or other plums, pitted and cut into wedges ½ inch (12 mm) wide

¼ cup (2 oz/60 g) granulated sugar, or more to taste

1 egg yolk whisked with 1 teaspoon water

1½ tablespoons crystal sugar

Serves 10

1 To make the dough in a food processor, combine the flour and salt and pulse to blend. Add the butter and pulse a few times to coat the butter with the flour. Add the shortening and pulse until the fat particles are coated with flour and are about the size of large peas. Transfer to a large bowl.

2 To make the dough by hand, place the flour and the salt in a large bowl and stir to blend. Add the butter pieces and, using a pastry blender or 2 knives, cut the butter into the flour until the pieces are the size of large peas. Add the shortening and cut into the flour until the pieces are coated with flour and also the size of large peas.

3 Sprinkle the flour-butter mixture with enough of the ice water while tossing with a fork, just until the dough begins to come together. Then gather up the dough with your hands and shape it into a thick disk. You may have to knead the dough a little to get it to hold together, but that is preferable to adding more water. Enclose the dough in plastic wrap and refrigerate for at least 2 hours.

4 Put a baking stone or baking tiles on the center rack of an oven and preheat to 425°F (220°C) for 45 minutes.

5 Put a large sheet of parchment (baking) paper on a work surface. Unwrap the dough and place it on the parchment. Top with another sheet of parchment. Roll out the dough into a 15-inch (38-cm) round between the parchment sheets. Occasionally you may need to lift the top parchment sheet, flour the dough lightly, and then replace the parchment. Once or twice, flip the dough over so that the bottom sheet is on the top, lift the sheet, flour the dough, and replace the sheet. If the parchment sheets are not at least 15 inches (38 cm) square, you may need to use a second, overlapping sheet. When the dough is rolled out to the desired size, slide a rimless baking sheet or pizza peel under the bottom parchment sheet. Remove the top parchment sheet.

6 Place the plums in a bowl, sprinkle with the ¼ cup granulated sugar, and toss to coat. Taste and add more sugar if desired. Scatter the plums over the surface of the dough, leaving a 2-inch (5-cm) rim uncovered. Slip an icing spatula or wide knife under the edge of the dough and gently fold it over the plums to make a wide border; make sure there are no cracks in the dough for juices to slip through. Brush the border with the yolk-water mixture, then sprinkle with the crystal sugar. Using scissors, cut away excess parchment.

7 Transfer the dough, still on the parchment sheet, onto the baking stone. Bake the galette until the crust is golden and the plums are tender, about 40 minutes. Using the rimless baking sheet or pizza peel, transfer the galette to a rack to cool briefly.

8 Transfer the galette to a flat serving plate. Cut into wedges and serve warm.

Blueberry Shortcakes

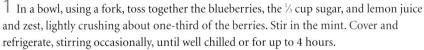

New England • America

During the summer, New England farm stands are loaded with ripe berries nearly bursting with juice, and it's a good thing: the New England cook's credo is to use the freshest fruits available to create the season's iconic desserts, such as these satisfying shortcakes.

3 pt (1½ lb/750 g) blueberries

⅓ cup (3 oz/90 g) plus
3 tablespoons sugar

2 teaspoons fresh lemon juice

½ teaspoon finely grated lemon zest

¼ cup (¼ oz/7 g) fresh mint leaves, cut into narrow strips

1⅔ cups (8 oz/250 g) all-purpose (plain) flour

1 tablespoon baking powder

¾ teaspoon salt

½ cup (4 oz/125 g) chilled unsalted butter, cut into ½-inch (12-mm) pieces

¾ cup (6 fl oz/180 ml) buttermilk

½ teaspoon vanilla extract (essence)

Sweetened whipped cream (page 225)

Serves 6

1 In a bowl, using a fork, toss together the blueberries, the ⅓ cup sugar, and lemon juice and zest, lightly crushing about one-third of the berries. Stir in the mint. Cover and refrigerate, stirring occasionally, until well chilled or for up to 4 hours.

2 Preheat the oven to 400°F (200°C). In a bowl, whisk together the flour, 3 tablespoons sugar, baking powder, and salt. Scatter the butter over the flour mixture and, using a pastry blender or 2 knives, cut in the butter until the pieces are no larger than peas. Add the buttermilk and vanilla and toss with a fork until the dry ingredients are just moistened and blended. Turn the dough out onto a work surface and press into a thick rectangle about 6-by-4-inches (15-by-10-cm). Using a knife, trim the edges even and cut the dough into 6 equal squares. Place on an ungreased baking sheet. Bake until puffed and brown, 15–18 minutes. Transfer to a wire rack.

3 Split the shortcakes in half horizontally. Place the bottom halves, cut sides up, on dessert plates. Spoon half of the blueberry compote, including the juices, over the halves, dividing it evenly. Top with whipped cream, dividing it evenly. Spoon on the remaining blueberries and top with the remaining halves.

COFFEE CULTURE

Not too long ago in the United States, coffee was coffee. It didn't matter much where it came from or what brand it was. But the early 1990s saw a major shift in coffee consciousness, and now consumers are able to choose from various types of beans and roasting styles for their daily cup. Nowhere has good coffee become so much a part of daily routine as it has in the Pacific Northwest.

Seattle alone boasts hundreds of coffee outlets, ranging from branches of international chains to small independent carts wheeled daily onto downtown street corners. A slew of inviting coffeehouse options prevails in the larger Northwest cities, from sleek cafés that look as if they were imported lock, stock, and espresso machine from Rome to no-frills neighborhood hangouts. Patronage tends to be split between the grab-and-go types and those who bring the newspaper so they can linger over their cappuccinos. Coffee loyalties are so strong in these parts that regulars show up with their own thermal cups, prompting an experienced barista to ask, "Same as usual?"

New York Cheesecake

The Mid-Atlantic • America

The original New York cheesecake is made with a sweetened pastry crust and an orange- or lemon-laced filling loaded with sweetened cream cheese and heavy (double) cream; it is legendary for its rich, dense taste. This version is enriched with sour cream and owes its bold flavor to vanilla beans. While the chocolate graham cracker crust definitely bucks tradition, it makes the cheesecake even more irresistibly delicious.

1 To make the cheesecake crust, preheat the oven to 400°F (200°C). Lightly butter a 9-inch (23-cm) springform pan.

2 In a bowl, combine the cookie crumbs, sugar, and melted butter. Stir until the mixture is well blended and the crumbs are evenly moistened. Transfer the crumb mixture to the prepared springform pan and press evenly onto the bottom and about 1½ inches (4 cm) up the sides of the pan. (A straight-sided, flat-bottomed coffee mug or cup works well for this step.) Bake for 10 minutes. Transfer the baked crust to a rack and let cool completely. Reduce the oven temperature to 300°F (150°C).

3 To make the filling, in a large bowl, combine the cream cheese, flour, and salt. Using a sharp paring knife, split each vanilla bean in half lengthwise. Using the tip of the knife, scrape out the vanilla seeds into the bowl. Using an electric mixer set on medium-high speed, beat until very smooth and fluffy, stopping frequently to scrape down the sides.

4 Add the sugar and sour cream to the cream cheese mixture and beat until well blended, again frequently scraping down the sides. Add the eggs one at a time, beating after each addition before adding the next egg. Pour the cheese mixture into the baked crust.

5 Bake the cheesecake until the center jiggles slightly when the pan is nudged back and forth, 60–65 minutes. The edges will be slightly puffed and will have a few little cracks.

6 Transfer the cheesecake to a wire rack and let cool to room temperature. Cover and refrigerate until well chilled, preferably overnight.

7 To serve, unclasp and remove the pan sides, then run a long, thin flexible metal spatula under the bottom crust. Carefully slide the cake onto a flat serving plate. To slice, before each cut run a thin-bladed knife under hot water and wipe it dry.

CRUST

1½ cups (4½ oz/140 g) chocolate graham cracker cookie crumbs (about 14 cookies)

2 tablespoons sugar

¼ cup (2 oz/60 g) unsalted butter, melted

FILLING

2 lb (1 kg) cream cheese, at warm room temperature

2 tablespoons all-purpose (plain) flour

¼ teaspoon salt

2 large vanilla beans

1½ cups (10 oz/315 g) sugar

½ cup (4 oz/125 g) sour cream

3 eggs, at room temperature

Serves 16

Baked Figs with Goat Cheese

Higos al Horno con Queso de Cabra · Coahuila · Mexico

This traditional recipe comes from northern Mexico, where figs are bountiful. Intensely sweet tree-ripened figs are often difficult to find in supermarkets. Look for them at their seasonal peak, in the summer, at farmers' markets.

12 ripe Mission figs

¼ cup (2 oz/60 g) firmly packed dark brown sugar

⅓ cup (1½ oz/45 g) walnut halves

¼ cup (2 oz/60 g) unsalted butter, cut into small cubes

¾ cup (4 oz/125 g) crumbled fresh goat cheese

Serves 4

1 Preheat the oven to 350°F (180°C). Butter a shallow baking dish in which the figs will fit snugly once they are cut.

2 Snip the stems from the figs and quarter them from the stem end down to, but not quite through, the bottoms. Spread the figs open and place, cut side up, in the prepared baking dish. Sprinkle evenly with the brown sugar, scatter the walnuts on top, and dot with the butter.

3 Cover and bake until the figs are heated through, about 20 minutes. Spoon some of the crumbled goat cheese onto each fig and, if desired, lightly toast the cheese in a broiler (griller) or very hot oven for just a few minutes.

4 Serve the figs warm or at room temperature on individual plates with some of the syrup that forms during baking spooned over the tops.

Key Lime Pie

The South • America

True key limes hail from the Florida Keys and the Caribbean Islands. About the size of a golf ball, they have yellowish (often two-toned) skin and lighter pulp and tarter juice than the more common Persian limes. If key limes are unavailable, you can use regular lime juice, but increase the amount to ¾ cup (6 fl oz/180 ml). Key lime pie filling is a pale lemon-yellow.

CRUST

28 gingersnaps, about 1½ inches (4 cm) in diameter

½ cup (2 oz/60 g) chopped pecans

1 tablespoon chopped crystallized ginger

3 tablespoons granulated sugar

⅛ teaspoon ground cinnamon (optional)

¼ cup (2 oz/60 g) unsalted butter, melted and cooled

FILLING

4 eggs, separated

¼ cup (1 oz/30 g) cornstarch (cornflour)

½ cup (4 oz/125 g) granulated sugar

1 can (14 oz/440 g) sweetened condensed milk

½ cup (4 fl oz/125 ml) fresh key lime juice

2 tablespoons finely grated key lime zest

½ teaspoon cream of tartar

½ teaspoon vanilla extract (essence)

TOPPING

1 cup (8 fl oz/250 ml) heavy (double) cream

⅓ cup (1½ oz/45 g) confectioners' (icing) sugar

⅛ teaspoon almond extract (essence)

8 thin key lime slices

Serves 8

1 Preheat the oven to 350°F (180°C). Lightly butter a 9-inch (23-cm) pie dish.

2 To make the crust, in a food processor, combine the gingersnaps, pecans, ginger, and granulated sugar, and the cinnamon, if using. Pulse until the mixture resembles finely ground crumbs, 1½–2 minutes. Transfer the mixture to a bowl and add the melted butter. Mix until the crumbs are evenly dampened and the mixture resembles a coarse meal, about 1 minute. Press the mixture in an even layer onto the bottom and up the sides of the prepared pie dish. (To make this step easy, place an empty pie dish of the same size on top of the crumbs and press down firmly, then lift off the dish.)

3 Place the crust in the oven and bake until it is lightly browned, about 10 minutes. Transfer the crust to a rack to cool.

4 To make the filling, in a large mixing bowl, using an electric mixer on high speed, beat together the egg yolks and 2 of the egg whites with the cornstarch, granulated sugar, and condensed milk until light and fluffy, about 5 minutes. Add the lime juice and zest and beat until smooth.

5 In a clean bowl, using clean beaters, whip the remaining 2 egg whites and the cream of tartar with an electric mixer on high speed for 1 minute. Continue beating until soft peaks form and the peaks hold their shape, 1–2 minutes. Whisk in the vanilla extract. Fold one-third of the egg whites into the key lime mixture to lighten it. Then fold the key lime mixture into the egg whites just until combined.

6 Transfer the filling into the cooled pie crust and smooth the top with a rubber spatula. Bake the pie until just firm, about 20 minutes. Transfer to a wire rack to cool completely, then cover and refrigerate for at least 4 hours or for up to overnight.

7 To make the topping, in a chilled bowl, using chilled beaters and the electric mixer on high speed, beat the cream until soft peaks form, about 2 minutes. Gradually add the confectioners' sugar and then the almond extract and beat until the peaks are thick and hold their shape, about 1 minute.

8 Spoon the whipped cream into a piping bag that is fitted with a rosette or star tip. Pipe 5 straight lines across the surface of the chilled pie, spacing them evenly. Then pipe 4 lines diagonally over the first lines to form a lattice pattern. At each intersection of the lines, pipe a small rosette or star. Alternatively, pipe the whipped cream around the rim of the pie. Refrigerate for up to 2 hours.

9 Remove the pie from the refrigerator. Cut the lime slices in half and arrange around the rim of the pie. Cut the pie into wedges and serve at once.

Hot Chocolate

Chocolate · Michoacán · Mexico

In Mexico, hot chocolate is traditionally made with water, but the practice of using milk is now widely accepted. Tablets made from chocolate ground together with sugar, cinnamon, and often almonds are put in a clay pot filled with hot water or milk. The cook rapidly rotates a *molinillo,* a wooden stick encircled with carved rings at its base, back and forth between his or her palms to create a thick layer of foam on the chocolate. Mexican chocolate tablets can be purchased in well-stocked food stores and in Hispanic markets.

4 cups (32 fl oz/1 l) milk or water

2 chocolate tablets, about ¼ lb (125 g) total, broken into small pieces

1 vanilla bean (optional)

Serves 4

1 In a saucepan over low heat, warm 1 cup (8 fl oz/ 250 ml) of the milk or water. Add the chocolate and stir with a wooden spoon until melted. Add the remaining 3 cups (24 fl oz/ 750 ml) milk or water and the vanilla bean, if using, and let simmer for several minutes.

2 Remove the pan from the heat. Lift out the vanilla bean and save for another use. Using a whisk or rotary beater, beat the chocolate milk vigorously until a thick layer of foam covers the surface. Pour into mugs or cups, distributing the foam evenly. Serve at once.

Peanut Clouds

Polvorones de Cacahuate · Mexico, D.F. · Mexico

To add a new dimension to these classic Mexican cookies, Laura Caraza Campos adds finely ground peanuts. Serve with cups of Hot Chocolate (above).

1 cup (5 oz/155 g) raw peanuts, skins removed and coarsely chopped

½ cup (4 oz/125 g) unsalted butter, at room temperature

½ cup (4 oz/125 g) solid vegetable shortening, at room temperature

½ cup (2 oz/60 g) confectioners' (icing) sugar, plus 1 cup (4 oz/125 g), sifted

1 tablespoon dark rum

2 cups (10 oz/315 g) all-purpose (plain) flour, preferably unbleached

¼ teaspoon sea salt

Makes about 36 cookies

1 In a spice grinder or food processor, finely chop the peanuts. Be careful not to over-process to a paste. In a bowl, using an electric mixer, beat together the butter and vegetable shortening until creamy. Add the ½ cup sugar and the rum and continue beating until the mixture is light and fluffy.

2 Place most of the flour and the salt in a sifter and sift into the bowl containing the butter-sugar mixture. Stir until well blended. Add the ground nuts and the remaining flour and mix well. Cover and refrigerate for at least 1 hour or as long as overnight.

3 Position a rack in the upper third of an oven and preheat to 325°F (165°C).

4 Using your hands, roll small pieces of the dough into ¾-inch (2-cm) balls. Place on an ungreased baking sheet, spacing them about 1 inch (2.5 cm) apart. Bake the cookies until light gold, about 15 minutes. If they are not browning evenly, rotate the pan halfway through the baking. Remove from the oven.

5 Spread the sifted confectioners' sugar in a shallow plate. While the cookies are still hot, roll them in the sugar, coating evenly, then set on a rack to cool completely. When the cookies are cooled, roll again in the sugar.

6 Serve the cookies, or store them between layers of parchment (baking) paper in a tightly covered container at room temperature for up to several weeks.

Fig and Pecan Pie

The South · America

Many southerners have a pecan tree or two growing on their property. Most cooks will use some of the nuts for the region's iconic pecan pie. In this version, fig preserves added to the pie filling make it less sweet than its traditional counterpart.

Pastry for a single-crust 9-inch (23-cm) pie (page 17)

⅓ cup (3 oz/90 g) sugar

3 tablespoons cornstarch (cornflour)

¼ teaspoon salt

½ cup (5 oz/155 g) light corn syrup

½ cup (6 oz/185 g) cane syrup or dark molasses

2 tablespoons vanilla extract (essence)

4 eggs, lightly beaten

1½ cups (6 oz/185 g) chopped pecans

¼ teaspoon ground cinnamon

Freshly grated nutmeg to taste

1 cup (8 fl oz/250 ml) fig preserves

Serves 8

1 On a lightly floured work surface, roll out the pastry disk into a round about 11 inches (28 cm) in diameter, dusting the rolling pin with flour to prevent sticking. Drape the pastry around the pin and ease it into a 9-inch (23-cm) pie pan, pressing it into the bottom and sides. Trim the overhang so that it extends about ¾ inch (2 cm) beyond the edge of pan. Roll the overhang under to shape a high edge that rests on top of the pan rim. Crimp attractively around the rim. Freeze for 30 minutes.

2 In a large bowl, stir together the sugar, cornstarch, and salt. Add the corn syrup, cane syrup or molasses, vanilla, and eggs. Whisk briefly to combine. Do not overmix. Stir in the pecans, cinnamon, nutmeg, and fig preserves. Pour into the chilled pie crust.

3 Bake the pie until the crust is golden brown and the center yields to slight pressure, 50–55 minutes. The filling will become firmer as the pie cools. Transfer to a wire rack to cool for at least 1 hour before serving.

THE SOUTHERN SWEET TOOTH

Sweets are so central to the southern supper table that many cafeterias display the dessert offerings before the main dishes. That way, customers know they had better leave enough room for a big wedge of cake or pie.

What is responsible for this love affair with sweets? The first reason is a practical one: sugarcane arrived in what is now St. Augustine, Florida, with the Spanish in 1565 (having been brought to Santo Domingo from the Canary Islands by Christopher Columbus in 1492). By the mid-1800s, the region's sugar refineries were so large and efficient that the sweetener fit into everyone's budget.

The second reason looks to the roots of the southern sweet tooth. The English contributed puddings and pies to the local dessert repertoire, but the majority of southern desserts seem to be based on French technique and tradition, a legacy due in large part to Thomas Jefferson, America's third president and the country's first serious food aficionado. Jefferson, who also served as the American minister to France, was a great champion of French cuisine and regularly served

French pastries, meringues, ice creams, pralines, cakes, and cookies at Monticello, his Virginia estate. The region's cooks copied Jefferson's lead.

Today, the southern sweet tooth is kept sated with a full schedule of bake sales throughout the year. Community groups from the children's theater to the neighborhood softball team, the local church to the high-school band, hold these traditional southern fund-raisers. The town's home bakers display their cakes, pies, cobblers, and cookies—each labeled with a price—on long tables, and the most prized sweets are purchased quickly by the savvy buyers who know which neighbor makes the best banana cream pie or Mississippi mud cake.

Come holiday time or a special occasion, elegant baked goods—a mile-high layer cake cloaked in buttercream frosting, a lemon meringue pie with a billowy, gold-tipped crown— are first set out on the sideboard for family and friends to admire. This is when a home baker gets to show off, and when the lucky guests, happy to sing the praises of the host, get to sit down and indulge in the baker's finest efforts.

Mulled Wine Poached Pears

The Pacific Northwest • America

Oregon and Washington are top producers of pears, including yellow and red Bartlett (Williams'), Bosc, Comice, Anjou, and even beautiful little Seckels. Bosc pears, with their firm texture even when ripe, are the ideal choice for this recipe, although you could use other pears that are ripe but not soft. The recipe brings together two favorite treats of late fall and early winter: sweet Northwest pears and aromatic mulled wine. The pears may also be halved and cored before poaching.

1 bottle (750 ml) Pinot Noir or other medium-bodied, fruity red wine

1 cup (8 fl oz/250 ml) water, or as needed

½ cup (4 oz/125 g) sugar

1 orange zest strip

2 cinnamon sticks

5 whole cloves

2 star anise

Few gratings of nutmeg

4 ripe but firm whole pears (see note), peeled

1 pint (500 ml) vanilla ice cream

Serves 4

1 In a large saucepan over medium-high heat, combine the wine, the 1 cup water, sugar, orange zest, cinnamon sticks, cloves, star anise, and nutmeg. Bring to a boil, stirring occasionally, until the sugar dissolves, then reduce the heat to medium so the liquid simmers gently.

2 Add the pears to the wine mixture along with enough water so that the pears are fully submerged in the liquid. Cover the pears with a round of parchment (baking) paper cut to fit just inside the pan and press directly onto the surface of the poaching liquid. Poach the pears gently until just tender when pierced with the tip of a knife, 20–30 minutes. Using a slotted spoon, transfer the pears to a bowl and let cool.

3 Raise the heat to medium-high and boil the poaching liquid until reduced by about two-thirds and slightly thickened, about 15 minutes. Scoop out and discard the orange zest and spices, and set the syrup aside to cool to room temperature.

4 For each serving, place a pear upright on a dessert plate and drizzle with the syrup. Serve with a generous scoop of ice cream.

Kahlúa and Rum Flan

Flan de Kahlúa y Ron • Guanajuato • Mexico

Flan traces its origins to the Spanish conquest, as do so many of Mexico's sweets. This version is updated with the addition of Kahlúa and rum.

1 In a large saucepan over medium-low heat, bring the milk, 1 cup (8 oz/250 g) of the sugar, and the cinnamon bark to a boil, stirring to dissolve the sugar. Reduce the heat to low. Simmer uncovered, stirring frequently, until the milk is reduced to about 4 cups (32 fl oz/1 l), about 45 minutes. (In order to judge accurately when the milk has reduced sufficiently, pour half of the milk into the pan before you add the remainder, to see where the final level should be.) Let the reduced milk cool slightly.

2 Place the remaining ⅔ cup (5 oz/155 g) sugar and the water in a small, heavy saucepan over medium-high heat and bring to a boil. Continue to boil without stirring until the syrup begins to color, about 15 minutes. Reduce the heat to a simmer, then swirl the pan until the syrup is a deep amber, about 1 minute. Immediately pour the caramel into a 2½-qt (2.5-l) soufflé dish or charlotte mold, or into individual molds, tilting to distribute the caramel evenly over the bottom. Some of the syrup may run up the sides of the mold, but try to keep most of it on the bottom. Set aside.

3 Preheat the oven to 350°F (180°C).

4 In a large bowl, beat the whole eggs, egg yolks, Kahlúa, rum, and vanilla until blended. Slowly beat in the reduced milk mixture. Pour the mixture through a fine-mesh sieve into the prepared mold(s). Place the mold(s) in a baking pan and pour in hot water to reach three-fourths up the side of the mold(s). Cover loosely with aluminum foil.

5 Bake until just set and a knife inserted in the middle comes out clean, 40–50 minutes. Remove the baking pan from the oven and let the flan cool in the water. (The flan can be covered and refrigerated for up to 2 days before serving.)

6 To unmold, run a knife around the edge of the mold(s) to loosen the custard. Invert a deep serving plate or individual plate over the top, and invert the flan and dish together. The flan should drop from the mold. If it resists unmolding, dip the mold(s) in hot water for just a few seconds, then invert. The flan should drop out easily. Sprinkle with ground cinnamon, if desired, and serve at once.

8 cups (64 fl oz/2 l) milk

1⅔ cups (13 oz/405 g) sugar

2-inch (5-cm) piece true cinnamon bark

¼ cup (2 fl oz/60 ml) water

6 whole eggs, plus 4 egg yolks

2 tablespoons Kahlúa or other coffee liqueur

1 tablespoon dark rum

1 teaspoon vanilla extract (essence)

Ground cinnamon (optional)

Serves 6–8

Plantains with Mexican Eggnog

Plátano con Rompope y Crema • Oaxaca • Mexico

Plantains are similar in appearance to large bananas, but unlike bananas, they are always cooked before eating. Select fully ripe, blackened plantains for this recipe. The eggnog recipe makes enough for other uses and is wonderful served over fruit or ice cream. Eggnog can be purchased in Hispanic grocery stores but lacks the richness of homemade.

2 cups (16 fl oz/500 ml) milk

½ cup (4 oz/125 g) sugar

1½-inch (4-cm) piece true cinnamon bark

⅛ teaspoon baking soda (bicarbonate of soda)

6 egg yolks

Ice cubes or crushed ice

¼ cup (2 fl oz/60 ml) brandy

2 black-ripe plantains (see note)

2 tablespoons unsalted butter, cut into small pieces

1 cup (8 fl oz/250 ml) *crema* (page 222)

Serves 4

1 In a saucepan over medium heat, stir together the milk, sugar, cinnamon bark, and baking soda. When it begins to boil, reduce the heat and simmer for about 20 minutes. Set aside to cool, then strain and discard the cinnamon bark.

2 Place the egg yolks in a bowl and whisk or beat with an electric mixer until thick and yellow, about 5 minutes. Continuing to beat, slowly pour the cool milk mixture into the yolks. Return to the saucepan and cook over low heat, stirring constantly, until the mixture thickens and lightly coats the back of a wooden spoon. Remove from the heat and stop the cooking by pouring the eggnog into a metal bowl set into a large bowl of ice cubes. Stir until cooled. Gradually stir in the brandy. You should have about 2 cups (16 fl oz/500 ml). (The eggnog can be stored, tightly covered, in the refrigerator for several weeks.)

3 Preheat the oven to 425°F (220°C). Lightly oil a baking dish. Cut the plantains in half lengthwise through the peels and lay the halves, cut sides up, in a single layer in the prepared dish. Dot with the butter. Bake until the plantains turn a dark golden brown, about 10 minutes.

4 Remove from the oven and transfer to a serving platter. Spoon the eggnog over the plantains, letting it puddle around them. Reserve any extra eggnog for another use (see note). Drizzle on the *crema* and serve very hot.

APPLE HARVEST

Autumn in the Northeast is known for Indian summer days, chilly nights, fiery-colored foliage, and, perhaps best of all, apple picking. Heading to the nearest orchard to gather a basket or two of the trees' best fruits is a fall tradition practiced by every true New Englander. A few orchard owners still allow folks to ramble among the trees and handpick the fruits themselves.

Despite the New Englander's—and seemingly every American's—love of the apple, buying the fruits can be confusing. New England and Mid-Atlantic apple varieties are many, and a number of them are available year-round both in supermarkets and in smaller specialty markets. The best thing to do is divide them into three categories: baking, eating, and juicing. The McIntosh apple, a New England classic, is among the best of the eating category. Along with its cousins, Jerseymac, Paulared, and Jonamac, the McIntosh is known for its crisp texture and juicy, full-flavored taste, characteristics that also make it an ideal apple for juicing.

Another New England favorite is the Macoun. Developed in New York in the early 1900s, the variety has a firm texture and a slightly tart taste that make it a wonderful choice for baking and eating. Other favorites for baking are the Jonathan, the Northern Spy, and the Baldwin. Finally, the all-purpose Roxbury Russet is an old but prized variety. It was first grown in New England in the mid-1600s, and the resurgence of interest in heirloom fruits has brought this wonderful old-timer back into farmers' markets.

Cranberry-Apple Pie

New England · America

European settlers, who saw the head and bill of a crane in the blossoms of its vines, gave the cranberry its name. At harvesttime, a small part of the crop is dry-picked for the fresh market. After that, the planting areas are flooded and one of the most unusual—and lovely—sights of a New England fall is visible: brilliant, glistening red berries float on the surface of the bogs, ready for wet-harvesting and then processing into sauces and juices.

PIE PASTRY FOR DOUBLE-CRUST PIE

2½ cups (12½ oz/390 g) all-purpose (plain) flour

2 tablespoons granulated sugar

1 teaspoon salt

½ cup (4 oz/125 g) chilled unsalted butter, cut into ¾-inch (2-cm) pieces

6 tablespoons (3 oz/90 g) chilled solid vegetable shortening, cut into ¾-inch (2-cm) pieces

6 tablespoons (3 fl oz/90 ml) very cold water

FILLING

2½ lb (1.25 kg) apples (see page 56), peeled, cored, and cut into slices ¼ inch (6 mm) thick

¾ cup (3 oz/90 g) cranberries

1 cup (7 oz/220 g) firmly packed dark brown sugar

¼ cup (1½ oz/45 g) all-purpose (plain) flour

1¼ teaspoons ground cinnamon

¼ teaspoon freshly grated nutmeg

1 teaspoon vanilla extract (essence)

Pinch of salt

Serves 8–10

1 To make the pastry in a food processor, combine the flour, granulated sugar, and salt and pulse to blend. Add the butter and shortening and pulse until the fats are in ½-inch (12-mm) pieces. Add the water and pulse until the dough just begins to come together in a rough mass.

2 To make the pastry by hand, stir together the flour, granulated sugar, and salt in a bowl. Add the butter and shortening pieces and toss to coat with flour. Using a pastry blender or 2 knives, cut the fats into the flour mixture until the pieces are no larger than small peas. Drizzle with the water and toss with a fork until the dough is evenly moist and begins to come together in a rough mass.

3 Turn the dough out onto a lightly floured work surface, divide in half, and shape each half into a 5-inch (13-cm) disk. Wrap the disks in plastic wrap and refrigerate until well chilled, at least 2 hours.

4 Preheat the oven to 425°F (220°C). Line a jelly-roll pan or baking sheet with aluminum foil. Have ready a 9-inch (23-cm) pie dish. On a lightly floured work surface, roll out 1 of the pastry disks into a 14-inch (35-cm) round, dusting the rolling pin with flour to prevent sticking. Drape the pastry around the pin and ease it into the pie dish, pressing it into the bottom and sides. Cover the pastry-lined dish with plastic wrap. Roll out the other pastry disk and drape a sheet of plastic wrap over it.

5 In a large bowl, combine the apples, cranberries, brown sugar, flour, cinnamon, nutmeg, vanilla, and salt. Toss with a fork or spoon until well blended.

6 Uncover the pastry. Pile the apple mixture into the lined pie dish along with any accumulated juices. Brush the dough around the edge of the pie dish with water. Drape the second pastry circle around the pin, and then center the dough over the filling. Press the bottom and top pastry edges together. Using scissors, trim the overhang to ½ inch (12 mm) beyond the edge of the dish. Roll the overhang under to shape a high edge that rests on top of the dish rim. Crimp attractively around the rim to seal the edges together. With a paring knife, cut 3 vents in the top crust.

7 Set the pie dish on the foil-lined pan. Bake for 15 minutes. Reduce the heat to 350°F (180°C) and continue to bake until the apples are very tender when pierced with a knife through the vents, about 50 minutes. Transfer to a rack and let cool. Serve the pie warm or at room temperature.

Mangoes Flambéed with Tequila

Mangos Flameados • Jalisco • Mexico

In this simple recipe, Paula Mendoza Ramos, longtime family cook for the Romo de la Peña family, combines the voluptuously sweet mango with the slightly tart flavor of white tequila. Ice cream served alongside provides a cool contrast.

6 ripe mangoes, about 3 lb (1.5 kg) total weight

3 tablespoons dark brown sugar

3 tablespoons unsalted butter, cut into small pieces

Finely shredded zest of 1 lime

Finely shredded zest of ½ orange

1 tablespoon fresh lime juice

1 tablespoon fresh orange juice

¼ cup (2 fl oz/60 ml) tequila blanco

1 qt (1 l) coconut or French vanilla ice cream

½ cup (2 oz/60 g) shredded unsweetened coconut, toasted (page 222)

Serves 6

1 Preheat the oven to 400°F (200°C). Lightly butter an attractive shallow baking dish measuring about 9-by-13-inches (23-by-33-cm).

2 Peel and pit each mango (page 223), cutting the flesh into slices. Arrange the slices, slightly overlapping them, in the prepared dish. Sprinkle with the brown sugar and dot with the butter. Scatter the lime and orange zests over the top, then drizzle with the lime and orange juices.

3 Bake, uncovered, until the mango slices begin to brown, about 20 minutes. Though best served immediately, the mangoes can be kept warm for about 30 minutes.

4 When ready to serve, sprinkle the tequila over the mangoes and carefully ignite with a long match. Jiggle the pan for a moment until the flames die out, then divide among individual plates. Add a scoop of ice cream to each plate and sprinkle with coconut.

Strawberry-Rhubarb Crisp

The Mid-Atlantic • America

Rhubarb and strawberries grow in abundance in the fertile farmland of New York and New Jersey. Using strawberries in this crisp softens the rhubarb's sour edge, and the addition of nuts and oats to the topping delivers crunch and flavor.

1 lb (750 g) strawberries, halved or quartered

¾ lb (375 g) rhubarb, cut into ¾-inch (2-cm) pieces

1 teaspoon vanilla extract (essence)

1¼ cups (10 oz/315 g) granulated sugar

½ cup (2½ oz/80 g) all-purpose (plain) flour

1½ teaspoons finely grated lemon zest

2 pinches of salt

½ cup (1½ oz/45 g) old-fashioned rolled oats

½ cup (3½ oz/105 g) firmly packed light brown sugar

¼ cup (1½ oz/45 g) all-purpose (plain) flour

½ teaspoon ground cinnamon

6 tablespoons (3 oz/90 g) lightly chilled unsalted butter, cut into ½-inch (12-mm) pieces

⅔ cup (2½ oz/75 g) chopped walnuts or pecans

Sweetened whipped cream (page 225) (optional)

Serves 6–8

1 Preheat the oven to 375°F (190°C). Butter a shallow 2-qt (2-l) baking dish. In a bowl, toss together the strawberries, rhubarb, and vanilla. Sprinkle the granulated sugar, ¼ cup (1¼ oz/40 g) of the flour, the lemon zest, and 1 pinch of the salt over the fruits and toss gently to coat. Spread evenly in the prepared dish.

2 In a bowl, combine the oats, brown sugar, remaining ¼ cup flour, the cinnamon, and the remaining pinch of salt. Add the butter and, using a pastry blender, cut in until the butter is in small pieces and the mixture begins to hold together. Add the nuts and mix just until combined. Scatter the topping over the rhubarb.

3 Bake the crisp until the filling bubbles and the topping is browned, about 45 minutes. Remove from the oven and spoon the crisp onto individual plates. Top with whipped cream, if desired.

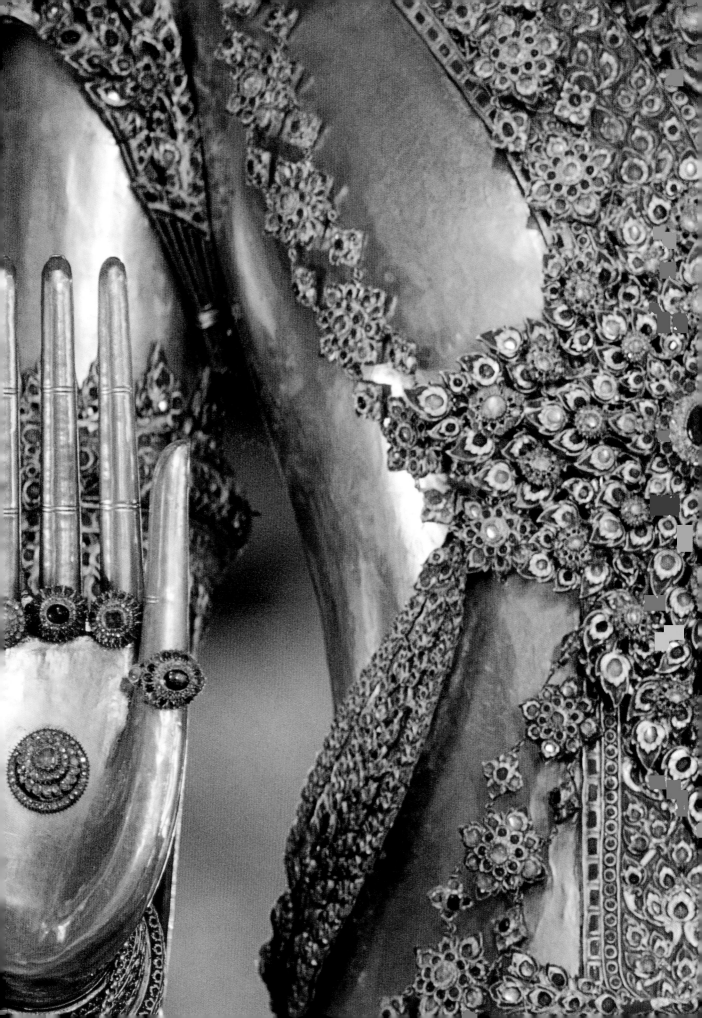

ASIA

N o cuisine is complete without its desserts, and Chinese, Indian, and Southeast Asian cuisines are no exception. The Chinese began refining cane sugar more than a millennium ago and have a history of making a wide range of confectionery, sweet pastries, dessert puddings, and candied fruit. But in devising their desserts, Chinese chefs had to work around what, to Western eyes, might seem to be two insurmountable obstacles. They had no ovens for baking and no dairy cattle (except in Muslim communities) to provide the butter, cream, and milk typically associated with the preparation of sweets. Instead, innovative Chinese cooks developed an impressive repertoire of steamed, fried, and griddle-baked pastries, including the pale sesame balls stuffed with lotus seed paste that remain popular in dim sum parlors today. For creaminess, coconut adds richness to steamed puddings

Iced sweet dishes have an interesting history as well. The Chinese have used refrigeration and freezing for thousands of years. In the far north, as far back as the Han dynasty (202 BC–AD 220), *bingshi* (ice chambers) were chipped into solid ice banks and rivers to make cold rooms for food storage. Block ice, packed in straw, was transported to the imperial residences and the homes of high officials in the south and west, so nobles in all parts of the country could serve exotic fruits over crushed ice. Serving a cone of shaved ice studded with fruit—a practice now common from Indonesia to Japan— began in that far-off time in China.

The desserts served after Indian meals are usually mellow, creamy preparations that are specially created to temper the effect of spicy food on the system. Rice pudding, which can be flavored with any number of ingredients, from coconut and cardamom to saffron and pistachios, is still the most common dish for the end of a meal, but fruit desserts such as mango fool—especially when made with the luscious Alphonso mango—are also very popular.

But what Indians are really passionate about are their *mithai*, or sweet snacks. These small bites, enjoyed throughout the day, are rich, syrupy, and sticky—just the

way Indians like them. Certain areas are famed for their expertise in preparing particular sweets; Gujarat, for example, is known for its candies, while the holy city of Varanasi has been renowned for centuries for its red fudge, made from long-cooked milk sweetened with jaggery. Sweet spices, sesame seeds, raisins, and cashews add flavor and texture in treats like saffron-sesame crunch and semolina halva. They are enjoyed whenever hunger pangs strike or when the heat in the mouth from a spicy snack needs to be neutralized. Sweet and spicy bites are often enjoyed together at teatime, washed down with a broad range of beverages from tea (especially the milky cardamom-laced brew known as chai) and coffee to fruit coolers and smooth yogurt drinks.

Fruit, of course, is available in staggering abundance throughout India. Even Western fruits like strawberries can be cultivated in the cooler, mountainous regions. Bananas are are found in abundance in southern India. Each of the four southern states has its own unique banana dessert or sweetmeat recipe, such as the delicate *kelapura*, pancakes of banana and coconut milk with a crisp exterior and a soft, spongy interior.

On the chains of islands and archipelagos that make up Thailand, Malaysia, Vietnam, Burma, Indonesia, and the Philippines, fruit is a central source of sweet refreshment. At home, most meals end with a cooling variety of seasonal fruit—perhaps a sunset-pink wedge of watermelon, a pale green serving of honeydew, or a bright platter of juicy, freshly cut orange wedges. Spectacular lichees, rambutan, dragon fruit, star fruit, and mangosteen all flourish in the tropical heat. The durian also makes its home here, inspiring euphoric devotion in some and nose-wrinkling revulsion in others. Strict rules prohibiting the bringing of durian into hotel rooms or onto trains or planes is proof of the truly powerful odor it emits. Despite its pungent reputation, shops that specialize in carefully chosen, trimmed and ready-to-eat durian can sell a single fruit for the price equivalent to a bottle of fine champagne.

Southeast Asians have a sweet tooth, but they usually satisfy it with snacks eaten between meals, bought from street vendors or bakeries. Brightly colored steamed cakes, made with glutinous-rice flour and coconut milk and flavored with jasmine, rose, or pandanus-leaf extracts, may be enjoyed with an iced Vietnamese coffee. Fried bananas are popular for breakfast or as an afternoon treat, as are bananas sliced into a "soup" of coconut milk and tapioca pearls. In restaurants, desserts are typically light, coconut puddings or custards, thickened with sago, tapioca, or, in the case of French-influenced Vietnam, eggs. Also, sweet soups are widespread in Asia and can be served either hot or cold. Like so many Asian treats, the finished dishes are refreshing, cooling, and intriguing all at once.

Left: At Calcutta's wholesale market, oranges are auctioned. The oranges of Nagpur, in Madhya Pradesh, are famous throughout India. **Above, left:** Peaches are native to China, originating near Xian. They have been cultivated for over three thousand years, but wild peach trees can still be found in remote areas of China. **Above, right:** The spire of Thatbyinnyu Temple in Bagan (Pagan), the capital of Myanmar (Burma) during its architectural golden age, is bathed in the reddish glow of the setting sun.

Coconut Caramel Flan

Banh Dua Ra Men • Vietnam

This is the Vietnamese version of classic French crème caramel. Here, it is made with the rich, tropical additions of creamy coconut milk and grated coconut.

CARAMEL

¾ cup (6 oz/185 g) sugar

½ cup (4 fl oz/125 ml) water

CUSTARD

1½ cups (12 fl oz/375 ml) milk

1½ cups (12 fl oz/375 ml) coconut milk (page 222)

⅓ cup (3 oz/90 g) sugar

4 eggs

1 teaspoon vanilla extract (essence)

¼ cup (1 oz/30 g) unsweetened grated dried coconut

Serves 8

1 Preheat the oven to 325°F (165°C). To make the caramel, put the sugar and water in a heavy saucepan over medium-high heat and heat, stirring, until the sugar dissolves. Cook without stirring until the mixture turns a rich caramel color, 8–12 minutes. Remove from the heat and immediately pour into eight ½-cup (4–fl oz/125-ml) custard cups. Tilt the dishes to coat the bottoms evenly. Set aside.

2 To make the custard, in a saucepan, combine the milk, coconut milk, and sugar. Place over medium heat and heat just until hot. Remove from the heat.

3 In a bowl, beat the eggs until blended. Slowly stir in the hot milk mixture, then mix in the vanilla. Pour the mixture through a fine-mesh sieve into a bowl. Gently fold in the dried coconut.

4 Place the caramel-lined dishes in a roasting pan. Pour enough hot water into the roasting pan to reach halfway up the sides of the dishes. Ladle the egg mixture into the dishes, dividing evenly.

5 Bake until the custard is set and a knife inserted into the middle of a custard comes out clean, 30–35 minutes. Remove the custards from the water bath and let cool. Cover and refrigerate to chill well before serving.

6 To serve, run a knife around the edge of the custards and invert onto individual plates.

VIETNAMESE COFFEE

In the city of Hanoi, cafés became part of the urban landscape with the French colonization of Vietnam, and today they offer good people watching as well as croissants, baguettes, and butter, and Vietnam's strong, fragrant coffee.

The Vietnamese tend coffee plants in the highlands and treat the harvested beans to a dark French roast. Coffee is brewed at the table in a metal filter that fits over a cup or glass, and it may take up to twenty minutes of agonizingly slow dripping before the last drop falls. An order of *ca phe* will deliver a cup of black coffee, while *ca phe sua* is coffee with sweetened condensed milk, *ca phe da* is iced coffee, and *ca phe da sua* is iced coffee with sweetened milk.

To make *ca phe sua*, unscrew the filter, lift off the top, place 2 tablespoons French-roast coffee into the bottom, then replace the filter top. Pour 3 tablespoons sweetened condensed milk into a cup, top with the filter, and moisten the grounds with a little hot water. Let steep for 30 seconds, then fill the filter to the top with hot water and allow it to drip slowly into the cup.

Saffron Sesame Crunch

Gajjak • Gujarat • India

Making candies is a special skill, and no region in India is as well known for the craft as Gujarat. Almost any combination of nuts and spices can be used in the Indian version of nut brittle. Almonds, walnuts, pecans, macadamias, pine nuts, pistachios, and cashew nuts are particularly tasty and attractive. Cardamom is the most common flavoring, although *gajjak* is occasionally flavored with ginger, clove, and cassia bud. A Persian influence can be seen here with the addition of rose water.

1 teaspoon unsalted butter

1½ cups (12 oz/375 g) sugar

1 cup (4 oz/125 g) sunflower seeds

½ cup (2½ oz/75 g) sesame seeds

1 teaspoon ground cardamom

½ teaspoon saffron threads

1 drop rose extract (essence) or
½ teaspoon rose water

Makes about 1 lb (500 g)

1 Use the butter to grease a rolling pin and a 10-inch (25-cm) square area on a large baking sheet. Set aside.

2 In a saucepan over medium heat, melt the sugar, stirring constantly with a wooden spoon to avoid the formation of hot spots that will make the sugar burn and taste bitter. As soon as the sugar turns caramel colored, after about 10 minutes, add the sunflower seeds, sesame seeds, cardamom, saffron, and rose essence or rose water and mix quickly.

3 Working swiftly, pour the contents onto the greased area of the baking sheet. Using the greased rolling pin, spread the mixture into as thin a sheet as possible, about 10 inches (25 cm) square.

4 Let cool completely, then cut or break the brittle into pieces about 2 inches (5 cm) wide. Store the pieces in an airtight container, separating each layer with parchment (baking) paper, for up to 6 months.

Banana Coconut Pancakes

Kelapura • Tamil Nadu • India

Kelapura (*kela* means "banana" and *pura* is "bread" or "pancake") are served all over southern India, where there is an abundance of banana and coconut palms. Any number of ingredients can be added to the basic batter: Indians like ripe mangoes, guava, and persimmon. You can also add nuts such as toasted cashews, pistachios, and pine nuts. If rice flour is unavailable, use an equal amount of cream of rice cereal and let the batter rest for fifteen minutes to soften the larger grains before making the pancakes.

1 In a medium bowl, combine the all-purpose flour, rice flour, coconut milk, milk, sugar, and baking powder. Beat with a whisk or electric mixer until a smooth, lump-free batter forms. Gently fold in the banana.

2 Pry open the cardamom pods, remove the seeds, and grind them to a powder. (This is best done using a mortar and pestle; you can also wrap the seeds in plastic wrap and crush them with a mallet or rolling pin.) Discard the skins. Add the ground cardamom to the batter and mix well.

3 In a nonstick frying pan, pour in oil to a depth of ¼ inch (6 mm) and place over high heat. When hot, add a heaping tablespoonful of batter to the pan to form each pancake. (The number of pancakes you can cook at one time will depend upon the size of the pan. You can also vary their size to suit your preference.) Cook until the undersides are brown and the edges begin to crisp, about 2 minutes. Turn and cook until the second side is nicely browned, about 1 minute longer.

4 If serving the pancakes immediately, keep them warm in a low oven while you cook the remaining batter in the same way, adding more oil as needed. If making the pancakes ahead of time, set aside, covered, until ready to serve. To reheat, place a nonstick frying pan over high heat. When hot, add the pancakes, one at a time, and warm them through for about 30 seconds. Alternatively, warm the pancakes, loosely wrapped in aluminum foil, in a preheated 375°F (190°C) oven for about 8 minutes.

½ cup (2½ oz/75 g) all-purpose (plain) flour

½ cup (2½ oz/75 g) rice flour

1¼ cups (10 fl oz/310 ml) coconut milk

½ cup (4 fl oz/125 ml) milk

⅓ cup (2½ oz/75 g) jaggery (page 223) or brown sugar

½ teaspoon baking powder

1 ripe banana, peeled and mashed

8 green cardamom pods

Vegetable oil for frying

Serves 8

Mango Pudding

Mang Guo Buding • Southern • China

Although Chinese cuisine is indisputably one of the most expansive in the world, little attention is paid to desserts. Members of the younger generations, however, have more of a sweet tooth. This pudding, an inspired borrowing from the kitchens of South Asia, has been absorbed into the dim sum repertoire in Hong Kong and Guangdong.

½ cup (3 oz/90 g) small pearl tapioca or sago pearls (page 225)

1 can (14 oz/440 g) sliced mango, drained, with liquid reserved, and the flesh puréed

⅓ cup (4 fl oz/125 ml) water

⅓ cup (3 oz/90 g) superfine (caster) sugar

½ cup (4 fl oz/125 ml) coconut cream

Serves 4–6

1 Pour the tapioca into a saucepan and rinse well with cold water. Drain. Measure out 1 cup (8 fl oz/250 ml) of the reserved mango liquid and add it to the saucepan (discard the remainder) along with the water and sugar. Bring to a boil over medium-high heat, reduce the heat to medium-low, and simmer, stirring frequently, until almost all of the tapioca pearls are translucent, about 20 minutes.

2 Add the coconut cream and simmer gently until the pudding is thick and no white pearls remain, about 6 minutes.

3 Stir in the mango purée, divide the mixture evenly among small individual serving bowls, cover, and refrigerate until firm. Serve the pudding chilled.

Semolina Halva with Raisins

Kesari · Tamil Nadu · India

Halva is a sweetmeat made of various syrup-soaked ingredients. Crushed sesame seeds are commonly used in the Middle East; this Indian version has a base of semolina. It gets its name from its principal flavoring, saffron (or *kesar* in Sanskrit).

4 tablespoons *usli ghee* (page 222)

½ cup (3 oz/90 g) raisins or golden raisins (sultanas)

½ cup (2½ oz/75 g) chopped cashew nuts or blanched almonds (page 223)

1 cup (5 oz/155 g) fine-grind semolina

6 green cardamom pods

2¼ cups (22 fl oz/680 ml) water

¾ cup (6 oz/185 g) sugar

½ teaspoon saffron threads, lightly crushed

Serves 8

1 In a large, shallow pan over medium-high heat, combine 2 tablespoons of the *usli ghee*, the raisins, and the cashews. Fry, stirring and tossing gently, until the nuts are golden, about 2 minutes. Transfer to a plate and set aside. Add the remaining *usli ghee* and the semolina to the pan and cook, stirring constantly, until the semolina is golden brown, about 4 minutes. Transfer to another plate and set aside.

2 Pry open the cardamom pods, remove the seeds, and grind them to a powder. (This is best done using a mortar and pestle; you can also wrap the seeds in plastic wrap and crush them with a mallet or rolling pin.) Discard the skins.

3 Wipe the pan clean, add the water and sugar, and bring to a boil over medium-high heat, stirring often. Continue stirring until the sugar dissolves, then cook, without stirring, for 5 minutes more until the liquid thickens to a syrupy consistency. Stir in the saffron. Reduce the heat to low, add the semolina, and cook, stirring, until the mixture thickens to the consistency of oatmeal, about 2 minutes. Continue to cook, stirring, until the semolina is fully cooked and soft, about 5 minutes. Add the cardamom and fried raisins and nuts. Mix well, remove from the heat, and let cool.

4 When cool enough to handle, firmly pack small portions of the halva into small, ungreased molds, such as mini muffin pans or tart shells. When completely cool, unmold and serve, or cover and refrigerate for up to 5 days.

TEA

Tea plants grow wild in the cool, wet climes of the northern Himalayas and are believed to date back to antiquity. Indians, who are generally associated with drinking black tea, also drink green tea—not just plain green tea, but aromatic varieties flavored with ingredients such as saffron, yak butter, *usli ghee,* mountain herbs, and salt.

Many families grow tea, just enough for their own consumption, in their backyard. The habit of drinking black tea with milk and sugar was introduced to India in the eighteenth century, during the British Raj.

The English are also credited with starting large-scale tea cultivation in Darjeeling and Assam, areas that are today considered to be the world's top producers of black tea. Among the most famous types of black tea is delicious Darjeeling orange pekoe.

Thoroughly Indianized by the addition of aromatic spices such as cinnamon, cardamom, clove, and ginger, tea—called *chai* in Hindi—is the beverage of choice in northern India. Coffee is popular in southern India, where it is roasted and freshly ground each day and served with milk.

Baked Semolina Pudding with Sesame Seeds

Sarnwin Makin • Myanmar (Burma)

The semolina (called *sooji* by the Indians, *shwegi* by the Burmese), cardamom, and ghee in this Burmese sweet reflect the Indian influence on local cooking.

1 cup (5 oz/160 ml) fine semolina flour

½ teaspoon ground cardamom

¼ teaspoon salt

2 cups (16 fl oz/500 ml) coconut milk

2 cups (16 fl oz/500 ml) water

¾ cup (5 oz/155 g) firmly packed palm sugar (page 224)

¼ cup (2 oz/60 g) ghee or unsalted butter

2 egg whites, lightly whisked

¼ cup (1½ oz/45 g) blanched almonds

2 tablespoons sesame seeds, toasted

Serves 8

1 In a dry frying pan over medium-low heat, toast the semolina flour, stirring frequently, until light golden brown, 8–10 minutes. Remove from the heat and let cool. Stir in the cardamom and salt.

2 Preheat the oven to 325°F (165°C). Lightly butter or oil an 8-by-13-inch (20-by-33-cm) cake pan.

3 In a saucepan over medium heat, combine the coconut milk, water, and palm sugar. Heat, stirring, until the mixture is smooth and well blended. Gradually pour in the semolina, whisking continuously to prevent lumping. When the mixture is smooth, continue cooking and stirring until you have a thick, dense mixture that pulls away from the sides and bottom of the pan, about 10 minutes. As you stir, you should be able to see the bottom of the pan easily. Beat in the ghee, a small amount at a time, and continue cooking until well incorporated. Remove from the heat and let cool slightly.

4 Add the egg whites and mix thoroughly. Pour the mixture into the prepared pan. Decorate with the almonds and then sprinkle with the sesame seeds.

5 Bake until golden brown and firm to the touch, about 1 hour. Transfer to a wire rack and let cool completely. Cut into diamonds and serve.

Bananas and Tapioca in Coconut Milk

Chuoi Chung • Vietnam

A sweet soup of bananas stewed in coconut milk is a popular afternoon snack in Vietnam. The pearl tapioca adds a satisfying texture. Serve this dessert hot or warm.

6 ripe bananas, peeled and cut crosswise into thirds

2 teaspoons salt

6 cups (48 fl oz/1.5 l) water

¾ cup (4 oz/125 g) pearl tapioca

⅔ cup (5 oz/155 g) sugar

1 tablespoon cornstarch (cornflour), mixed with 3 tablespoons water

1 can (13½ fl oz/420 ml) coconut milk (page 222)

Serves 6

1 Place the bananas in a large bowl and add water to cover and ½ teaspoon of the salt. Set aside.

2 In a saucepan over high heat, bring the 6 cups (48 fl oz/1.5 l) water to a boil. Add the pearl tapioca, reduce the heat to low, and simmer until the pearls are clear, about 10 minutes. Add the sugar and the remaining 1½ teaspoons salt and stir to dissolve.

3 Stir in the diluted cornstarch until the liquid is lightly thickened, 2–3 minutes. Drain the bananas and add to the saucepan along with the coconut milk. Cook over medium heat until the bananas are tender but firm, about 5 minutes.

4 Remove the pan from the heat and divide the bananas and liquid evenly among individual bowls and serve.

"Open Mouth Laughs"

Kou Xiao Gao • Northern • China

Once you've tasted these sugar-dusted balls, you won't stop at one! Be sure to cook them in oil that is not too hot. In order for them to burst open into "laughing mouths," they must heat and expand from the inside before the outer surface has sealed.

½ cup (3½ oz/105 g) superfine (caster) sugar

1 tablespoon butter or lard, at room temperature

1 egg

2 tablespoons water

1¼ cups (9 oz/280 g) all-purpose (plain) flour

1½ teaspoons baking powder

Oil for deep-frying

2–3 tablespoons superfine (caster) or confectioners' (icing) sugar

Makes 18; serves 6–8

1 In a food processor, combine the ½ cup sugar, butter or lard, egg, and water and process until smooth. Slowly add the flour and baking powder, using the pulse control, to make a soft dough. Alternatively, in a bowl, beat the sugar and butter or lard until creamy. Beat in the egg and then slowly work in the flour, baking powder, and water to make a soft dough. With wet hands, form the dough into 18 balls, each about 1 inch (2.5 cm) in diameter.

2 Pour the oil to a depth of 2 inches (5 cm) into a wok or deep, heavy frying pan, and heat over high heat to 300°F (150°C). Reduce the heat to medium-high, add all of the balls, and fry them slowly, pushing them under the oil to encourage them to rise and split. The oil will gradually increase in temperature to about 350°F (180°C). Cook the balls until golden brown, 2½–3 minutes. Using a wire skimmer or slotted spoon, transfer to paper towels to drain.

3 Sprinkle the balls with the 2–3 tablespoons sugar, and serve warm or cold.

CHINESE FESTIVALS

Spring heralds the first of China's annual festivities, as the vast nation celebrates the arrival of the new lunar year. The flying of kites in Waifang (Shandong), the lighting of torches in Yunnan, the ripening of the grapes in Turpan (Xinjiang), and the mass singing of folk songs in Xining (Qinghai) are all events that have shaped China's packed calendar of festivals. The joy of life, the beauty of nature, and obeisance to gods and ancestors are the enduring themes.

The New Year's Eve feast is the first of many celebratory meals of the Chinese lunar year. New Year falls in late January to early February according to the moon, and within the annual holiday of up to two weeks are three days of energetically observed festivities, enjoyed with feasting and visiting. The kitchen god's mouth is smeared with honey to sweeten his report on the state of the house. Rice is washed and eaten to bring prosperity. Gifts of food are offered to gods and friends, and sweet puddings and pastries are presented to and shared with loved ones.

The Lantern Festival originated in Chengdu in Sichuan province in the Tang dynasty some fifteen hundred years ago. On the fifteenth day of the first lunar month, pagodas and pavilions are hung with strings of lights. Thousands of candle-illuminated lanterns are floated on lakes and rivers or carried in procession to the highest point, to represent the return of the sun after the winter months. Glutinous rice and taro dumplings are distributed to children and friends.

On the fifth day of the fifth moon, the Dragon Boat Festival is celebrated wherever there are convenient waterways in which to hold the symbolic boat races and toss tributes of leaf-wrapped, sticky rice cakes.

The Moon Festival is celebrated in August, when the moon is at its fullest. Melons and other round fruits symbolic of the moon's round face are placed outdoors as tributes. Moon cakes of flaky or shortcrust pastry filled with sweet lotus or bean paste, or spicy ground (minced) meat, are stamped with traditional insignia and offered as symbols of friendship and appreciation.

The solemn ritual of the Tomb-Sweeping Festival turns into an enjoyable springtime outing for the family. Everyone proceeds to the graveside of the family ancestors to sweep, weed, and tidy the tombs. Obeisance is made, incense is lit, and offerings are set out, then everyone returns home to a lavish family feast in which pork is a tribute to the ancestors and rice or another grain represents continuance and growth.

Sago in Coconut Milk Pudding with Palm Sugar

Sago Gula Melaka • Malaysia

In Malaysia, *gula Melaka* translates literally as "Malacca sugar." But when you ask for *gula Melaka* in a Malaysian restaurant, you will get this popular pudding of sago pearls, thick and creamy coconut milk, and a drizzle of palm sugar syrup.

1 cup (6 oz/185 g) sago pearls (page 225) or pearl tapioca

8 cups (64 fl oz/2 l) water

SYRUP

¼-lb (125-g) block dark palm sugar, shaved

2 tablespoons treacle or dark molasses

¾ cup (6 fl oz/180 ml) water

1 pandanus leaf, scraped with the tines of a fork (page 224)

Pinch of salt

1 cup (8 fl oz/250 ml) thick coconut milk (page 222)

Serves 6

1 If using sago, pick over for any large impurities, then place in a sieve and shake to release any dust and dirt. If using pearl tapioca, you do not have to clean it. In a saucepan, bring the water to a boil. Add the sago or tapioca in a steady stream, stirring continuously to keep the pearls separated. Continue cooking until the pearls swell and become transparent, about 10 minutes. Pour into a fine sieve and rinse thoroughly with cold water. Divide the sago among 6 small custard cups, cover, and refrigerate until set, about 1½ hours.

2 To make the syrup, in a saucepan, combine the palm sugar, treacle, water, pandanus leaf, and salt. Bring to a boil over high heat, stirring continuously until the sugar is dissolved. Continue cooking until the mixture reduces to 1 cup (8 fl oz/ 250 ml), 5–8 minutes. Remove from the heat and let cool. Remove and discard the pandanus leaf.

3 To serve, unmold each custard cup into a shallow bowl. Pour an equal amount of the coconut milk and syrup over each portion. Serve immediately.

Cardamom Cheese Cake

Paneer Mithai • Maharashtra • India

Paneer mithai was traditionally made as a *barfi,* or fudge, using the Indian *chenna* cheese. With the introduction of Western-style ovens during the British Raj, Indian cooks began baking it like a cheesecake. If kewra extract is unavailable, use an equal amount of either rose or vanilla extract. Commercial breadcrumbs are unsuitable for this recipe because the bread is not trimmed and the crusts give the crumbs an uneven brown color.

12 green cardamom pods

2 lb (1 kg) ricotta cheese

2 cups (4 oz/125 g) fresh bread crumbs, made from about 8 slices of white bread, trimmed of crusts and processed in a food processor to produce fluffy crumbs

⅔ cup (5 oz/155 g) sugar

7 tablespoons (3½ oz/105 g) unsalted butter, melted

½ teaspoon *each* almond extract (essence) and kewra extract (essence) (page 223)

½ cup (2 oz/60 g) sliced (flaked) almonds

Strawberry Sauce (optional; page 87)

Serves 6–9

1 Preheat the oven to 325°F (165°C). Butter a 9-inch (23-cm) square baking pan.

2 Pry open the cardamom pods, remove the seeds, and grind them to a powder. (This is best done using a mortar and pestle; you can also wrap the seeds in plastic wrap and crush them with a mallet or rolling pin.) You will need 1½ teaspoons ground cardamom. Discard the skins.

3 In a large bowl, stir together the ricotta, bread crumbs, sugar, melted butter, cardamom, almond extract, and kewra extract. Spoon into the prepared pan. Smooth the top and sprinkle with the almonds.

4 Bake until the top is golden, about 1¼ hours. Remove and let cool completely. Cut into 3-inch (7.5-cm) squares and serve with the Strawberry Sauce, if desired.

Sesame Lotus Balls

Zhima Lianzi Qiu • Eastern • China

The edible oval seeds of the lotus plant are ground and cooked with sugar to make a sweet paste used for filling buns and pastries. Lotus seed paste is sold ready-made in cans.

2 cups (8 oz/250 g) glutinous rice flour

3 tablespoons superfine (caster) sugar

¾ cup (6 fl oz/180 ml) water

1 cup (10 oz/315 g) sweetened lotus seed paste (see note)

⅔ cup (2 oz/60 g) sesame seeds

Vegetable oil for deep-frying

Makes 15

1 In a large bowl, combine the rice flour, sugar, and water and stir until well mixed. Then, using your hands, knead the dough in the bowl until it is soft and smooth. Turn out onto a lightly oiled work surface and, using your palms, roll the dough into a log 15 inches (38 cm) long. Cut into 15 equal pieces each 1 inch (2.5 cm) thick. Roll out each piece into a round about 2½ inches (6 cm) in diameter.

2 Divide the lotus paste into 15 equal pieces, and roll each piece into a ball. Place a ball of paste in the center of each dough round, and draw the dough up around it to form a ball, pinching the edges together at the top. Lightly oil your hands and gently roll each ball into a smooth, round sphere.

3 Spread out the sesame seeds onto a plate. One at a time, roll the balls in the sesame seeds to coat evenly.

4 Pour the oil to a depth of 2 inches (5 cm) into a wok or deep, heavy frying pan, and heat to 325°F (165°C), or until a small cube of bread dropped into the oil begins to turn golden after about 1 minute. Add the balls all at once and fry until puffed and golden, about 2½ minutes. Using a wire skimmer or slotted spoon, transfer to paper towels to drain. Serve warm or at room temperature.

THE LOTUS

The lotus is an elegant water plant that proliferates in lakes throughout China. Some of the most majestic examples grow in the famed West Lake waterways beside the city of Hangzhou. Buddha ascribed a sacred status to the lotus, making it a symbol of purity and fertility: Purity can be attained from the lowliest beginnings, as shown by the beautiful lotus growing from the sludgy mud of a pond or lake. That the lotus is highly prolific is indisputable. One small plant can grow to cover a massive waterway in a very short time.

But if the lotus plant takes something for itself, it gives back tenfold. Blossoms of fragile beauty in yellow, pink, white, blue, and lavender are inedible, but are used as garnishes. Leaves as big as rafts can be employed as umbrellas against a sudden downpour, or dried for use as food wrappers. Delve beneath the mud in which the lotus has taken root and you will find long, hollow tubers that can be cooked as a tender but crunchy vegetable, or sugar-coated as candy.

As if all of that were not enough, the edible seeds of the plant also have many popular culinary uses. The nutty flavor of lotus seeds is utilized and appreciated in both sweet and savory dishes, and they can also be boiled with sugar and mashed to a thick paste to fill sweet buns and pastries.

Candied Apples

Basi Pingguo • Northern • China

Long before red eating apples were introduced to China, quinces and crabapples were available. In Kaifeng, the sugared and honeyed fruit was being sold by street vendors one thousand years ago, and a few hundred years before that, during the Tang dynasty, crabapples steeped in honey and cinnabar were eaten as an elixir of life. Here, tart apples are coated in hot toffee; diners dip the hot pieces in ice water before eating.

1 Fill a bowl three-fourths full of lightly salted water, add the apple wedges, and let soak for 10 minutes. Drain and spread to dry on a kitchen towel.

2 Place ⅓ cup (1¾ oz/50 g) of the flour in a paper or plastic bag, add the apple wedges, close the top of the bag, and shake well to coat the apple wedges evenly with the flour.

3 In a bowl, beat the egg lightly until well blended. Beat in the remaining ⅓ cup (1¾ oz/50 g) flour, the cornstarch, and the water to make a thin batter.

4 Pour the oil to a depth of 2 inches (5 cm) into a wok or deep, heavy frying pan, and heat to 350°F (180°C), or until a few drops of the batter dropped into the oil almost immediately float to the surface. Dip half of the apple wedges into the batter, coating evenly, and add to the oil. Fry, stirring and turning the pieces with a slotted spoon to prevent them from sticking together, until golden, about 1½ minutes. Using a wire skimmer or slotted spoon, transfer to a serving plate. Repeat with the remaining apple wedges and batter and add to the first batch.

5 Pour off the oil into a heatproof container. Add the sugar, sesame oil, and the lard, if using, to the pan and cook, stirring continually, until the sugar is golden brown, 3–4 minutes. Carefully add the water and allow it to bubble briefly, then add the fried apple wedges and quickly turn to coat them with the toffee. Using the wire skimmer or slotted spoon, return the apple wedges to the plate.

6 Immediately place the ice cubes in a bowl, fill it with water, and set the bowl on the table with the plate of apple wedges. Using chopsticks or a dessert fork, each guest selects a piece of hot apple and holds it in the iced water for 10 seconds until the toffee hardens before eating it.

2 tart apples, peeled, cored, and cut into wedges ⅓ inch (9 mm) thick

⅔ cup (3½ oz/100 g) all-purpose (plain) flour

1 egg

⅓ cup (1½ oz/45 g) cornstarch (cornflour)

½ cup (4 fl oz/125 ml) water

Vegetable oil for deep-frying

⅓ cup (2½ oz/75 g) superfine (caster) sugar

2 teaspoons sesame oil

2 teaspoons vegetable shortening (optional)

1½ tablespoons water

Ice cubes

Serves 6–8

Lotus and Tangerine Sweet Soup

Juzi Lianzi Xingren · Eastern · China

Clear sweet soups are an important category of Chinese desserts. They are considered cooling and sometimes medicinally beneficial. An imaginative variety of ingredients can be added such as crunchy-textured white fungus, scarlet wolfberries, and gelatinous edible bird's nest. Gingko nuts, red dates, and cherries are also favorite additions. Indeed, nearly any fresh fruit can be served in a sweet soup. Fresh lotus root must be well scrubbed and thickly peeled before use. If unavailable, substitute water chestnuts.

⅓ cup (1½ oz/45 g) dried lotus seeds, soaked in water for 2 hours and drained

4 cups (32 fl oz/1 l) cold water

¾ cup (6 oz/185 g) crushed rock sugar or superfine (caster) sugar

3-oz (90-g) piece lotus root, peeled and thinly sliced crosswise

3 tangerines, peeled and sectioned

Serves 6–8

1 In a small saucepan over high heat, combine the soaked lotus seeds with hot water to cover. Bring to a boil, reduce the heat to low, and simmer, uncovered, until partially tender, about 15 minutes.

2 In another saucepan over medium heat, combine the cold water and sugar and bring to a boil, stirring to dissolve the sugar. Add the drained lotus seeds and simmer, uncovered, for 15 minutes. Add the lotus root and continue to simmer until the lotus root and seeds are tender, 10 minutes longer.

3 Carefully remove the white pith and seeds from the tangerine sections. Add the sections to the syrup. Simmer over low heat, uncovered, until the tangerine is slightly transparent, about 10 minutes. Let cool and serve at room temperature, or chill before serving.

Banana Fritters on a Stick

Pisang Goreng • Indonesia

Most visitors to Southeast Asia think of banana fritters as dessert. In Indonesia, however, they are also enjoyed for breakfast or as a snack. The fritters are best when made with the small thin-skinned bananas found in Southeast Asia. Thais prefer a small, firm banana called *gluay nam wah,* which tends to be particularly sweet, is the perfect size, and stays fairly firm when cooked. Indonesians are partial to the larger sweet king banana, or *raja.*

1 cup (5 oz/155 g) all-purpose (plain) flour, or as needed

½ cup (2 oz/60 g) rice flour

2 teaspoons baking powder

½ teaspoon salt

1 cup (8 fl oz/250 ml) water, or as needed

Vegetable oil for deep-frying

8 small, firm bananas, peeled

Confectioners' (icing) sugar or ground cinnamon

2 limes, cut into wedges

Serves 4

1 In a bowl, sift together the 1 cup all-purpose flour, rice flour, baking powder, and salt. Stir in the 1 cup water to make a smooth, thick pancakelike batter. Adjust the consistency by adding more all-purpose flour or water.

2 Pour the oil to a depth of 2 inches (5 cm) in a wok or deep frying pan and heat to 350°F (180°C) on a deep-frying thermometer. Spear one end of a banana with a bamboo skewer, running the skewer all the way through to the other end, then dip it into the batter, coating evenly. Carefully lower the battered banana into the hot oil, leaving the skewer in. Repeat with as many more bananas as will fit in the pan without crowding. Deep-fry the bananas until they are crisp and golden, about 3 minutes. Using a slotted utensil, transfer to paper towels to drain.

3 Serve the bananas hot, still on their skewers. Dust with confectioners' sugar or cinnamon. Each diner squeezes lime juice over his or her serving.

TROPICAL FRUITS

Southeast Asians treasure their bountiful variety of fruits, tropical and subtropical specimens that delight the eye and the palate. The Vietnamese delight in the dragon fruit, a stunning sphere with a reddish pink exterior that has the texture of banana skin and a handful of spikes tipped with emerald green. The white flesh has a subtle crispness, much like an Asian pear, and is flecked with tiny black seeds. It can be difficult to eat because it is so beautiful.

Although the local favorite throughout the region is the big, spiky durian, many simply can't get beyond its notorious odor and strong flavor. Fortunately, there are many other choices: crisp, tart, juicy star fruits and red-husked, deliciously sweet mangosteens; lichees, with their strawberry-red skins and shiny white translucent flesh; full-flavored stubby finger bananas and large cooking bananas; and football-sized papayas and golden mangoes that are the sweetest in the world. There is also the blush-colored, faintly sweet rose apple;

the teardrop-shaped *salak*, also called snake fruit for the brown triangular scales that make up its skin; the rambutan, a bright red or yellow-green fruit with hairy spikes and juicy, tart pulp; and the more commonplace watermelon and pineapple.

When in the mood for a cooling snack, many Southeast Asians head for a fresh-fruit vendor at a hawker center, who makes up a plate from whatever the customer points out in the usually large display. If they are thirsty, they order a glass of freshly squeezed star-fruit, watermelon, or sugarcane juice. And many Southeast Asians can almost never pass a stand with young, green coconuts without stopping. The vendor whacks off the top of the nut and sticks a straw in the hole, through which one slowly sips the cool liquid contained inside—guaranteed to hit the spot on even the hottest day. Fruits are also the everyday dessert for Southeast Asians. They are healthful and satisfying and just the right finish to a meal of highly seasoned dishes.

Rum and Cashew Nut Ice Cream with Strawberry Sauce

Kaju Ice Cream • Goa • India

Strawberry ka Sas • Uttaranchal • India

Cashew nuts, introduced to Goa in the fifteenth century, are a favorite Goan ingredient. This dessert will be slightly grainy and crystalline if not made with an ice-cream maker.

ICE CREAM

2 teaspoons *usli ghee* (page 222) or walnut oil

½ cup (3 oz/90 g) chopped cashew nuts

3 cups (24 fl oz/750 ml) light (single) cream

⅔ cup (5 oz/155 g) sugar

4 eggs, separated

1 teaspoon vanilla extract (essence)

¼ cup (2 fl oz/60 ml) Indian rum or good-quality Caribbean rum

STRAWBERRY SAUCE

3 pints (24 oz/750 g) strawberries, stemmed and cut into 1-inch (2.5-cm) pieces

7 tablespoons (3½ oz/105 g) sugar

2 tablespoons cashew fenni or any fruit-flavored brandy

1 tablespoon crème de cassis or black currant syrup

Makes 2½ pints (40 fl oz/1.25 l) ice cream and 3½ cups (28 fl oz/875 ml) sauce; serves 8

1 To make the ice cream, in a small frying pan over medium-high heat, warm the *usli ghee* or oil. When hot, add the cashews and fry, stirring constantly to ensure that it browns evenly, until light brown, about 4 minutes. Using a slotted spoon, transfer to paper towels to drain. Set aside.

2 In a large, heavy pan over medium-high heat, bring the cream and sugar to a boil, stirring constantly, then immediately remove from the heat.

3 In a bowl, lightly beat the egg yolks. Gradually whisk in 1 cup (8 fl oz/250 ml) of the hot cream until blended and smooth. Stir this mixture into the cream remaining in the pan. Cook over medium-low heat, stirring constantly, until the custard is thick enough to coat the back of a metal spoon, about 10 minutes. Remove from the heat.

4 In a large bowl, beat the egg whites until soft peaks form. Fold in the hot custard until the mixture is well blended. Stir in the vanilla and let the mixture cool completely.

5 The ice cream can be made in an ice-cream maker or food processor. If using an ice-cream maker, pour the cooled custard into the machine and freeze according to the manufacturer's instructions. Add the rum and the fried cashews halfway during the freezing, before the ice cream begins to harden and set.

6 If using a food processor, stir the rum into the cooled custard, then pour the mixture into ice-cube trays and place in the freezer until completely frozen, about 4 hours. Transfer the frozen cubes to zip-lock freezer bags and return them to the freezer. When ready to serve, transfer 8 frozen ice-cream cubes to a food processor and process quickly until the cubes are thoroughly crushed and creamy. Add some cashew nuts in the last 5 seconds of processing, to avoid them being completely pulverized. (Further mixing can be done while scooping the ice cream for serving.) Working swiftly, spoon the ice cream into dessert bowls. Repeat with the remaining cubes and cashews.

7 To make the Strawberry Sauce, place the strawberries in a nonaluminum pan. Add the sugar, toss to combine, and let the berries sit for 15 minutes to draw out the juices.

8 Place the pan over medium heat and cook, stirring frequently, until the fruit is soft and the syrup is bubbling, about 6 minutes. Remove from the heat and stir in the fenni and cassis. If not serving immediately, pour into warmed jars, let cool, then cover and keep refrigerated for up to 5 days.

9 Scoop the ice cream into dessert bowls and top with the strawberry sauce.

Steamed Sponge Cake

Ma La Gao • Southern • China

Anyone trained in conventional baking arts may be surprised at the light texture of this steamed sponge cake. Beneath its delicate honey taste is a subtle flavor drawn from the bamboo steamer. This classic dish appears on the menu in many dim sum restaurants.

2 teaspoons plus ½ cup (4 oz/125 g) butter or margarine, at room temperature

½ cup (3½ oz/105 g) superfine (caster) sugar

½ cup (6 oz/185 g) honey

4 eggs

1 teaspoon vanilla extract (essence)

2½ teaspoons baking powder

1½ cups (7½ oz/235 g) all-purpose (plain) flour

½ cup (4 fl oz/125 ml) milk, at room temperature

Serves 6–8

1 Cut out a piece of parchment (baking) paper to fit the bottom of a 9-inch (23-cm) steamer basket precisely, place in the basket, and thickly grease the parchment with the 2 teaspoons butter or margarine.

2 Set a steamer base half filled with hot water over high heat, and bring to a boil.

3 Meanwhile, in a food processor, combine the sugar, honey, eggs, the ½ cup butter or margarine, and the vanilla extract and blend until smooth. Add the baking powder, flour, and milk and beat until a smooth, thick batter forms. Pour the batter into the prepared steamer basket.

4 Place the basket over the boiling water, cover, and reduce to a steady simmer. Cook, replenishing with extra boiling water as needed to maintain the original level, until the cake looks spongy and well risen and feels dry on the surface, about 30 minutes.

5 Remove from the steamer, allow to cool for about 5 minutes, and then cut the cake into wedges to serve.

Mango Fool

Aamphal · Maharashtra · India

This dessert comes from Bombay, home to the superb Alphonso mango. Its bright orange pulp is buttery smooth with a liquorlike aroma. The English believe that mango fool is an Indian interpretation of their classic pudding, but Indians think the name is a mispronunciation of *manga phal*. *Manga* is the original Sanskrit name for mango, and *phal* means "fruit."

4 cups (32 fl oz/1 l) milk

6 tablespoons (3 oz/60 g) custard powder (page 222)

½ cup (4 oz/125 g) sugar

1 teaspoon vanilla extract (essence)

1 cup (8 fl oz/250 ml) fresh mango purée, from Alphonso mangoes if possible, or canned purée

½ cup (4 fl oz/125 ml) heavy (double) cream, whipped to stiff peaks

¼ cup (1 oz/30 g) sliced pistachios

Serves 8

1 In a small bowl, combine ½ cup (4 fl oz/125 ml) of the milk with the custard powder. Mix with a fork until the custard powder is fully dissolved.

2 In a large, heavy pan over medium-high heat, bring the remaining 3½ cups (28 fl oz/875 ml) milk to a boil, stirring constantly. Remove from the heat.

3 Add 1 cup (8 fl oz/250 ml) of the hot milk to the custard powder solution and gradually whisk until blended and smooth. Return the mixture to the hot milk in the pan. Cook over medium-low heat, stirring constantly, until the custard is thick enough to coat the back of a metal spoon, about 10 minutes. Add the sugar and vanilla and cook for 1 minute longer.

4 Remove from the heat, stir in the mango purée, and let cool. Fold the whipped cream into the mango mixture and spoon into dessert glasses. Sprinkle with the pistachios, cover, and refrigerate. Serve well chilled.

FRANCE

*N*o matter how simple or how elaborate a French meal might be, dessert is an essential part. Something sweet, as the French like to say, brings closure to the repast. For fancier meals, fruit is a course in itself, offered after cheese and before a sweet, but often a bowl of fruit is served as the dessert, especially at home. Thus a dessert can range from a single apple or orange, peeled at the table, to glamorous confections of chocolate and intricate cream-filled pastries. Between the two extremes are homemade cakes and tarts, custards and puddings, cookies, ice creams, and sorbets.

In every French region, city, town, and village, one finds that French institution, the pâtisserie. Virtually every day of the year, pastry shops supply the ornate creations that few French men or women make at home. They don't need to: They can be assured of a fine cake or tart from the pâtisserie, made with top-quality eggs, cream, chocolate, sugar, and fruit that will satisfy the desire for a delectable and beautiful dessert.

Walking the streets of any French town or city is a call to pause before the windows of the many pâtisseries, as each one seems to compete with the next in an effort to entice with layered mille-feuilles, brilliantly colored berry tartlets, and dark, intense-looking chocolate gâteaux, some decorated with paper-thin slices of chocolate or masses of chocolate curls. Browsing through the many cake displays, one can find such regional delicacies as *tarte Tropezienne*, a sugar-topped brioche cake split in half and filled with a pastry cream lightly flavored with almond, or the famous *gâteau Basque*, a wonderfully dense cake filled with *crème pâtissière* or cherry jam. The port of Brest has its own specialty, a cake made of *pâte à choux* in the shape of a wheel, topped with sugar and almonds and filled with cream. The people of Languedoc favor their local chestnut cake, while those of Alsace have *Kugelhopf*, a yeast-raised almond-and-raisin sweet bread. A variety of cookies—such as buttery madeleines or crunchy macaroons—is always on hand as well, the smaller ones sold by weight, the larger ones by the piece.

Even more than a love and respect for elegant pastries, the French have a deep appreciation and enthusiasm for seasonal fruits. They are aware that the fruit's moment is brief and fleeting and that locally produced, perfectly ripe fruits are available for only a short period each year. A bowl or tart of strawberries, just picked in May from a Savoyard strawberry patch, will relinquish its place to wild berries in summer and to the apples and pears of fall. The pattern varies only with the ripening times and varietal nuances of each region.

The majority of homemade desserts in France are fruit-based, with poached fruits, tarts, and fruit pastries among the favorites. Poached fruits may be served with ice cream or with a purée of contrasting fruit, such as a fresh raspberry coulis. Raspberry purée is also a delight in the cavity of a melon or spooned over lightly poached Cotignac figs from the Var or small, whole Bartlett (Williams') pears from the Bouches-du-Rhône. Almost as easy are rustic tarts made with packaged puff pastry (available from most supermarkets) unwound on a baking sheet and topped with fresh sliced fruit tossed with sugar and a bit of flour. The pastry edges are folded around the filling to make a free-form tart. In a hot oven, it bakes quickly and comes to the waiting table still warm, golden, and crisply puffed, rich with the season's flavor. For a fancier presentation, pastry dough is fitted into a tart pan before being filled with wedges of plums, apricots, or nectarines, sprinkled with vanilla sugar, and dotted with butter before baking. More simple than fruit pastries are flans, gratins, and custard cakes. Cherry *clafouti* remains the most popular, especially in its birthplace of Limousin, the richly agricultural heart known as *la France profond*.

Of course, not all desserts are fruit-based. Among the most popular sweets are eggy custards and airy puddings, such as chocolate mousse, pot de crème, crème caramel, and crème brûlée. In the south, these dishes are often customized with popular regional ingredients like lavender flowers, fresh oranges, marzipan, and honey. When cheese is offered as a course in its own right, it is served by presenting two or three varieties, chosen for contrast, on a platter. They arrive before the dessert and after the main dish, while the red wine is still on the table. Local cheeses are given pride of place, but a special occasion may call for cheeses of high pedigree from all over the country.

A special treat is handmade ice cream from a *glacier*, whether it is an expensive, pint from the famous Berthillon on the Ile Saint-Louis in Paris, whose silky *glaces* are touted by quality cafés and restaurants throughout the capital, or a dripping cone from a village shop in Provence whose chalkboard sign proudly displays local flavors like lavender honey, licorice, almond macaroon, candied fennel, and nougat.

Left: In the mountains of the Luberon, graceful plane trees shade Cucuron's central Place de l'Etang, the pleasant site of a weekly market.
Above, left: Le Flore en l'Ile, one of the most famous cafés in Paris, boasts a breathtaking view of Notre Dame, just across the water.
Above, right: In France, the first cherries of the season ripen near the small town of Céret, a center of Catalan culture with a very mild Mediterranean climate that nurtures the local grapes as well.

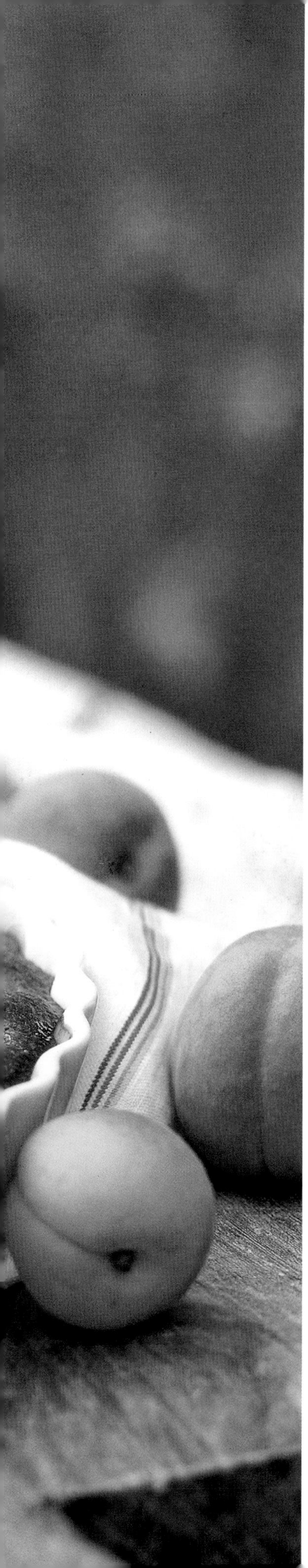

Apricot-Almond Tart

Croûte d'Abricots • Provence • France

This dessert comes from Saint-Saturnin-les-Apt, deep in the region that produces the best stone fruits in France. Although the consistency is a little firmer than that of a *clafouti*, the tart is not unlike that well-known rustic dessert of the Limousin. The combination of luscious fresh apricots and lavender flowers is totally seductive.

About 2 teaspoons unsalted butter, plus 6 tablespoons (3 oz/90 g), melted and cooled

Confectioners' (icing) sugar for dusting tart dish, plus 3 tablespoons

1¾ cups (7 oz/220 g) ground almonds

3 eggs

Pinch of salt

¼ cup (3 oz/90 g) lavender honey

1 teaspoon pesticide-free fresh lavender flowers, without stems

12 large apricots, halved, pitted, then each half halved again

Serves 8

1 Preheat the oven to 350°F (180°C). Butter a 9-inch (23-cm) fluted porcelain tart dish or a metal tart pan with about 2 teaspoons butter. Dust with the confectioners' sugar and tap out the excess.

2 In a bowl, combine the ground almonds, eggs, 6 tablespoons (3 oz/90 g) melted butter, 3 tablespoons confectioners' sugar, salt, honey, and lavender flowers and stir to mix well. Spread the mixture in the bottom of the prepared dish or pan.

3 Arrange the apricots in concentric circles on top of the almond mixture; press lightly to embed them but leave their edges protruding above the surface. Bake the tart until it is bubbling and the edges of the apricots are brown, about 45 minutes, rotating the dish 180 degrees after 20 minutes and then again after another 15 to ensure even browning.

4 Transfer to a rack and use a paper towel to blot up some of the moisture from the top of the tart. Let cool and serve warm or at room temperature.

Champagne Sorbet

Sorbet au Champagne • Champagne • France

Only sparkling wines made in specified areas of Champagne under rigorous state-controlled regulations can legally bear the name Champagne, but for this sorbet other sparkling wines may be used. This is a stylish way to finish a meal, as the flavor of Champagne is foremost. Add a drop or two of crème de cassis or other fruit liqueur for color and flavor—some good choices are pear, raspberry, and peach. Garnish the sorbet with candied violets or rose petals and serve in bowl-shaped Champagne glasses.

1 bottle (24 fl oz/750 ml) Champagne or sparkling wine

¼ cup (2 oz/60 g) sugar

Serves 4

1 In a shallow metal bowl or pan, stir together the Champagne or sparkling wine and the sugar. Cover tightly with plastic wrap or aluminum foil and place in the freezer. Freeze, whisking every 30 minutes, until the mixture becomes firm and granular, about 4 hours.

2 Once the mixture is granular, transfer it to a food processor or blender and process to break up the chunks. This will create a lighter texture.

3 Put the mixture back in the shallow bowl or pan, cover with plastic wrap or aluminum foil, and refreeze until ready to serve. For optimum flavor, the sorbet should be served within 48 hours of being prepared.

4 To serve, spoon into Champagne flutes, wine glasses, or other dessert dishes.

Red Wine Granita with Berries

Granité de Vin Rouge aux Fruits Rouges · Provence · France

Summer would not be summer in Provence without fresh berries. The small, vividly colored strawberries from Carpentras, which are always labeled as such, are pungent and sweet. Here they are mixed with other berries atop a cool granita.

GRANITA

¾ cup (6 oz/185 g) sugar

¾ cup (6 fl oz/180 ml) water

2 cups (16 fl oz/500 ml) dry red wine

Juice of 1 orange

About 4 cups (1 lb/500 g) mixed berries such as raspberries, blueberries, blackberries, loganberries, and small strawberries

1 tablespoon sugar

8 fresh mint sprigs

Serves 8

1 To make the granita, in a saucepan over medium heat, combine the sugar and water. Bring to a boil, stirring to dissolve the sugar. Remove from the heat, pour the syrup into a bowl, and refrigerate until cold, about 30 minutes.

2 Add the red wine and orange juice to the sugar syrup and mix well. Pour into a nonreactive metal pan about 8 by 12 inches (20 by 30 cm) and 1 inch (2.5 cm) deep. The mixture should be about ½ inch (12 mm) deep. Place in the freezer until the mixture starts to thicken, 1½–2 hours. Remove from the freezer, stir with a fork to break up the crystals, and then return to the freezer. Repeat this process every 30 minutes until the mixture begins to firm, then every 15 minutes until all of the liquid has turned into well-separated granules. The granita should be ready in 4–5 hours.

3 Place the berries in a bowl, sprinkle with the sugar, and stir gently to combine. Set aside.

4 To serve, chill individual bowls in the freezer. Spoon some of the granita into each chilled bowl and top with the berry mixture. Garnish with the mint sprigs.

Blackberry Upside-Down Cake

Gateau de Mûre • The Pyrenees and Gascony • France

In the mountains, summertime is wild-berry time. In August, in the Pyrenees, buckets of fresh berries are perfectly suited to recipes like this cake. Serve it warm with a scoop or two of vanilla ice cream from a local *glacier* (ice cream shop).

⅓ cup (3 oz/90 g) unsalted butter, plus 1 tablespoon, melted and cooled

2 cups (1 lb/500 g) granulated sugar

1 pint (8 oz/250 g) blackberries

4 eggs

1 cup (5 oz/155 g) all-purpose (plain) flour

1 teaspoon baking powder

¼ teaspoon salt

Serves 6–8

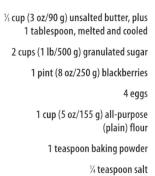

1 Preheat the oven to 350°F (180°C). Put the ⅓ cup (3 oz/90 g) butter in a 9- or 10-inch (23- or 25-cm) round baking dish with 2½-inch (6-cm) sides. Place in the oven to melt, about 5 minutes. Remove from the oven and add 1 cup (8 oz/250 g) of the sugar. Stir and return to the oven for 5 minutes, stirring once or twice, then remove from the oven. Spread the berries in a single layer on the sugar.

2 Separate the eggs, putting the whites into a large bowl and the yolks into a smaller one. Whisk the 1 tablespoon melted butter into the yolks and set aside. In another bowl, sift together the flour, baking powder, and salt. Set aside. With an electric beater set on medium speed or with a whisk, beat the egg whites just until they form firm peaks. Do not overbeat. Fold the remaining 1 cup (8 oz/250 g) sugar into the egg whites, about one-fourth at a time. Then fold in the egg yolk mixture about one-fourth at a time. Finally, fold in the flour mixture about ¼ cup (1½ oz/45 g) at a time. Pour the batter over the berries and spread to cover evenly.

3 Bake until a toothpick inserted into the center comes out clean, about 30 minutes. Let stand for at least 10 minutes before unmolding, then slide a knife along the inside edge of the dish. Invert a large plate over the top. Holding the plate and dish firmly together, turn them over and lift off the dish. Serve the cake warm, cut into wedges.

CONFITURES

Confitures, delicious French preserves, jams, and jellies made from cherries, raspberries, quinces, blackberries, apricots, blueberries, plums, and other seasonal fruits, play nearly as important a role in dessert making as they do at the breakfast table, where they are spread onto bread and croissants. Thick preserves, such as apricot or cherry, are used to fill deep-fried pastries. Jellies are melted and thickened to glaze fruit tarts large and small. Confitures top fresh cheese and are spooned alongside ice cream and sweet

pain perdu. In the pâtisserie, you will find them hidden between layers of cakes and pooled atop freshly-baked cookies.

Many people still make a few jars of their favorite confiture at home, perhaps with fruit brought back from an August vacation in the mountains or countryside. They are served for special occasions, such as Christmas morning breakfast, and the label begins the story: *confiture de figues sauvages, fait à Moustiers-Ste-Marie, août 1998* (wild-fig jam, made at Moustiers-Ste-Marie, August 1998). The rest of the story—where the figs were gathered, what the weather was like, who was along on the trip—is told during the meal, amid exclamations of how good the jam tastes.

Little Pots of Orange Cream

Petits Pots de Crème à l'Orange • Provence • France

Petits pots de crème can be had all over France, in practically every flavor from vanilla to passion fruit to chocolate. In Saint-Raphaël, a town said to have been a holiday resort since Roman times and the haunt of such writers as Alexandre Dumas in the mid-nineteenth century, this dessert is so popular that porcelain factories make dainty individual pots with lids designed expressly for the cream.

1 orange

2 cups (16 fl oz/500 ml) milk

6 tablespoons (3 oz/90 g) sugar

3 eggs

Few drops of vanilla extract (essence)

Boiling water, as needed

1 cup (8 fl oz/250 ml) water

1 cup (8 fl oz/250 ml) heavy (double) cream, whipped (optional)

Serves 8

1 Using a small knife with a flexible blade, remove the zest from the orange in strips ¾ inch (2 cm) wide and as long as possible. Reserve 3 of the strips to infuse the custard. Turn the other strips over and, using a small, sharp knife, remove any residual white pith. Cut the strips into fine julienne for the garnish and set aside. (Reserve the orange flesh for another use.)

2 Pour the milk into a saucepan and add the reserved zest strips. Let stand for 30 minutes.

3 Preheat the oven to 400°F (200°C). Select a baking dish large enough to hold 8 small pots or ½ cup (4 fl oz/125 ml) ramekins. Set the molds in the dish.

4 Add 4 tablespoons (2 oz/60 g) of the sugar to the saucepan holding the milk, place over medium heat, and stir to dissolve the sugar. Bring just to a boil and remove from the heat.

5 In a bowl, whisk the eggs until blended. Pour half of the hot milk over the eggs, whisking constantly. Then pour the egg-milk mixture into the saucepan of milk, place over medium heat, and cook, stirring constantly, until the mixture coats the back of a spoon, about 2 minutes. Do not let boil. An instant-read thermometer inserted into the custard should read 180°F (82°C).

6 Add the vanilla, whisk to blend, and then quickly pour the custard through a sieve into the pots or ramekins, dividing it evenly. Discard the zest strips. Place the baking dish on an extended oven rack, add boiling water to the dish to reach nearly to the rims of the pots or ramekins, and carefully slide the rack into the oven.

7 Bake the custards until set, about 20 minutes. To test, insert a metal skewer into the center of a custard; it should come out clean. Transfer the baking dish to a work surface and remove the pots or ramekins. Let cool and refrigerate until set, 2–3 hours.

8 Meanwhile, place the reserved julienned zest in a small saucepan with the 1 cup (8 fl oz/ 250 ml) water. Add the remaining 2 tablespoons sugar and bring to a boil, stirring to dissolve the sugar. Boil rapidly until the zest becomes flexible and shiny from the sugar, about 2 minutes. Drain and spread out on a plate.

9 To serve, top each custard with a dollop of whipped cream, if using, and a few strands of the julienned zest.

Caramelized Oranges with Orange Flower Water

Oranges Caramélisées à l'Eau de Fleur d'Oranger • Provence • France

The orange flower water made in Grasse in the Cannes hinterlands has become a favorite flavoring ingredient of the Provençaux. Here it enhances simple navel oranges.

6 navel oranges or blood oranges

2 teaspoons orange flower water, or to taste

½ cup (4 oz/125 g) plus 1 tablespoon sugar

¾ cup (6 fl oz/180 ml) water

Serves 6

1 Using a citrus zester, remove the zest from 1 orange in long threads. Using a sharp knife, cut a thin slice off the top and bottom of each orange to expose the flesh. Stand the orange upright and slice the remaining peel in strips, carefully following the contour of the orange and removing all the white pith and membrane. Then cut each orange crosswise into slices about ⅛ inch (3 mm) thick. Spread the orange slices on a serving plate, arranging them in 2 or 3 layers. Scatter the zest over the top and drizzle with the orange flower water.

2 No more than 45 minutes before serving the oranges, combine the sugar and water in a small saucepan and place over medium heat, stirring constantly to dissolve the sugar. When the mixture reaches a boil, continue to boil without stirring until it turns a light beige. Lift and swirl the pan to distribute the color and return to medium heat. Using a pastry brush dampened with water, brush down the pan sides to release the sugar crystals. Continue to boil until the sugar turns a dark caramel color. The whole process should take about 15 minutes.

3 Immediately pour the caramel over the oranges, working from the center outward, but not quite to the edges, and distributing the caramel evenly. It will set quickly. Using a spoon and fork, "crack open" the caramel in front of the diners, then serve the orange slices on individual plates.

Crepes with Armagnac-Quince Filling

Crêpes aux Coings à l'Armagnac • Provence • France

Crepes, paper-thin pancakes, seem to be synonymous with France, and crêperies abound throughout the country. Most serve the pancakes in both sweet and savory versions so that you can make a complete meal of them, but some—especially the open-air stands—serve only sweet crepes with butter and sugar or jam. Raw quince are pale, highly astringent, and flavorless. Once cooked, they turn a soft amber-rose and become richly flavorful.

CREPE BATTER

4 eggs

1¾ cups (14 fl oz/430 ml) milk, or more if needed

⅓ cup (2 oz/60 g) all-purpose (plain) flour

1 teaspoon sugar

½ teaspoon salt

FILLING

3 tablespoons unsalted butter

4 large quinces, peeled, cored, and cut lengthwise into slices ¼ inch (6 mm) thick

2 tablespoons sugar

¼ cup (2 fl oz/60 ml) water

2 tablespoons Armagnac

About ¼ cup (2 oz/60 g) unsalted butter

1 cup (8 fl oz/250 ml) heavy (double) cream

1½ tablespoons sugar

Serves 8

1 To make the crepe batter, in a large bowl, whisk together the eggs and 1¾ cups (14 fl oz/ 430 ml) milk until blended. Then, a little at a time, whisk in the flour, sugar, and salt to make a thin, lump-free batter. If, despite your best efforts, there are still lumps, strain the batter through a sieve lined with several layers of cheesecloth (muslin). Cover and refrigerate for 2 hours.

2 To make the filling, in a frying pan over medium heat, melt the butter. When it foams, add the quince slices and cook until glistening, 1–2 minutes. Add the sugar and continue cooking until lightly browned on the first side, 2–3 minutes. Turn the slices and continue to cook until lightly browned on the second side, another 2–3 minutes. Add the water and continue to cook until the quince slices are tender, 2–3 minutes longer. Pour the Armagnac over the quinces and ignite with a match. When the flames subside, cover and keep warm until ready to serve.

3 Place a 12-inch (30-cm) frying pan, preferably nonstick, over medium-high heat. When a drop of water flicked into the pan sizzles and spatters, the pan is ready. Drop in 1 teaspoon butter. When it melts, tip the pan from side to side to coat the bottom evenly. If the batter seems too thick (it should be the consistency of heavy (double) cream), thin it by beating in a little milk. Then pour a scant ¼ cup (2 fl oz/60 ml) of the batter into the pan, quickly tipping and rotating the pan to coat the bottom evenly. Pour off any excess. In a very short time, only about 30 seconds, bubbles will begin to appear on the surface and the edges will begin to dry and pull away from the pan sides. Using a spatula, turn over the crepe and cook just a moment longer on the other side. Transfer to a plate, stacking as you go, and cover to keep warm. Repeat until all the batter has been used, adding more butter as needed. You should have about 16 crepes.

4 In a bowl, using an electric mixer set on high speed, beat the cream until it begins to thicken, about 2 minutes. Slowly add the sugar, continuing to beat until soft peaks form.

5 To serve, place 1–1½ tablespoons of the quince filling in the center of a crepe. Fold the crepe in half, and then into quarters. Place on an individual plate. Repeat until all the crepes are filled and folded, placing 2 crepes on each plate. Top each crepe with a spoonful or two of whipped cream. Serve at once.

Peach Gratin

Gratin de Pêches • Pays de la Loire • France

Fruit gratins are some of the easiest fruit desserts to make. Just enough thin, crepe-like batter is used to hold the fruit together when it is sliced. All sorts of fruits can be used, from figs to berries to apricots. Serve the gratin on its own or with crème fraîche or ice cream.

1 teaspoon plus 1 tablespoon unsalted butter, cut into small bits

4 tablespoons (2 oz/60 g) sugar

¼ cup (2 fl oz/60 ml) milk

1 egg

⅛ teaspoon salt

¼ cup (1½ oz/45 g) all-purpose (plain) flour

2 lb (1 kg) peaches, peeled (page 224), halved, and pitted

2 tablespoons coarsely chopped almonds

Serves 4–6

1 Preheat the oven to 425°F (220°C). Using the 1 teaspoon butter, grease an 8- or 9-inch (20- or 23-cm) gratin dish or other shallow baking dish, then sprinkle it with 1 tablespoon of the sugar.

2 In a bowl, whisk together the milk, egg, 1 tablespoon of the sugar, and the salt. Gradually whisk in the flour. Pour this creamy batter into the gratin dish and top with the prepared peaches. Sprinkle the remaining 2 tablespoons sugar and the nuts over the top and dot with the 1 tablespoon butter.

3 Bake until the batter is set, the butter is melted, and the peaches are cooked through, 12–15 minutes. Remove from the oven and let stand for about 10 minutes, then serve.

SEASONAL FRUIT

Fruit is often served as dessert in France, a particularly healthful habit, and seasonal fruits (*fruits de saison*) are considered highly desirable. In winter it might be oranges, apples, and dried fruits, and in spring cherries or apricots. Of course, in summer, the fruit bowl will be heaped with peaches, plums, nectarines, grapes, and melons. Come fall, figs and pears are the main attractions.

The home orchard, or *verger*, is the counterpoint of the *potager*, or vegetable garden, and whenever possible people will plant as many fruit trees as they can, even in small city backyards. It is considered a true luxury to be able to serve fresh fruit to guests from one's own trees. Failing that, people seek out the best of what is available from the local market.

Fruits form the basis of many simple desserts. *Clafouti*, a cakelike pudding classically made with cherries, is also fashioned with apricots, peaches, figs, plums, or nectarines. A fruit gratin, in which fruit is put in a buttered gratin dish, then sparsely covered with a light batter and sugared, is one of the easiest desserts to put together—yet it makes an elegant appearance when served.

Seasonal fruits such as peaches, cherries, or grapes can be used to fill crepes or to top pound cake or ice cream, and they are especially good if first poached in a sugar syrup flavored with vanilla. The best pâtisseries tempt passers-by with their displays of exquisite tarts constructed of seasonal fruits, such as blackberries in spring, oranges and lemons in winter, and prune plums in fall.

Chocolate Mousse

Mousse au Chocolat • Burgundy and Lyon • France

Chocolate mousse is almost synonymous with French dessert. Unfortunately, one often finds poor imitations of the real thing in France and elsewhere. A good chocolate mousse is so rich, so chocolatey, that one might only want to eat half of what would be a normal dessert portion. Styles of mousse range from gooey to firm. This version falls into the latter group. If you'd like, garnish it with chocolate shavings.

¼ lb (125 g) bittersweet chocolate, chopped into very small pieces

3 tablespoons unsalted butter, cut into small pieces

3 eggs

⅛ teaspoon salt

2 tablespoons confectioners' (icing) sugar

Serves 4

1 Place the chocolate in a heatproof bowl. Set over (not touching) barely simmering water in a saucepan. Heat, stirring, until the chocolate melts, about 2 minutes. Add the butter and continue to stir until the butter melts and is incorporated, 30–60 seconds.

2 Separate 1 egg, placing the white in a large bowl and adding the yolk to the chocolate. Quickly whisk in the yolk, fully incorporating it. Repeat with the remaining 2 eggs. Remove the bowl from over the saucepan and let cool to lukewarm.

3 Add the salt to the egg whites. Using an electric mixer set on medium-high speed, beat the whites until they form stiff peaks, then beat in the sugar. Using a rubber spatula, gently fold the egg whites into the chocolate, being careful not to deflate the whites.

4 Spoon the mixture into a large bowl or individual glasses. Cover and refrigerate until very firm, at least 6 hours or for up to 24 hours. Serve well chilled.

Walnut Tart

Tarte aux Noix • Franche-Comté and the Alps • France

Walnut liqueur, *vin de noix*, is used to flavor this classic nut tart, but if it isn't available, Cointreau or another orange liqueur makes a good substitute.

PASTRY

1½ cups (7½ oz/235 g) all-purpose (plain) flour

¼ cup (2 oz/60 g) granulated sugar

½ cup (4 oz/125 g) unsalted butter, cut into ½-inch (12-mm) chunks

1 egg

FILLING

2 tablespoons unsalted butter, melted and cooled

½ cup (3½ oz/105 g) firmly packed light brown sugar

2 eggs

¼ cup (2 fl oz/60 ml) walnut liqueur or Cointreau

1 teaspoon vanilla extract (essence)

1½ cups (6 oz/185 g) walnut halves, toasted (page 224)

Serves 12

1 Position a rack in the lower third of an oven and preheat to 350°F (180°C).

2 To make the pastry, in a bowl, stir together the flour and granulated sugar. Add the butter and work it in with your fingertips until the mixture becomes crumblike. Add the egg and mix it with a fork. Press the dough evenly into an 11-inch (28-cm) tart pan with a removable bottom. Set aside.

3 To make the filling, in a bowl, combine the melted butter, brown sugar, eggs, liqueur, and vanilla. Beat with a wooden spoon until blended. Stir in the toasted nuts. Pour the filling into the tart pan.

4 Bake until the crust and the filling are golden brown, about 50 minutes. Transfer to a rack to cool briefly. Remove the pan rim and slide the tart, on the metal base, onto a plate. Serve warm or at room temperature.

Iced Terrine of Fig and Ginger

Nougat Glacé aux Figues et Gingembre · Provence · France

This frozen terrine from the Alpes-Maritimes may be served as is, but it looks even more beautiful when garnished with fresh berries, orange slices, fresh figs, or sweet cherries.

7 tablespoons (3½ oz/105 g) superfine (caster) sugar

5 tablespoons (2½ fl oz/75 ml) water

4 egg yolks

6 plump, moist dried figs, each cut into 3 or 4 pieces

2 tablespoons candied ginger, coarsely chopped

1 tablespoon *each* candied orange peel and candied lemon peel

6 candied red cherries, halved

⅓ cup (2 oz/60 g) pistachios

½ teaspoon ground cinnamon

¼ teaspoon ground cardamom

1¼ cups (10 fl oz/310 ml) heavy (double) cream, whipped

2 tablespoons kirsch

Serves 8–10

1 In a saucepan over medium heat, combine the sugar and water. Heat, stirring to dissolve the sugar, then raise the heat to high and bring to a boil. Boil without stirring until the mixture reaches 240°F (116°C), the soft-ball stage, on a candy thermometer.

2 Meanwhile, in a bowl, beat the egg yolks with a handheld electric mixer. When the sugar mixture is ready, pour onto the eggs slowly while beating constantly. Beat until the mixture has cooled and has doubled in volume. Fold in the figs, ginger, citrus peels, cherries, pistachios, and spices, then carefully fold in the whipped cream. Fold in the kirsch.

3 Pour the mixture into a 4-cup (32–fl oz/1-l) rectangular ceramic terrine or loaf pan. Cover with plastic wrap and freeze for at least 8 hours or up to 4 days.

4 Run a knife blade around the sides of the mold and invert the mold onto a plate. Soak a kitchen towel with hot water, wring out, place on the bottom of the mold to release the nougat, and lift off the mold. Return to the freezer to refirm. Cut into slices ½ inch (12 mm) thick and serve.

CANDIED FRUITS

Candying fruit is the art of gently bathing flawless fruits in up to a dozen basins of successively more dense sugar syrup until the original water content of the fruits has been replaced with the sugary liquid. Apt, in the Lubéron, is now the world capital of this six-centuries-old art, closely followed by Carpentras and Oraison, both important centers with a reputation for high-quality handmade *fruits confits*.

The Provençaux love to champion artisans who make things by hand, where it is the eye, rather than the machine, that is in charge, and the Jouvauds are an excellent example of such an artisanal tradition. Each year, the family produces more than 4,000 pounds (2,000 kg) of preserved fruits in its small pâtisserie in Carpentras. The family creates some of the most beautifully symmetrical candied fruits imaginable, each piece revealing no change in texture when cut through to the center, each firm and with no crystallization. Frédéric Jouvaud, with his "retired" father, Gilbert, and son Pierre by his side, uses only fruit from his *département*, except for the large Corsican melons and whole pineapples he loves to spend up to four months completing.

Plum Custard Cake

Flognard · Central · France

Various regions of France have a custard-like cake or flan, served either plain or with fruits. Prune plums are especially popular to use. In the Auvergne, the preparation is called *flognard,* and is made with sliced local fruits such as pears or plums. In the Limousin, the custard cake is made with cherries and called *clafouti.*

4½ tablespoons (2½ oz/67 g) unsalted butter

¼ cup (1½ oz/45 g) all-purpose (plain) flour

¼ cup (2 oz/60 g) sugar, plus extra for sprinkling

3 eggs

½ cup (4 fl oz/125 ml) milk

¼ teaspoon plum brandy or vanilla extract (essence)

6 red, purple, or green plums, pitted and cut into slices ¼ inch (6 mm) thick, or 12 prune plums, pitted and halved (about ¾ lb/375 g total weight)

Serves 4

1 Preheat the oven to 400°F (200°C). Using ½ tablespoon of the butter, heavily grease a 10-inch (25-cm) quiche dish or other shallow baking dish.

2 In a bowl, using a whisk or electric beater, beat together the flour, sugar, eggs, milk, and brandy or vanilla to make a thin batter. Beat vigorously for 1–2 minutes to incorporate air. Pour the batter into the prepared baking dish. Arrange the plums on top in a single, tightly packed layer. Sprinkle with a thin layer of sugar. Cut the remaining 4 tablespoons (2 oz/ 60 g) butter into small bits and use to dot the top.

3 Bake until the top puffs up and the edges turn a deep golden brown, about 30 minutes. Remove from the oven, tent loosely with foil, and let stand for about 5 minutes. The cake will deflate slightly.

4 Serve hot, warm, or at room temperature.

Honey Madeleines

Madeleines au Miel • Provence • France

The rich, golden interiors of madeleines, one of the classic small cakes of France, are made more succulent by the addition of a choice local honey. Honey from orange flowers goes well with the grated orange zest, but lavender honey is the most recognizably Provençal.

5 tablespoons (3 oz/90 g) unsalted butter, at room temperature, plus melted butter for greasing molds

Scant ⅓ cup (2½ oz/75 g) superfine (caster) sugar

2 teaspoons light brown sugar

Pinch of salt

1 tablespoon honey (see note)

½ cup plus 2 tablespoons (3 oz/90 g) all-purpose (plain) flour

Scant 1 teaspoon baking powder

2 eggs

1 teaspoon grated orange zest

Confectioners' (icing) sugar (optional)

Makes 12 large or 24 miniature madeleines

1 In a bowl, using a wooden spoon, beat the 5 tablespoons (3 oz/90 g) butter until creamy. Beat in the superfine and brown sugars. Stir in the salt and honey. Sift the flour and baking powder into a separate bowl. Add the eggs to the butter mixture one at a time, beating well after each addition. Then add the flour mixture and orange zest and beat well.

2 Preheat the oven to 375°F (190°C). Brush a tray of 12 standard madeleine molds or 24 miniature molds with melted butter and place in the refrigerator for 2 minutes. Brush again with melted butter and coat with flour, tapping out the excess.

3 Spoon the batter evenly into the prepared molds; do not overfill. Bake until golden, 6–7 minutes for miniature madeleines, 8–9 minutes for standard. Let rest for a few seconds, and then invert the pan and tap on a work surface. Transfer the madeleines to a rack to cool. If desired, dust with confectioners' sugar.

Prune and Armagnac Soufflé

Soufflé aux Pruneaux à l'Armagnac • Gascony • France

Soufflés are traditional desserts throughout France, and you will often find that a particular region has a special version that calls for its local products. The presence of prunes and Armagnac identify this example as a specialty of Gascony.

½ lb (250 g) pitted prunes

1 cup (8 fl oz/250 ml) warm water

2 tablespoons Armagnac

1½ tablespoons unsalted butter

1½ teaspoons plus 6 tablespoons (3 oz/90 g) granulated sugar

7 egg whites

⅛ teaspoon salt

Confectioners' (icing) sugar

Serves 6

1 In a bowl, combine the prunes, warm water, and 1 tablespoon of the Armagnac. Let stand at room temperature overnight until nicely plumped.

2 The next day, preheat the oven to 350°F (180°C). Using the butter, generously grease an 8-inch (20-cm) soufflé dish. Sprinkle with the 1½ teaspoons sugar, then rotate the mold to coat the bottom and sides evenly.

3 Drain the prunes, reserving 2 tablespoons of the liquid. In a blender, combine the prunes, the reserved liquid, and the remaining 1 tablespoon Armagnac. Process until a thick purée forms. Set aside.

4 In a large bowl, combine the egg whites and salt. Using an electric mixer set on medium-high speed, beat until soft peaks form. Gradually beat in the 6 tablespoons granulated sugar until stiff peaks form. Using a rubber spatula, fold in the prune purée, a little at a time, being careful not to deflate the egg whites. Pour into the prepared dish.

5 Bake until puffed above the rim, about 20 minutes. Remove from the oven and, using a fine-mesh sieve, dust the top of the soufflé with confectioners' sugar. Serve immediately.

DIGESTIFS

Just as aperitifs are the prelude to a meal, a digestif is the conclusion, its purpose to aid in digestion—a distinctly pleasurable assistance. Sometimes it is taken with an after-dinner coffee, but more often it follows it.

Unlike aperitifs, digestifs are typically products of distillation, either of wine or of fruits, and virtually all the regions of France have their own specialties. No doubt the most well-known digestif is Cognac, distilled from wine in the area around the city of Cognac in Charentes. In Gascony, Armagnac is the choice digestif, which, like Cognac, is made from distilled wine. Marc, made by distilling the grape skins, stems, and seeds left behind after pressing grapes for wine, also has its regional aficionados, and you can find marc de Bourgogne, marc de Champagne, d'Auvergne, d'Alsace—the list goes on and on. Calvados, a specialty of Normandy, is made from distilled apple juice and pulp. One can readily find eaux-de-vie of raspberries, pears, and other fruits made by first fermenting the fruit, then distilling it, which is a different process than that used for marc, although both of these digetifs can be quite good.

All of the digestifs, with their complex flavors, are excellent in cooking, where they are frequently ignited, burning off the alcohol but leaving the flavor.

Bread and Butter Pudding

Pain Perdu • Provence • France

Meaning "lost bread" or "hidden" bread, *pain perdu* was originally invented as a way to use up stale bread. It has become such a favorite, however, that only crème caramel rivals it as the most popular cooked family dessert in France. This country recipe comes from Digne, northeast of Marseilles. Other flavors of jam may be used, but raspberry is probably the most common. More sophisticated versions substitute a raspberry coulis (sauce of puréed sweetened raspberries) for serving as a sauce at the table.

About 20 thick slices day-old bread from a square-cornered loaf

⅓ cup (3 oz/90 g) unsalted butter, at room temperature

About 5 tablespoons (3 oz/90 g) raspberry jam or red currant jelly

2 cups (16 fl oz/500 ml) milk

1 vanilla bean, split lengthwise

3 whole eggs, plus 2 egg yolks

½ cup (4 oz/125 g) plus 2 tablespoons granulated sugar

Boiling water, as needed

Confectioners' (icing) sugar (optional)

Serves 6

1 Preheat a broiler (grill). Spread 1 side of each bread slice with butter and then cut in half on the diagonal. Working in batches if necessary, arrange the slices, buttered side up, on a baking sheet and slip under the broiler (grill) close to the heat source to brown. This should take 30–45 seconds. Remove from the broiler and turn the oven to 400°F (200°C).

2 Arrange the toasted slices, buttered side up, points facing the same direction, and each slice slightly overlapping another, in a rectangular gratin dish 12 inches (30 cm) long and 8 inches (20 cm) wide. The dish should hold 2 or 3 slices across and 6–8 slices along the length. As the dish is being filled, spoon or spread a little raspberry jam or red currant jelly here and there among the slices.

3 Pour the milk into a saucepan, add the vanilla bean, and place over medium heat until small bubbles appear along the edges of the pan. Remove from the heat and let cool. While the milk is cooling, in a bowl, whisk together the whole eggs, egg yolks, and granulated sugar until creamy and the mixture lightens.

4 Remove the vanilla bean from the cooled milk and discard. Whisk the milk into the egg mixture until well blended, then pour it over the bread slices.

5 Place the gratin dish in a large baking pan and add hot water to the pan to reach halfway up the sides of the gratin dish. Place the pan on an extended oven rack, add boiling water to the pan to reach almost to the rim of the gratin dish, and carefully slide the oven rack into the oven.

6 Bake the pudding for 5 minutes, then, using a wide metal spatula, press on the bread slices to embed them in the custard fully before it sets. Continue to bake until the custard is set and the top is golden, about 25 minutes longer.

7 Carefully remove the baking pan from the oven and let stand for 30 minutes. Remove the gratin dish from the pan. If desired, dust the top of the pudding with confectioners' sugar before serving.

Cherry Custard Cake

Clafouti aux Cerises · Limousin · France

Clafouti, a custardlike pudding thick with locally grown tart, dark cherries, originated in the Limousin, in the center of France. The delectable dish has been taken up all over the country, however, and now not only are different varieties of cherries used, but different fruits as well. The cherries are typically left unpitted, so be sure to warn your guests.

1½ teaspoons unsalted butter

1 cup (8 fl oz/250 ml) milk

¼ cup (2 fl oz/60 ml) heavy (double) cream

⅔ cup (3½ oz/105 g) all-purpose (plain) flour, sifted

3 eggs

¼ cup (2 oz/60 g) granulated sugar

1 tablespoon vanilla extract (essence)

¼ teaspoon salt

4 cups (1 lb/500 g) stemmed sweet or tart cherries, pitted if desired

1 tablespoon confectioners' (icing) sugar

Serves 6–8

1 Preheat the oven to 350°F (180°C). Using the butter, grease a 9- to 10-inch (23- to 25-cm) round baking dish. In a bowl, combine the milk, cream, flour, eggs, granulated sugar, vanilla, and salt. Using an electric mixer set on medium speed, beat until frothy, about 5 minutes.

2 Pour enough of the batter into the prepared baking dish to cover the bottom with a layer about ¼ inch (6 mm) deep. Put the dish in the preheated oven for 2 minutes, then remove it. Cover the batter with a single layer of the cherries. Pour the remaining batter over the cherries. Return to the oven and bake until puffed and browned and a knife inserted into the center comes out clean, 30–35 minutes.

3 Dust the top of the *clafouti* with confectioners' sugar. Serve warm.

Apple-Pine Nut Tart with Almond Cream

Tarte Moelleuse aux Pommes • Provence • France

Since the days of the Roman Empire, pine nuts have been harvested along the coastline of Provence, and since medieval times, Digne and Aix-en-Provence have been at the heart of a thriving almond industry. Here the two are combined in a simple apple tart.

PASTRY

1¼ cups (6½ oz/200 g) all-purpose (plain) flour

7 tablespoons (3½ oz/105 g) unsalted butter, at room temperature, cut into small pieces

1 egg yolk

3 tablespoons superfine (caster) sugar

3 tablespoons water

ALMOND CREAM

6 tablespoons (3 fl oz/90 ml) milk

1 whole egg, plus 1 egg yolk

2 tablespoons granulated sugar

2 tablespoons cornstarch (cornflour)

½ teaspoon vanilla extract (essence)

3 tablespoons unsalted butter, at room temperature

½ cup (2 oz/60 g) ground almonds

¼ cup (1 oz/30 g) confectioners' (icing) sugar

1 tablespoon dark rum

¼ cup (2 oz/60 g) fig or apricot jam

3 tablespoons water

1 large Granny Smith apple, peeled, cored, and cut into ½-inch (12-mm) dice

1 cup (5 oz/155 g) pine nuts

Serves 8

1 To make the pastry, in a food processor, combine the flour and butter and pulse until blended. Add the egg yolk, superfine sugar, and 1 tablespoon of the water and then pulse until the pastry gathers in a mass on the blade. Add some of the remaining 2 tablespoons water if it is too dry. Transfer to a floured work surface and form into a ball. Cover the pastry with plastic wrap and refrigerate for at least 30 minutes or for up to 2 hours.

2 On a floured work surface, roll out the pastry into a 12-inch (30-cm) round, about ⅛ inch (3 mm) thick. Drape it around the rolling pin and transfer to an 11-inch (28-cm) tart pan with a removable bottom. Ease the pastry into the bottom and sides of the pan and make a small lip of pastry at the top edge. Cut away the excess pastry, then use your fingers to round the top edge attractively.

3 To make the almond cream, pour the milk into a saucepan and heat over medium heat until small bubbles appear along the edges of the pan. Remove from the heat. In a bowl, whisk together the whole egg and egg yolk until well blended. Whisk in the granulated sugar, and then whisk in 1 tablespoon of the cornstarch. Pour about half of the hot milk over the egg mixture while whisking constantly. Then pour the egg-milk mixture into the saucepan holding the remaining milk, place over medium heat, and cook, stirring constantly, until the mixture thickens and comes to a boil, 1½–2 minutes. Remove from the heat, stir in the vanilla, and immediately pour back into the bowl and set aside to cool.

4 Preheat the oven to 375°F (190°C). In another bowl, using a wooden spoon, beat the butter until creamy. Stir in the ground almonds. Using a fine-mesh sieve, sift in the confectioners' sugar and then stir to mix. Whisk in the rum and the remaining 1 table-spoon cornstarch. Fold the cooled custard into the almond mixture until fully combined.

5 In a small saucepan, combine the fig or apricot jam and the water. Place over low heat and stir constantly until the jam dissolves and is fluid. Brush a thin layer of the dissolved jam on the bottom of the pastry-lined pan. Spread the almond cream over the jam layer, smoothing the top to cover evenly. Spread the diced apple over the custard layer, again distributing evenly. Press the apple pieces lightly so they sit well in the custard but do not sink. Cover the entire surface with the pine nuts, again making sure they adhere but not immersing them in the cream.

6 Place the tart in the oven and immediately reduce the heat to 350°F (180°C). Bake until the top is golden, about 40 minutes, rotating the pan 180 degrees after about 30 minutes to ensure even browning. Transfer to a rack and let cool completely. Remove the pan sides, slide the tart onto a serving plate, and serve at room temperature, cut into wedges.

Crème au Caramel

Crème au Caramel • Ile-de-France • France

Like chocolate mousse, *crème au caramel* appears in many versions in restaurants of all persuasions. An elegant dessert, it is easy and rewarding to make at home.

1 cup (8 oz/250 g) sugar

2 cups (16 fl oz/500 ml) milk

2 cups (16 fl oz/500 ml) heavy (double) cream

8 eggs

¼ teaspoon salt

1 teaspoon vanilla extract (essence)

Boiling water, as needed

Serves 8

1 Put ½ cup (4 oz/125 g) of the sugar in a 10-inch (25-cm) cake pan with 1½-inch (4-cm) sides and place it on the stove top over medium-low heat. Holding the edge of the pan with a hot pad, tilt the pan from side to side as the sugar melts and caramelizes. When all the sugar has melted and become a golden brown liquid, remove the pan from the stove. Tip the pan so that the sides and bottom are evenly coated with the syrup. Set aside.

2 Preheat the oven to 325°F (165°C). In a saucepan over medium heat, combine the milk and cream and heat until small bubbles appear along the edges of the pan. Meanwhile, in a bowl, beat the eggs until blended. Add the remaining ½ cup (4 oz/125 g) sugar, the salt, and the vanilla and beat until blended. Slowly pour the hot milk mixture into the egg mixture while stirring continuously.

3 Place the caramel-lined cake pan in a shallow baking pan. Pour the custard into the cake pan, filling it to the rim. Pour boiling water into the baking pan to reach halfway up the sides of the cake pan. Bake until a small, sharp knife inserted into the center comes out clean, 35–45 minutes. Remove from the oven and let cool to room temperature.

4 To unmold, slide a knife along the inside edge of the pan. Invert a shallow serving plate on top of the custard. Holding the cake pan and the plate firmly together, turn them over so the plate is on the bottom. Give the pan a shake and then lift it off. The custard should drop smoothly to the serving plate. Serve at room temperature or chilled.

L'AFFINEUR

Except for very fresh cheeses, all cheeses are aged. The longer a cheese ages, the drier and more flavorful it becomes. However, each type has its optimum point of ripeness, the point at which it has fully matured. *Affineurs,* or master cheese maturers, buy cheeses of all kinds from producers and then age them in caves.

In Bordeaux, there is one such *affineur,* Jean d'Alos, whose shop and cave are near the river on the rue Montesquieu. His cave was hewn out of the rock hundreds of years ago and originally used by a wine merchant for storing casks. Looking at its cheese-laden shelves today, which are on three levels beneath the

shop, is like taking a trip to all the regions of France. The subterranean walls are lined with hundreds of cylinders, pyramids, wheels, disks, and squares from Savoy, Auvergne, the north and Pas-de-Calais, Normandy, Lorraine and Alsace, Burgundy, the Alps, and Provence, each cheese carefully tended by M. d'Alos and his white-smocked staff. Upstairs in the light-filled, intensely aromatic shop, his clients come to request a cheese for the night's dinner or for a midday meal two days hence. M. d'Alos selects a cheese from the vast display in his shop or cave that will be perfectly ripe at the specified moment.

Rum and Orange Babas

Babas au Rhum • Alsace-Lorraine • France

Babas are cakes that are soaked in a sugar-and-rum syrup until saturated and spongy. Three things are especially important in making babas: the rising temperature must be very warm, you must continue to work with the very sticky dough until it becomes elastic, and both the cakes and the syrup must be warm when you pour the syrup over them.

DOUGH

3 tablespoons granulated sugar

¼ cup (2 fl oz/60 ml) warm water

2½ teaspoons (1 package) active dry yeast

3 tablespoons milk

5 tablespoons (2½ oz/75 g) unsalted butter

2½ cups (12½ oz/390 g) all-purpose (plain) flour, sifted

2 large eggs

¼ teaspoon salt

SYRUP

¾ cup (6 oz/185 g) granulated sugar

1½ cups (12 fl oz/375 ml) water

1 tablespoon fresh orange juice

⅓ cup (3 fl oz/80 ml) dark rum

TOPPING

1 cup (8 fl oz/250 ml) heavy (double) cream

2 tablespoons confectioners' (icing) sugar

½ teaspoon vanilla extract (essence)

2 tablespoons finely julienned orange zest

Serves 6

1 To make the dough, in a small bowl, combine 1 tablespoon of the sugar and the water. Sprinkle the yeast over the water and put in a very warm place (80°–100°F/27°–38°C) until the mixture has more than doubled in size, about 10 minutes.

2 In a small saucepan over medium heat, combine the milk and 4 tablespoons (2 oz/60 g) of the butter and heat until the butter melts. Set aside.

3 Sift the flour again into a bowl and make a well in the center. Add the eggs, salt, the remaining 2 tablespoons granulated sugar, the yeast mixture, and the warm (not hot) milk mixture. Beat with a whisk until blended. The dough will be so sticky that it cannot yet be kneaded in the traditional sense. Instead, using your hands and leaving the dough in the bowl, pull it high and slap it back into the bowl. Continue doing this until it becomes so elastic that you can pull it into ropes without it tearing, about 5 minutes. Gather the dough into a ball, cover the bowl with a damp kitchen towel, put in a very warm place, and let the dough rise until doubled in size, 1½–2 hours. Gently roll the edges of the dough over the center and push the dough down.

4 With the remaining 1 tablespoon butter, grease 6 baba cups or standard muffin cups. Divide the dough equally among the cups, filling each one-third full. Cover with a damp kitchen towel and again put in a very warm place to rise for about 1 hour. The dough should be just peeking over the rims. While the dough is rising, position a rack in the upper third of an oven and preheat to 375°F (190°C).

5 Meanwhile, make the syrup: In a saucepan over medium-high heat, bring the granulated sugar and water to a boil, stirring to dissolve the sugar. Add the orange juice and cook, stirring, until a thick syrup forms, 4–5 minutes. Let cool slightly, then stir in the rum. Keep warm.

6 Remove the kitchen towel and place the cups in the oven. Bake until the babas are nicely golden and pull away from the sides of the cups, about 15 minutes. Remove from the oven, let stand for 10–15 minutes, then unmold them. Set upright on a rack.

7 To soak the babas in the syrup, poke them all over with a wooden skewer. Put them in a shallow baking dish and spoon the syrup over them. As it drains into the dish, spoon it over again. Let stand for 4–5 minutes, then spoon it over again. Repeat several times until the babas are soft and spongy. Put a rack on a baking sheet and place the babas on the rack. Let drain until they stop dripping, then transfer the babas to another plate or dish, cover, and refrigerate for at least several hours or for up to 24 hours.

8 To make the topping, beat the cream until soft peaks form. Add the confectioners' sugar and the vanilla and beat until stiff peaks form.

9 To serve, place the babas on individual plates. Spoon the topping onto each baba and sprinkle with the orange zest. Serve at once.

Poached Quinces

Coings Pochés • Provence • France

Quince trees thrive in household gardens throughout the south of France. Although quinces may be cooked much more quickly, here they are slowly poached to a glorious deep hue the color of carnelian. The technique is one passed on by the wise grandmothers of Provence. The poached quinces can also be used for making a tart, in which case you should cut them into thick wedges rather than quarters.

4 large quinces

2¼ cups (18 oz/560 g) sugar

4 cups (32 fl oz/1 l) water

Zest from 1 large lemon, cut into strips ¾ inch (2 cm) wide

1 orange zest strip, ¾ inch (2 cm) wide

Serves 6

1 Peel, quarter, and core the quinces. Place the cores and peels on a piece of cheesecloth (muslin), bring the corners together, and tie with kitchen string. In a large nonaluminum saucepan, combine the sugar and water. Add the quince pieces, lemon and orange zests, and cheesecloth bundle and reduce the heat to very low.

2 Cut a round of parchment (baking) paper the diameter of the pan, place over the quinces, and top with a heatproof plate. Cover the pan and cook very slowly for 6–7 hours, using a heat diffuser if cooking on a gas burner. The quinces will be tender and a lovely red. Alternatively, place the covered pan in a 200°F (95°C) oven for 8–9 hours.

3 Remove the pan from the stove top or the oven, carefully remove the plate and parchment, and discard the cheesecloth bundle. Let the quinces cool in their cooking liquid. Transfer to a large serving bowl. Serve in bowls with a few tablespoons of the juice spooned over the top. The quinces can be stored in the refrigerator for up to 10 days.

Oven-Roasted Figs with Crème Fraîche

Figues Rôties à la Crème Fraîche • Southwestern • France

When figs are roasted or grilled, their natural sugars begin to caramelize slightly, and their already sweet taste takes on a deeper, richer flavor. Here that heightened intensity is further enhanced by the addition of a little crème fraîche. Any fig variety may be used as long as the fruits are very ripe and soft. The small, nearly black Violette de Bordeaux, which tastes like sweet berry jam, works particularly well here.

1 teaspoon unsalted butter

16 very ripe figs

2 tablespoons granulated sugar

1 teaspoon fresh lemon juice

½ cup (4 fl oz/125 ml) crème fraîche

1 tablespoon grated lemon zest

1 tablespoon firmly packed brown sugar

Serves 8

1 Preheat the oven to 400°F (200°C). Using the butter, grease a shallow roasting pan just large enough to hold the figs.

2 Place the figs in the prepared pan and turn them once or twice to coat with the butter. Sprinkle with the granulated sugar.

3 Bake just until the figs are cooked through, 10–12 minutes. Remove from the oven, drizzle with the lemon juice, and let stand for 5 minutes.

4 Divide the figs among warmed dessert plates. Serve hot, garnished with a little crème fraîche, lemon zest, and brown sugar.

Apple and Goat Cheese Galette

Galette de Pommes au Fromage • Normandy • France

One of the nice things about apples is that because a number of varieties store well, the fruit is in season from fall through spring. The French have made good use of this bounty, and consequently dishes incorporating apples are abundant and inventive. Here, creamy sweetened goat cheese complements the tart crispness of the apples.

1 sheet frozen puff pastry, about 12 by 14 inches (30 by 35 cm) and ¼ inch (6 mm) thick, thawed in the refrigerator

¼ lb (125 g) fresh goat cheese

½ cup (4 oz/125 g) plus 2 tablespoons sugar

1 egg

½ cup (4 fl oz/125 ml) heavy (double) cream

¼ teaspoon vanilla extract (essence)

2 large apples such as Granny Smith, Gala, or Golden Delicious, peeled, cored, and cut lengthwise into slices ¼ inch (6 mm) thick

Serves 6

1 Preheat the oven to 375°F (190°C).

2 Unfold the sheet of puff pastry. Using a sharp knife, trim off the corners to make a round about 12 inches (30 cm) in diameter. Transfer the pastry to an ungreased baking sheet. Pinch the edges up to form a generous ¼-inch (6-mm) rim.

3 In a bowl, whisk together the goat cheese, the ½ cup (4 oz/125 g) sugar, the egg, cream, and vanilla until a smooth paste forms. Spread the paste evenly over the bottom of the pastry. Arrange the apple slices in a concentric circle on top. Sprinkle the 2 tablespoons sugar evenly over the apples.

4 Bake until the pastry is puffed and browned and the apples are lightly golden, about 30 minutes. Remove from the oven, cover loosely with aluminum foil, and let stand for about 10 minutes.

5 Serve the galette warm or at room temperature, cut into wedges.

THE CHEESE COURSE

There are several ways to compose a classic platter for a cheese course. The simplest is an offering of five to seven cheeses from different regions and families. The families include fresh cheeses, such as *petit-suisse* and *fromage frais;* soft cheeses with a coated rind, usually soft and white, such as Camembert; and soft cheeses with a washed rind, such as Meunster. The rinds of these latter cheeses are typically orange-red from the frequent washings they receive as they age. Veined cheeses, those with blue veining or marbling, form another family. Hard uncooked cheeses, which are aged from three to six months, make up a group that includes Morbier and Saint-Nectaire, and hard cooked cheeses constitute yet another family. From this latter cluster come Comté and Beaufort, which are aged for up to two years. Goat cheese can belong to any of the families, depending upon how it was made.

Another way to compose your cheese board is to choose three cheeses from the same region and accompany them with a wine, cider, or beer of that region. With goat cheese, you can serve a "flight" from very fresh to aged cheeses. In every case, for the best flavor, you should remove your cheeses from the refrigerator at least an hour and a half before serving.

Pears in Puff Pastry with Lavender Custard

Feuilleté de Poires et Crème Anglaise à la Lavande • Provence • France

The pear halves look beautiful framed in their puff pastry casings. These pastries are usually served with a custard; one perfumed with lavender keeps the dish Provençal.

LAVENDER CUSTARD

2 cups (16 fl oz/500 ml) milk

4 egg yolks

½ cup (4 oz/125 g) sugar

1 tablespoon pesticide-free fresh or dried lavender flowers, without stems

PEAR PASTRIES

3 pears, with stems intact

2 cups (1 lb/500 g) sugar

4 cups (32 fl oz/1 l) plus 3 tablespoons water

3 tablespoons sweet white wine

1 vanilla bean, split lengthwise

6 teaspoons marzipan or 6 pitted dates or prunes (optional)

¾ lb (375 g) frozen puff pastry

1 egg beaten with 1 tablespoon milk

¼ cup (2 oz/60 g) apricot jam

Serves 6

1 To make the custard, pour the milk into a saucepan and place over medium heat until small bubbles appear along the edges of the pan. In a bowl, beat together the egg yolks and sugar until creamy. Pour about ½ cup (4 fl oz/125 ml) of the hot milk into the egg mixture while whisking constantly. Return the milk-egg mixture to the saucepan and stir constantly over medium heat with a wooden spoon until the mixture thickens and lightly coats the back of the spoon, about 1 minute. Do not allow it to boil. An instant-read thermometer inserted into the custard should read 180°F (82°C).

2 Remove from the heat and stir in the lavender flowers. Pour into a pitcher, place plastic wrap directly on the surface to prevent a skin from forming, and refrigerate overnight.

3 The next day, pour the custard through a fine-mesh sieve. Return the custard to the pitcher, cover with clean plastic wrap again pressed directly on the surface, and refrigerate for up to 2 days before serving.

4 To make the pastries, peel the pears, leaving the stems intact. In a saucepan large enough to hold the pears snugly, combine the sugar, 4 cups (32 fl oz/1 l) water, the wine, and vanilla. Bring to a boil over high heat, stirring to dissolve the sugar. Add the pears, reduce the heat to low, and simmer until the pears are tender, 15–20 minutes. Let the pears cool in the liquid, then transfer to paper towels to drain well. Split each pear in half lengthwise, splitting the stem, if possible. Remove the cores gently without disturbing the stems. If you like, place 1 teaspoon of the marzipan or a date or prune in the hollow left in each half after the removal of the core.

5 Make a template by tracing a pear half, including its stem, on a piece of cardboard. Cut out the shape, leaving an extra ¾ inch (2 cm) outside the tracing.

6 Preheat the oven to 400°F (200°C). Remove the custard from the refrigerator and bring to room temperature.

7 On a floured work surface, roll out the puff pastry into a large rectangle no more than ⅛ inch (3 mm) thick. Using the template, cut out 6 pieces of pastry and transfer to 2 ungreased baking sheets. Dry the pear halves well on paper towels and place a pear half, rounded side up, in the center of each piece of pastry. Brush the exposed pastry edges with the egg-milk mixture. Place 1 sheet in the oven and bake, rotating the sheet 180 degrees after 15 minutes to ensure even coloration, until the pastry is puffed up and golden brown, 20–25 minutes.

8 Meanwhile, in a small saucepan, combine the apricot jam and the remaining 3 tablespoons water. Place over low heat and stir constantly until the jam dissolves.

9 Remove the pastries from the oven, slide onto a rack, and brush with half of the apricot glaze. Repeat the process with the second baking sheet of pastries. Serve warm or at room temperature, on individual plates, with some lavender custard spread around each pastry.

Gratinéed Peaches with Honey Cake

Pêches Gratinées au Pain d'Épices • Provence • France

This dessert is ideal at the beginning of the peach season, when the fruits need cooking to bring out their full flavor. *Pain d'épices* is a soft, gingerbread-like loaf cake sold internationally by Dutch companies under the name "honey cake." If it is unavailable, pound cake may be substituted. Nectarines or pears can be used in place of the peaches. Peel the pears prior to cooking and allow up to 15 minutes of poaching for most varieties.

1 Select a saucepan large enough to hold the peaches snugly. Combine the water and granulated sugar in the pan and place over high heat, stirring constantly to dissolve the sugar before the water comes to a boil. Add the peaches (they should be fully immersed) and bring to a boil over high heat. Reduce the heat to low and simmer, uncovered, until the peaches are just tender, 5–8 minutes. Do not overcook, or the peaches will be difficult to slice neatly.

2 Drain the peaches and, when cool enough to handle, peel, halve, and remove the pits. Cut the halves lengthwise into slices ¼ inch (6 mm) thick.

3 Preheat a broiler (griller) or preheat the oven to 450°F (230°C). Roughly crumble the *pain d'épices* or pound cake onto the bottom of individual dessert dishes, ideally small oval or round white porcelain dishes. The dishes must be flameproof or ovenproof. Arrange the peach slices concentrically, overlapping the slices slightly, over the cakes.

4 In a bowl, beat together the egg yolks and 2 tablespoons brown sugar until creamy. Fold in the whipped cream and ground hazelnuts. Flavor to taste with the liqueur. Spread the mixture over the peach slices, leaving a border ½–¾ inch (12 mm–2 cm) wide uncovered.

5 Sprinkle the cream topping with the chopped hazelnuts and then with a light coating of brown sugar. Slip under the broiler until the tops are lightly browned, about 1 minute, or bake in the oven for 2–3 minutes. Serve at once.

4 cups (32 fl oz/1 l) water

1½ cups (12 oz/375 g) granulated sugar

6 medium-ripe peaches

½ loaf *pain d'épices* (see note) or pound cake

2 egg yolks

2 tablespoons brown sugar, plus more for topping

1 cup (8 fl oz/250 ml) heavy (double) cream, whipped until stiff

1 tablespoon ground toasted hazelnuts (filberts) (page 224)

1½–2 tablespoons amaretto or peach liqueur

6 tablespoons (2 oz/60 g) hazelnuts (filberts), toasted (page 224) and chopped

Serves 4

Pine Nut Crescents

Croissants aux Pignons • Provence • France

These cookies, said to have originated in Nice, have gained a reputation that has taken them farther afield. Many of the pine trees that once grew along the coast have been cleared to make way for houses and for plantings of eucalyptus, which are less vulnerable to fire. This makes the *pignolats,* as the cookies are also called in Nice, even more special.

1 cup (5 oz/155 g) pine nuts

1 whole egg, plus 3 egg whites

2¼ cups (9 oz/280 g) ground almonds

1 cup (7 oz/220 g) plus 3 tablespoons superfine (caster) sugar

Makes 16–20 cookies

1 Preheat the oven to 375°F (190°C). Butter a baking sheet.

2 Spread the pine nuts in an even layer on a plate or wooden board. Break the whole egg into a wide, shallow bowl and beat with a fork until blended.

3 In a bowl, combine the ground almonds, sugar, and egg whites. Using a whisk or handheld electric mixer, beat until a firm dough forms. Using the palms of your hands, form the dough into walnut-sized balls. Roll each ball first in the beaten egg and then in the pine nuts to coat evenly. Press each coated ball against the work surface with your fingers to elongate it into a crescent with a flattened underside, then place on the prepared baking sheet. Bake the crescents until golden, 15–20 minutes. Let cool completely on the sheet. Using a metal spatula, slide them onto a plate and serve.

Figs Stuffed with Marzipan

Figues Sèches au Marzipan • Provence • France

Fig trees are nearly as dominant in the landscape of Provence as olive trees. The recipe for these marzipan-stuffed delicacies from the papal city of Avignon includes two versions: a moister one for use as a dessert and a sweeter and stickier one for use as a sweetmeat.

3 cups (24 fl oz/750 ml) water

1 cup (8 oz/250 g) sugar

3 whole cloves

3 orange zest slices

18–20 dried figs, moister if for dessert and drier if for a sweetmeat

4 tablespoons (2 fl oz/60 ml) Cognac or Armagnac

1 package (6½ oz/200 g) marzipan paste

Serves 6 as a dessert, or 10 as a sweetmeat

1 In a small saucepan over medium heat, combine the water, sugar, cloves, and orange zest. Bring to a boil, stirring to dissolve the sugar. Add the figs and 3 tablespoons of the Cognac or Armagnac. Reduce the heat to as low as possible and simmer gently for 2 hours to plump the figs. Let cool for 30–45 minutes.

2 Remove the figs from the cooking liquid, reserving the liquid. Using a small knife, make a slit at the center of each fig. Using a small spoon or your fingers, press a scant teaspoon of marzipan into each fig, smoothing the surface of the marzipan. Pinch the slit closed, but leave a little marzipan visible. Return the figs to the liquid in the saucepan. Stir in the remaining 1 tablespoon Cognac or Armagnac, mixing well, and then stir the figs to coat them with the liquid. Using a slotted spoon, transfer the figs to a bowl.

3 To serve the figs as a dessert, boil the liquid in the pan, stirring often, until it is a good sauce consistency, then pour over the figs. To use the figs as a sweetmeat, reduce the liquid to a thick syrup, stirring constantly. Transfer the figs and syrup to a bowl or jar, cover, and refrigerate for up to 4 weeks. Remove from the refrigerator at least 1 hour before serving.

LES CALISSONS D' AIX

For more than four centuries, the *calisson d'Aix* has been the unrivaled champion of Provençal confectionery. Nowadays, the sweetmeat is manufactured in fewer than half a dozen local factories, although a handful of artisans, laboring in spaces behind their family pâtisseries, continue to make *calissons* by hand in the time-honored manner.

Georges Touzet is a fourth-generation pâtissier from Maison Béchard on Cours Mirabeau, the beautiful plane tree–lined main street of Aix-en-Provence. Each day, Georges and his octogenarian father, Raymond, oversee the production of 100–110 pounds (50–60 kg) of the classic confection, shaping them in cast-iron diamond-shaped molds that hold just thirty-six at a time.

Following rules that guarantee both quality and regional integrity, the Touzets painstakingly build the *calissons*. First they prepare the traditional paste center, a mixture of ground blanched almonds, at least 40 percent of which must come from Mediterranean trees; the famed candied Presco melon of Apt; candied orange peel; honey; and orange flower water. The almond mixture is molded upon a thin rice-paper base, the top is lightly brushed with apricot jam, and then a snow-white fondant is applied. Once the finished confections are slipped from their molds, they are briefly dried and then carefully packed for sale.

Berry Tartlets

Tartelettes aux Fruits • Ile-de-France • France

Rows of fruit tarts are presented like glittering multicolored jewels in pâtisserie windows all over France. For a large tart, substitute a 10-inch (25-cm) tart pan for the tartlet molds.

PASTRY DOUGH

2 cups (10 oz/315 g) all-purpose (plain) flour

1 teaspoon salt

½ cup (4 oz/125 g) plus 3 tablespoons chilled unsalted butter, cut into ½-inch (12-mm) chunks

6 tablespoons (3 fl oz/90 ml) ice water

PASTRY CREAM

1 cup (8 fl oz/250 ml) milk, plus 1 tablespoon (optional)

½ cup (4 oz/125 g) sugar

3 egg yolks

⅓ cup (2 oz/60 g) all-purpose (plain) flour

1 tablespoon unsalted butter, at room temperature

1½ teaspoons vanilla extract (essence)

½ cup (5 oz/155 g) red currant jelly

1½ cups (6 oz/185 g) blueberries

1½ cups (6 oz/185 g) raspberries

Serves 12

1 To make the pastry dough, in a large bowl, stir together the flour and salt. Using a pastry blender or 2 knives, cut in the butter until pea-sized balls form. Add the ice water 1 tablespoon at a time while turning the dough lightly with a fork and then with your fingertips. (Do not overwork the dough, or it will become tough.) Gather the dough into a ball (it will be a little crumbly), wrap in plastic wrap, and refrigerate for 15 minutes.

2 Preheat the oven to 425°F (220°C).

3 Divide the dough into quarters and roll out 1 piece at a time, keeping the others refrigerated. On a floured work surface, roll out the first piece of dough a scant ¼ inch (6 mm) thick. Place a 2-inch (5-cm) round or other shape mold face down on the dough and, using a knife, cut out the same shape ½ inch (12 mm) larger than the mold. Continue until as much dough as possible has been used. Slip a knife or icing spatula under each cutout and gently press into a mold, trimming the edges as needed. Gather together the dough scraps and roll out again. Cut out as many shapes as possible, but do not rework the scraps a second time. Continue until all the dough has been used and the molds lined. Cut out a piece of parchment (baking) paper for each mold and use to line the molds. Fill the lined molds with pie weights or dried beans.

4 Bake for 10 minutes, then lift out the weights and paper. With a fork, prick the bottoms of the tarts, return to the oven, and bake until golden, 4–5 minutes longer. Let cool completely on a rack.

5 To make the pastry cream, pour the 1 cup (8 fl oz/250 ml) milk into a large saucepan and place over medium heat until small bubbles form at the edges of the pan. Meanwhile, in a large bowl, using an electric beater set on medium speed, beat together the sugar and egg yolks until lemon-colored. Beat in the flour to form a thick paste. When the milk is ready, gradually pour it into the sugar mixture, beating constantly. When the warm milk is incorporated, pour the mixture back into the saucepan and bring to a boil over medium-high heat, beating continuously. When the mixture thickens, after 1–2 minutes, immediately remove it from the heat and whisk vigorously until very thick, about 1 minute. Whisk in the butter and vanilla. Let cool slightly. If the pastry cream thickens too much to spread upon cooling, add the 1 tablespoon milk and whisk until smooth.

6 In a saucepan over low heat, warm the jelly, stirring until melted. Remove from the heat. Pour just enough of the warm melted jelly into a cooled pastry shell to glaze the bottom, tipping the mold from side to side to coat evenly. Continue until all the pastries are glazed, reheating the jelly gently if needed to thin it.

7 Spoon enough of the pastry cream over the glaze in each shell to make a layer ¼–⅓ inch (6–9 mm) thick. Cover the cream layer with the blueberries and raspberries. Spoon just enough glaze over the berries to coat them. Cover and refrigerate for at least 1 hour or for up to 12 hours.

8 Let the tartlets stand at room temperature for 15–20 minutes before serving.

Jam-Filled Pastries

Rissoles d'Abricots • Provence • France

These *rissoles* resemble ravioli that have been deep-fried and dusted with sugar. Vendors in markets sometimes offer savory versions as well, with fillings such as spinach or potato and cheese. The pastry is the same for the sweet and savory versions.

1 To make the dough, put the flour, egg yolks, olive oil, and water, in that order, in a food processor. Process until a sticky ball forms. Transfer the dough to a floured work surface and knead until it is elastic and can be rolled out, about 7 minutes. Loosely wrap the dough in plastic wrap and let stand at room temperature for 30 minutes.

2 Divide the dough into 2 equal pieces. On a large, well-floured work surface, roll out 1 ball of dough into a 16-by-20-inch (40-by-50-cm) rectangle about ⅛ inch (3 mm) thick. Visually divide the dough sheet into 4-inch (10-cm) squares. Place 3 tablespoons of the jam filling in the center of each square, smoothing and spreading it out to within ½ inch (12 mm) of the edges of the squares.

3 Roll out the remaining ball of dough into the same-sized sheet. Lay the second sheet over the top of the first. With the edge of your hand, press the upper sheet to the lower one, making lines between the mounds of filling to seal the edges of the squares.

4 With a pastry cutter or a sharp knife, cut along each sealing line, dividing the filled dough sheets into 4-inch (10-cm) squares. (At this point, you can cook the squares, or you can arrange them in a single layer, not touching, on a flour-dusted kitchen towel or piece of waxed paper, dust them well with flour, and cover them with another towel or piece of waxed paper. They will keep for several hours.)

5 In a deep frying pan, pour in oil to a depth of 1 inch (2.5 cm) and heat over medium heat to 350°F (180°C) on a deep-frying thermometer, or until a drop of water flicked into the pan sizzles. Add the squares, a few at a time; do not allow them to touch. Cook on the first side until golden brown, about 2 minutes. Using tongs, turn them over and cook on the second side until golden brown, about 1½ minutes longer. Using tongs, transfer to paper towels to drain. Keep warm in a low oven until ready to serve, or serve as they are prepared, a few at a time.

6 Just before serving, using a fine-mesh sieve, dust the pastries with sugar. Serve hot.

DOUGH

2 cups (10 oz/315 g) all-purpose (plain) flour

2 egg yolks

1 tablespoon extra-virgin olive oil

2 tablespoons water

2 cups (1¼ lb/625 g) thick apricot jam with chunks of fruit

Canola or other light oil for deep-frying

Confectioners' (icing) sugar

Makes about 20 pastries; Serves 5 or 6

French Toast with Warm Cherries

Pain Perdu aux Cerises Tièdes • Pays de la Loire • France

Although this dessert is humble farmhouse fare, the combination of tastes, textures, and colors makes it a splendid sweet. Be sure to alert your guests about the unpitted cherries.

¼ cup (2 oz/60 g) sugar

½ cup (4 fl oz/125 ml) water

1 star anise

1 tablespoon kirsch (optional)

1 cup (6 oz/185 g) stemmed yellow Rainier cherries or other large, sweet cherries

4 eggs

2 tablespoons milk or water

4 slices day-old brioche or other sweet bread, each ½ inch (12 mm) thick

3 tablespoons unsalted butter

Confectioners' (icing) sugar

Serves 4

1 In a saucepan over medium heat, combine the sugar and water. Bring to a boil, stirring until the sugar dissolves. Add the star anise and the kirsch, if using. Cook, stirring occasionally, until a thin syrup forms, 4–5 minutes. Add the cherries and continue to cook, stirring often, until softened, 7–8 minutes. Remove from the heat and cover to keep warm.

2 In a shallow baking dish just large enough to hold the brioche slices in a single layer, whisk together the eggs and milk or water until blended. Add the brioche slices and let soak for 1–2 minutes. Turn them over and let soak on the second side until all the liquid has been absorbed.

3 In a frying pan over medium heat, melt the butter. Add the bread and cook, turning once, until golden, 6–8 minutes total.

4 Transfer a slice of the brioche to each of 4 warmed individual plates. Spoon an equal amount of the warm cherries and their sauce over each slice. Dust with confectioners' sugar and serve.

Lavender Honey Ice Cream

Glace au Miel de Lavande • Provence • France

Although fields of cultivated lavender are common today in Provence, wild lavender was gathered commercially until the late 1940s. Here, lavender blossoms are combined with honey, another significant product of the region, to make a lusciously rich ice cream.

3 cups (24 fl oz/750 ml) heavy (double) cream

1 cup (8 fl oz/250 ml) milk

½ cup (6 oz/185 g) lavender, orange blossom, or clover honey, plus honey for serving

½ cup (3½ oz/105 g) firmly packed brown sugar

1 teaspoon dried lavender blossoms

1 piece vanilla bean, 2 inches (5 cm) long

¼ teaspoon salt

4 egg yolks

¼ teaspoon ground cloves

Makes about 1 qt (1 l)

1 In a heavy saucepan over medium-high heat, combine the cream, milk, ½ cup honey, brown sugar, lavender blossoms, vanilla bean, and salt. Bring to a boil, stirring often until the sugar dissolves completely.

2 In a bowl, whisk the yolks until they are lemon-colored. Slowly whisk 1 cup (8 fl oz/ 250 ml) of the hot cream mixture into the yolks. Now, whisk the yolk mixture into the hot cream mixture. Continue to cook, stirring constantly, until the mixture thickens enough to coat the back of a spoon, 5–6 minutes. Do not allow it to boil. Remove from the heat and let cool to lukewarm. Pour through a fine-mesh sieve placed over a bowl, discarding the lavender and vanilla bean. Stir in the cloves.

3 Freeze in an ice cream maker according to the manufacturer's directions, then allow to cool completely. Scoop into small bowls and drizzle with honey.

HONEY

Wherever you go in the French countryside, you are likely to find locally produced honey, or *miel*. In spring and summer, beehives dot orchards, forests, meadows, and fields, and the bees feed on whatever is blooming. Once a particular bloom is over, that honey is gathered and the bees are set elsewhere to feast on another nectar. Small producers may depend upon three or four different kinds of honey, while larger ones usually focus on a single product. Each honey displays distinct characteristics, and it is a treat to sample different ones as you travel through France. On country roads you may come across hand-lettered signs reading *Miel à vendre ici*, or "Honey for sale here." It is well worth stopping, as chances are that you will find farmhouse honey made the old-fashioned way by small producers.

Honey turns up in a variety of guises on the French table. You will find it spread on the morning tartines, used as a glaze in such savory preparations as roast duck or chicken, and added to sweets of all kinds. A truly extraordinary dessert is an utterly simple one: a stream of mountain honey spooned over fresh cheese and served with bread.

ITALY

I s there a sight more evocative of the rustic pleasures of the Italian table than a fig tree heavy with late-summer fruit? Carefully tended in front yards or growing wild along the roadside, warmed by the relentless sun, the trees dip their branches toward the ground under the weight of plump fruit oozing honey-like juice. Even in the city, each fruttivendolo displays its fruit with painterly care, often with the leaves still attached as a sign of freshness.

With such an abundance of luscious choices, meals in Italy often end with fruit. Even when more elaborate pastries or cakes are to follow, most diners expect to have some fruit as a palate cleanser and *digestivo*. Fragrant peaches or berries may be doused with a glass of dessert wine or baptized with a few drops of syrupy balsamic vinegar and a pinch of freshly ground pepper—a surprising combination that works brings out the sweetness of ripe strawberries. Whole fruits may be poached in syrup or sliced and layered in parfaits with mascarpone and crushed amaretti cookies. As each season's abundance of plums, cherries, apricots, or raspberries reaches its peak, the overflow is simmered down into *marmellate* and *conserve*. Later, the jewel-colored jars will be opened and their sweet contents spread between layers of golden pastry to make

crostate, or tarts. Other desserts, like a buttery apple cake from Friuli, contain fresh fruit baked right into the pastry.

Nuts, too, figure prominently in desserts: Apulia produces sweet, cakelike almond biscotti and Siena makes *castagnaccio*, a flat, deep cake made with chestnut flour and pine nuts. Piedmont is known for growing particularly delicious hazelnuts (filberts), which are mixed with chocolate to make *gianduja* (sometimes spelled *gianduia*). You can find *gianduja* ice cream, cakes, and candies, including Perugina's famous Baci, little "kisses" of hazelnut-studded chocolate topped with a hazelnut.

In the south, the options in the *pasticcerie* change dramatically, becoming sweeter and richer and making extravagant use of the sharply aromatic oranges and lemons that grow along the Amalfi coast. Neapolitans

make delicious *bignè*, or cream puffs, often with a lemon cream filling, while cannoli—pastry tubes fried and filled with sweetened sheep's milk ricotta—are a classic Sicilian sweet. Sicilians also bake *biscotti all'arancia*, using the region's famous oranges.

Gelato is perhaps the finest ice cream in the world. No wonder you will see everyone from infants to grandparents licking cones all day long, especially during the hot summer months. When visiting Italy, look for a *gelateria* that displays a sign indicating *produzione propria*—meaning "made by the proprietor"—for a superior product.

Holidays, usually connected with saints' days, seem to occur more frequently in Italy than anywhere else, and each festivity has a special sweet associated with it. In February, during *Carnevale*, a four-week period of revelry ending on the day before Lent, pastry shops in Florence are filled with trays of *schiacciata alla fiorentina*, a golden yellow cake dusted with confectioners' (icing) sugar that beckons Italians in from the cold for a slice of cake and a cup of thick, bittersweet *cioccolata calda* (hot chocolate) topped with whipped cream. During Lent, lavish cakes are replaced by *quaresimali*, dark brown, crunchy cookies cut into alphabet shapes. At Easter, no pastry shop is without *la colomba*, a light, yeast-raised sweet bread similar to the *panettone* served at Christmas, only formed in the shape of a dove and decorated with almonds. By *ferragosto* (the Feast of the

Assumption, in mid-August) businesses all over Italy shut down as their proprietors flee to the beach towns along the Mediterranean and Adriatic. Here, the evening *passeggiata* always includes a stop at the local *gelateria* for a scoop of watermelon-mint *sorbetto* or refreshing *granita di caffè*.

Come autumn, grapes hang lush and sweet in vineyards, and whatever isn't made into wine is baked into *schiacciata all'uva*, a sweet focaccia studded with wine grapes and fresh rosemary. Chestnuts encased in prickly outer shells fall from leafy branches, ready to be roasted with fennel seed and doused with flaming grappa to make Lucca's *bruciate ubriache*, or drunken chestnuts.

As autumn gives way to Christmas, and holiday sweets line the windows of pastry shops, decorated by boxes of *panetonne*, a tall sweet bread studded with dried fruit. In Siena, the most famous dessert is *panforte*, a dense, chewy fruitcake laden with honey, nuts, candied fruits, and spices. In Sicily, a similar confection of chopped figs and walnuts is rolled into a rich paste with honey, orange zest, cloves, and cinnamon and surrounded by a fancifully decorated ring of pastry.

No matter what the time of year, you can savor the end of any meal the Italian way with a tumbler of sweet, amber-colored *vin santo*, a wedge of cheese or piece of perfectly ripened fruit, and a couple of crunchy biscotti to dunk in the glass between sips.

Left: Piedmont boasts a wide range of desserts, from simple butter cookies to *ciliegie al Barolo*, sour cherries simmered with wine and sugar and topped with whipped cream. **Above, left:** Taormina's spectacularly situated Greek theater offers a magnificent view of Mount Etna, one of the world's largest active volcanoes. **Above, right:** When perfectly ripened, late-summer figs make a simple yet sensuous dessert.

Blackberry Jam Tart

Crostata di Marmellata · Tuscany · Italy

Tuscans generally do not eat elaborate desserts. But when blackberries are in season, fruit tarts made with homemade blackberry jam suddenly appear in pastry shop windows. The berries grow wild all over the Tuscan countryside and are eaten with sugar and lemon juice or turned into a warm sauce for spooning over ice cream.

PASTRY

2¾ cups (14 oz/440 g) all-purpose (plain) flour

½ cup (4 oz/125 g) sugar

1½ teaspoons baking powder

½ teaspoon salt

Grated zest of 1 lemon

¾ cup (6 oz/185 g) chilled unsalted butter, cut into bits

1 whole egg, plus 1 egg yolk

1 teaspoon vanilla extract (essence)

2 cups (1¼ lb/625 g) blackberry jam

Confectioners' (icing) sugar

Serves 8

1 To make the pastry, in a large bowl, stir together the flour, sugar, baking powder, salt, and lemon zest. Using a pastry blender or a fork, work in the butter until the mixture resembles coarse crumbs.

2 In a small bowl, whisk together the egg, egg yolk, and vanilla. Pour over the dry ingredients and stir just until the liquid is incorporated. If the mixture seems dry, add a teaspoon or so of cold water, just enough to bring the dough together. Divide the dough into 2 disks, one slightly larger than the other. Wrap the disks separately in plastic wrap and refrigerate for at least 30 minutes or for up to overnight.

3 Position a rack in the lower third of an oven and preheat to 350°F (180°C).

4 Place the larger dough disk between 2 sheets of plastic wrap and roll out into a 12-inch (30-cm) round. Transfer to a 10-inch (25-cm) tart pan with a removable bottom, pressing it smoothly against the bottom and sides. Trim the edges, leaving a ½-inch (12-mm) overhang. Fold the overhang over against the inside of the rim of the pan.

5 Spread the jam evenly in the pastry shell.

6 Roll out the remaining dough disk between 2 sheets of plastic wrap into a 10-inch (25-cm) round. Using a pastry wheel, cut the dough into strips ½ inch (12 mm) wide. Arrange half of the strips across the top of the tart, spacing them about 1 inch (2.5 cm) apart. Give the pan a quarter turn and place the remaining dough strips across the top, again spaced 1 inch (2.5 cm) apart, to form a lattice pattern. If the strips break, simply patch them together. Press the ends of the strips against the sides of the tart shell to seal.

7 Bake until the pastry is golden brown, about 55 minutes. Transfer to a wire rack to cool for 10 minutes. Remove the pan rim and let the tart cool completely.

8 Just before serving, slide the tart off the base onto a serving plate. Place confectioners' sugar in a small sieve and dust the top of the tart.

Lent Alphabet Cookies

Quaresimali · Tuscany · Italy

These chocolate alphabet cookies were traditionally eaten in Florence during the forty days of Lent and were made with very little sugar or fat, in keeping with the abstemious nature of the religious period. *Quaresimali* have gone somewhat out of fashion, and when you find them, they are usually made from a slightly richer recipe, like the one here.

½ cup (4 oz/125 g) unsalted butter, at room temperature

¾ cup (6 oz/185 g) sugar

1 egg

1 teaspoon vanilla extract (essence)

1¾ cups (9 oz/280 g) all-purpose (plain) flour

½ teaspoon grated orange zest

½ teaspoon salt

¼ cup (¾ oz/20 g) unsweetened cocoa powder

Makes about 36 cookies

1 In a large bowl, using an electric mixer, beat together the butter and sugar until creamy. Add the egg and vanilla and beat until light and fluffy. Stir in the flour, orange zest, salt, and cocoa until well combined. Transfer the dough to a sheet of plastic wrap, shape into a ball, and flatten to a disk. Wrap well and refrigerate until very firm, about 2 hours.

2 Preheat the oven to 350°F (180°C). Line 2 baking sheets with parchment (baking) paper.

3 On a work surface, place the dough disk between 2 sheets of plastic wrap. Roll out to a thickness of ⅛ inch (3 mm). Using a sharp knife, cut out letters 2 inches (5 cm) tall. Using a metal spatula, transfer them to the prepared baking sheet, spacing them about 2 inches (5 cm) apart. Place the sheet in the freezer for 10 minutes before baking. Gather the dough scraps and refrigerate if too soft to roll easily, then roll out and cut more cookies.

4 Bake until firm to the touch, 10–12 minutes. Transfer to a wire rack to cool on the pan for 2 minutes, then transfer the cookies to the rack and let cool completely. Store in an airtight container at room temperature for up to 1 week.

Vin Santo Ice Cream

Gelato di Vin Santo · Tuscany · Italy

A twentieth-century addition to Tuscan cuisine, this version of gelato is eaten at a wine maker's estate outside the beautiful hill town of Montepulciano. Serve light, buttery cookies, such as *quaresimali* (above), to complement this delicate treat.

2 cups (16 fl oz/500 ml) heavy (double) cream

2 cups (16 fl oz/500 ml) milk

4 egg yolks

¾ cup (6 oz/185 g) sugar

¼ cup (2 fl oz/60 ml) *vin santo*

Makes about 1 qt (1 l); Serves 4

1 In a saucepan over medium heat, combine the cream and milk and heat until small bubbles appear along the edges of the pan.

2 Meanwhile, in a bowl, using an electric mixer, beat together the egg yolks and sugar until the mixture is thick and a creamy pale yellow. Whisking continuously, slowly add ½ cup (4 fl oz/125 ml) of the warm milk-cream mixture to the eggs. Then pour the resulting mixture into the saucepan with the remaining milk and cream. Place over low heat and heat gently, stirring continuously, until the mixture is thick enough to coat the back of a spoon, about 8 minutes. Do not allow it to boil.

3 Pour the mixture through a fine-mesh sieve placed over a bowl. Stir in the *vin santo*, cover, and refrigerate to chill thoroughly.

4 Freeze the mixture in an ice-cream maker according to the manufacturer's instructions. Transfer to an airtight container and chill in the freezer for 1 hour before serving.

Tuscan-Style Trifle

Zuppa Inglese • Tuscany • Italy

Translated literally as "English soup," *zuppa inglese* is not a soup, of course, but a dessert so named because of its resemblance to English trifle. Homemade with high-quality ingredients, it is not only delicious but also a perfect primer on standard dessert-making techniques. Those who lack the time to make the cake can use store-bought sponge cake (cut into ¼-inch/6-mm strips) or ladyfingers, also known as *savoiardi*.

1 Preheat the oven to 350°F (180°C). Lightly butter a 9-inch (23-cm) round cake pan, then dust with flour, tapping out the excess.

2 To make the cake, in a bowl, using an electric mixer, beat together the egg yolks and sugar until pale and creamy, 5 minutes. Stir in the lemon zest.

3 In another bowl, using clean beaters, beat the egg whites until frothy. Add the cream of tartar and salt and continue to beat until stiff peaks form.

4 Add one-third of the egg whites to the egg yolk mixture and stir until fully incorporated. Add the remaining egg whites and fold in gently just until combined. Sift the flour and baking powder over the top and fold it into the batter until fully incorporated. Pour the batter into the prepared pan.

5 Bake until golden, about 25 minutes. Transfer to a wire rack and let cool in the pan for 5 minutes. Invert onto the rack and let cool for at least 3 hours.

6 To make the custard, in a saucepan over medium heat, warm the milk until small bubbles appear along the edges of the pan. In a bowl, using an electric mixer, beat together the egg yolks and sugar until light and creamy. Sprinkle in the flour and beat until the mixture is pale yellow and thick, about 5 minutes. Slowly pour in the warm milk while stirring constantly with a wooden spoon. Pour the contents of the bowl into the saucepan, place over low heat, and stir in the lemon zest. Heat gently, stirring continuously, until the mixture is thick enough to coat the back of the spoon, about 5 minutes. Do not allow it to boil. Pour the custard through a fine-mesh sieve placed over a bowl. Stir in the vanilla. Cover the bowl with plastic wrap, pressing it directly onto the surface of the custard. Set aside to cool.

7 To assemble the trifle, using a serrated knife, cut the cake into slices ¼ inch (6 mm) thick. Line an 8-cup (64–fl oz/2-l) dessert bowl with a layer of the slices, trimming them as necessary to fit the bowl. Douse the cake layer with one-third of the rum or brandy, if using, then spread with one-third of the custard. Repeat to make 2 more layers. Cover and refrigerate for 2–3 hours.

8 In a bowl, whip the cream until stiff peaks form. Remove the trifle from the refrigerator. Spoon the whipped cream attractively over the top and serve.

CAKE
3 eggs, separated

½ cup (4 oz/125 g) sugar

1 teaspoon minced lemon zest

¼ teaspoon cream of tartar

¼ teaspoon salt

¾ cup (3 oz/90 g) cake (soft-wheat) flour

1 teaspoon baking powder

CUSTARD
2 cups (16 fl oz/500 ml) milk

4 egg yolks

½ cup (4 oz/125 g) sugar

1 tablespoon all-purpose (plain) flour

1 teaspoon minced lemon zest

1 teaspoon vanilla extract (essence)

1 cup (8 fl oz/250 ml) rum or cherry brandy (optional)

2 cups (16 fl oz/500 ml) heavy (double) cream

Serves 6

Panna Cotta with Mixed Berries

Panna Cotta · Piedmont · Italy

These delicate creams are a specialty of Piedmont, where they have been made since medieval times to take advantage of the abundant fresh milk from the region's cows. The name *panna cotta,* or "cooked cream," is thought to be a joke, since the cream is in fact not cooked. Serve the cream with fresh fruit, caramel, or warm chocolate sauce.

2½ teaspoons (1 package) unflavored gelatin

¼ cup (2 fl oz/60 ml) milk

2 cups (16 fl oz/500 ml) heavy (double) cream

¼ cup (2 oz/60 g) sugar

½ vanilla bean

1 small lemon zest strip

4 cups (1 lb/500 g) mixed berries such as blackberries, sliced strawberries, blueberries, and raspberries, in any combination

Serves 4

1 In a large bowl, sprinkle the gelatin over the milk. Let stand for 2 minutes to soften.

2 In a saucepan over medium heat, stir together the cream, sugar, vanilla bean, and lemon zest. Cook, stirring occasionally, until small bubbles appear around the edges of the saucepan. Remove from the heat.

3 Remove the vanilla bean and let cool briefly, then slit it open lengthwise with a sharp knife and scrape the seeds into the cream with the tip of the knife. Discard the lemon zest.

4 Slowly add the cream to the gelatin mixture, stirring until completely dissolved. Pour into four ¾-cup (6–fl oz/180-ml) ramekins or custard cups, dividing evenly. Cover and chill for 4 hours, or for up to overnight.

5 When ready to serve, run a small knife blade around the inside of each ramekin to loosen the cream. Invert each ramekin onto a serving plate.

6 Arrange the berries around the creams and serve immediately.

Strawberries in White Wine

Fragole al Vino Bianco • Lazio • Italy

White wine, sugar, and lemon zest bring out the sweet perfume of fresh strawberries. A bowlful of these berries can be hidden away in the back of the refrigerator, waiting to satisfy the any cravings for a refreshing late-night snack.

1 cup (8 fl oz/250 ml) dry white wine

2 tablespoons sugar, or to taste

2 lemon zest strips

2 pints (1 lb/500 g) strawberries, hulled and quartered or sliced if large

Serves 4

1 In a large bowl, combine the wine, sugar, and lemon zest. Stir to dissolve the sugar. Add the berries and toss well.

2 Cover and refrigerate for 1 hour, tossing the berries occasionally. Serve in shallow glass bowls or stemmed glasses.

Orange Biscotti

Biscotti all'Arancia • Sicily • Italy

Fine yellow cornmeal gives these biscotti a pleasant crunch, while fresh and candied orange peel add a zesty flavor. Enjoy them with coffee, dessert wine, or fresh fruit.

2 cups (10 oz/315 g) all-purpose (plain) flour

¾ cup (4 oz/125 g) fine yellow cornmeal

1½ teaspoons baking powder

1 teaspoon salt

3 eggs

1 cup (8 oz/250 g) sugar

1 tablespoon grated orange zest

⅓ cup (2 oz/60 g) very finely chopped candied orange peel

Makes about 6 dozen

1 Preheat the oven to 325°F (165°C). Butter 2 large baking sheets. Dust the baking sheets with flour and tap out the excess.

2 In a large bowl, stir together the flour, cornmeal, baking powder, and salt. In another bowl, using an electric mixer set on medium speed, beat together the eggs and sugar until foamy. Beat in the orange zest. Reduce the speed to low and stir in the flour mixture and the candied orange peel just until blended. The dough should be soft and sticky.

3 Using 2 rubber spatulas, scoop the dough into 3 logs about 12 inches (30 cm) long and placed about 2 inches (5 cm) apart on the prepared baking sheets. Moisten your hands with cool water and pat the surface of the dough until smooth.

4 Bake until lightly browned, 25–30 minutes. Remove the baking sheets from the oven, leaving the oven on. Slide the logs onto a cutting board. With a heavy chef's knife, cut the logs on the diagonal into slices ½ inch (12 mm) thick. Stand the slices on a cut side on the baking sheets, arranging them about ½ inch (12 mm) apart.

5 Return the baking sheets to the oven and bake until the slices are lightly toasted, about 15 minutes. Transfer the biscotti to racks to cool completely. Store in an airtight container at room temperature for up to 2 weeks.

STRAWBERRIES

The little town of Nemi, not far from Rome, has long been famous for its strawberries, which grow practically year-round in the rich volcanic soil of the green hillsides that surround the nearby lake of the same name. Just twenty families are said to hold the secret to cultivating the legendary dark-red fruits, a secret that they carefully pass down through the generations.

The locals will proudly tell you that the Emperor Caligula journeyed to Nemi to worship at the temple of Diana and to eat the berries. Visitors still come to the town to see the placid lake, known as the Mirror of Diana, to visit the ruins of the temple, and, of course, to sample the legendary strawberries.

Each year in June, a festival honoring the town's most important product is held. A charming parade of children turned out in imaginative strawberry costumes is part of the festivities, as are young women who walk through the streets carrying baskets filled with ripe, fragrant berries. Attendees consume their fill of the fruits, either fresh from the bush or folded into a rich and creamy gelato, and then pack shopping bags with wonderful strawberry jams and liqueurs. Romans and other savvy visitors also know to stop at the street-side vendors selling slabs of peppery *porchetta* from the nearby town of Ariccia.

Flat Bread with Wine Grapes

Schiacciata all'Uva • Tuscany • Italy

Delicious *schiacciata all'uva* is a sweet, chewy flat bread dotted with wine grapes and rosemary. The herb may seem an odd ingredient for a dessert, but the piney taste lends a surprisingly pleasant note and an element of intrigue to otherwise predictable flavors. Wine grapes are generally smaller than table grapes, with dense skins and tart seeds. You can substitute table grapes, which will eliminate the seeds but also some of the flavor.

1 cake (1 oz/30 g) fresh yeast or 2½ teaspoons (1 envelope) active dry yeast

1 cup (8 fl oz/250 ml) lukewarm water (110°F/43°C)

½ teaspoon plus 1 tablespoon sugar

4½ cups (22½ oz/700 g) all-purpose (plain) flour

5 tablespoons (2½ fl oz/75 ml) extra-virgin olive oil

1 teaspoon salt

¾ lb (375 g) red wine grapes

Leaves from 2 fresh rosemary sprigs

Sugar for dusting

Serves 12

1 In a small bowl, sprinkle the yeast over the lukewarm water and stir gently. Stir in the ½ teaspoon sugar and let the mixture stand until creamy, about 5 minutes.

2 In a large bowl, mound the flour and make a well in the center. Pour the yeast mixture and 4 tablespoons (2 fl oz/ 60 ml) of the extra-virgin olive oil into the well and sprinkle in the salt. Stir in a circular motion, slowly incorporating all of the flour until the ingredients are well mixed and a rough dough has formed.

3 Turn the dough out onto a lightly floured work surface and knead until smooth and soft, about 10 minutes. If the dough is very sticky, add small amounts of flour as you work the dough. Shape the dough into a ball and place it in a well-oiled bowl. Turn to coat with oil, cover the bowl with a damp kitchen towel, and set in a warm place to rise until the dough has doubled in volume, about 1 hour.

4 Preheat the oven to 375°F (190°C). Oil a 9-by-13-by-2-inch (23-by-33-by-5-cm) baking pan.

5 Punch down the risen dough. Return it to the floured surface and knead it for another 10 minutes. Divide the dough in half. Roll out half of the dough into a size that roughly matches the size of the prepared pan. Transfer the rolled-out dough to the prepared pan and scatter one-half of the grapes and one-third of the rosemary leaves evenly over the surface. Sprinkle with the 1 tablespoon sugar.

6 Roll out the second half of dough on the floured surface into a sheet of the same size and lay it on top of the grape-and-herb-covered dough. Cover evenly with the remaining grapes and rosemary and drizzle with the remaining 1 tablespoon extra-virgin olive oil. Cover the pan with a damp kitchen towel and set in a warm place to rise until the dough has doubled in volume, about 30 minutes.

7 Bake until a soft gold on top, 30–35 minutes. Remove the pan from the oven and transfer to a wire rack to cool until warm. Remove the bread from the pan, dust the surface with sugar, and cut into squares to serve. The bread can be stored, well wrapped, for up to 2 days and reheated or served at room temperature.

SEASONAL FRUIT

After dinner at a small trattoria in Florence, a man is brought a whole peach on a plate, along with a knife. With the precision of a surgeon, he slices the velvet skin from the fruit in one long strip, then slowly eats the peach, wedge by perfectly cut wedge. Most non-Italians rarely eat fruit with such care, and except for the occasional bowl of wild berries, rarely see, much less order, fruit for dessert at a restaurant.

Fruit is not eaten casually in Tuscany. It appears less often as a snack than as a full-fledged dessert at the end of a simple lunch or dinner. Springtime is for cherries and strawberries—often tossed with sugar and lemon, or scattered over vanilla ice cream—and for tart, apricot-hued medlars. Summer brings apricots, plums, peaches, and melons, although cantaloupe is served at the beginning of a meal with slices of cured prosciutto, rather than as dessert. Plump, tart gooseberries and delicate red currants are made into jams and tortes. Sweet black and green figs ripen in late summer and are eaten at the end of a meal or at the beginning with slices of mild salami. Harvest season brings grapes (lushly flavorful and full of seeds), pears, apples, and chestnuts, and winter delivers glossy persimmons and juicy tangerines.

Perhaps the Tuscan reverence for fruit can be explained by the fact that it is almost always of exceptional quality. Fruit is generally eaten only in season, with locally grown fruit, denoted by the word *nostrale,* almost always preferred over something shipped from a distant continent. Also, Tuscans are far more concerned about how a fruit tastes than what it looks like, and will regard with suspicion anything that looks unnaturally perfect. In fact, children are told that an orchard apple lightly pecked at by a bird is likely to be far sweeter than the untouched (and presumably less ripe) fruits from the same tree. As the Tuscans say, the bird knows better than the eye.

Strawberries with Custard

Fragole in Coppa • Tuscany • Italy

Fragoline di bosco, wild strawberries that grow in the Apennines above Lucca and Pistoia, taste like the essence of springtime. Here, cultivated strawberries are soaked in rum before being dressed with a simple custard and a dollop of whipped cream.

2 pints (1 lb/500 g) strawberries, stems removed, sliced lengthwise

¼ cup (2 fl oz/60 ml) rum

1 cup (8 fl oz/250 ml) milk

2 egg yolks

¼ cup (2 oz/60 g) sugar

2 teaspoons all-purpose (plain) flour

½ teaspoon grated lemon zest

½ teaspoon vanilla extract (essence)

Whipped cream for serving (page 225)

Serves 4

1 Place the strawberries in a bowl, add the rum, and mix gently. Cover and set aside at room temperature or in the refrigerator for 3–4 hours, but no longer.

2 In a saucepan over medium heat, warm the milk until small bubbles appear along the edges of the pan. In a bowl, beat the egg yolks and the sugar until light and creamy. Sprinkle in the flour and beat until the mixture is pale and thick, about 5 minutes. Slowly pour in the warm milk, stirring constantly. Pour the contents of the bowl into the saucepan, place over low heat, and stir in the lemon zest. Heat gently, stirring continuously, until the mixture is thick enough to coat the back of a spoon, about 5 minutes. Do not allow to boil. Pour the custard through a fine-mesh sieve placed over a bowl. Stir in the vanilla. Cover with plastic wrap, pressing it directly onto the surface of the custard. Set aside to cool.

3 Divide half of the strawberries among 4 goblets and top with the custard, dividing it evenly. Top with almost all of the remaining berries, reserving some for garnish. Cover and refrigerate for about 2 hours. Just before serving, top with whipped cream and garnish with the reserved berries.

Chocolate Kisses

Baci · Veneto · Italy

These chocolate-filled cookie sandwiches are a favorite in Verona, a city perhaps best known for being Shakespeare's setting for *Romeo and Juliet*. In many of the local bakeries, the cookies are known as *baci di Giulietta*, or "Juliet's kisses."

1 cup (8 oz/250 g) plus 2 tablespoons unsalted butter, at room temperature

½ cup (2 oz/60 g) confectioners' (icing) sugar

½ teaspoon salt

1 tablespoon rum

2 cups (10 oz/315 g) all-purpose (plain) flour

2 oz (60 g) semisweet (plain) chocolate such as Perugina or Callebaut

Makes about 2 dozen

1 In a large bowl, using an electric mixer set on medium speed, beat together the 1 cup (8 oz/250 g) butter, the confectioners' sugar, and the salt until light and fluffy. Beat in the rum. Stir in the flour and well blended. Cover and chill until firm, about 1 hour.

2 Preheat the oven to 350°F (180°C).

3 Scoop up the dough by the teaspoonful and roll each nugget into a ball. Place the balls about 1 inch (2.5 cm) apart on ungreased baking sheets.

4 Bake the cookies until firm but not browned, 10–12 minutes. Transfer to wire racks to cool completely.

5 Place the chocolate and the remaining 2 tablespoons butter in a small heatproof bowl. Set the bowl over (not touching) simmering water in a saucepan and heat until the chocolate softens. Remove from over the water and stir until smooth. Let cool slightly.

6 Using a butter knife, spread a small amount of the chocolate on the bottom of a cookie. Place the bottom of a second cookie against the chocolate, sandwich style, and press the halves together. Repeat with the remaining cookies. Let cool on the wire racks until the filling is set. Store in an airtight container in a cool place for up to 1 week.

Florentine Carnival Cake

Schiacciata alla Fiorentina • Tuscany • Italy

This cake appears in pastry shops throughout Florence in the late-winter Carnival season. There are a few popular variations worth noting: A pinch of saffron is sometimes added to bring color and exotic flavor. Also, pastry shops will occasionally split the *schiacciata* through the middle, filling it with whipped cream or custard. Making this cake with lard, as is traditional, gives it a wonderfully tender texture, but butter is a fine substitute.

1 In a small bowl, sprinkle the yeast over the lukewarm water and stir gently. Stir in the granulated sugar and let the mixture stand until creamy, about 5 minutes.

2 In a large bowl, mound the flour and make a well in the center. Pour the yeast mixture into the well. Stir in a circular motion, incorporating all of the flour until well mixed. Cover the bowl with a kitchen towel and set in a warm place to rise until the sponge has doubled in volume, about 1 hour.

3 Butter a 13-by-9-inch (33-by-23-cm) baking pan.

4 To make the dough, in a small saucepan over low heat, melt the lard or butter with the salt, then remove from the heat and let cool for 10 minutes.

5 In a bowl, using an electric mixer, beat together the eggs and the granulated sugar until light yellow. Stir in the citrus zests and vanilla.

6 Add the egg mixture to the sponge, stirring vigorously with a wooden spoon to mix thoroughly. Stir in the cooled lard or butter. Add the flour, 2 tablespoons at a time, incorporating each new addition fully before adding the next. The resulting batter will be rather thick and sticky, more like a bread dough than a cake batter. Pour the batter into the prepared pan, cover with a kitchen towel, and let the batter rise until almost doubled in volume, about 1 hour.

7 Preheat the oven to 375°F (190°C).

8 Remove the towel and bake the cake until the surface is a soft gold, 30–35 minutes. Transfer to a wire rack and let cool completely.

9 Just before serving the cake, using a fine-mesh sieve, heavily dust the top with confectioners' sugar. Cut into squares to serve.

SPONGE

1 cake (1 oz/30 g) fresh yeast or
2½ teaspoons (1 envelope)
active dry yeast

1 cup (8 fl oz/250 ml) lukewarm water
(110°F/43°C)

½ teaspoon granulated sugar

3 cups (12 oz/375 g) cake
(soft-wheat) flour

DOUGH

½ cup (4 oz/125 g) lard or unsalted butter

1 teaspoon salt

4 eggs

½ cup (4 oz/125 g) granulated sugar

½ teaspoon grated orange zest

½ teaspoon grated lemon zest

1½ teaspoons vanilla extract (essence)

1½ cups (6 oz/185 g) cake
(soft-wheat) flour

Confectioners' (icing) sugar for dusting

Serves 12

Baked Custard with Cherries and Almonds

Focaccia Dolce di Ciliege e Mandorle · Tuscany · Italy

In spring in Pistoia, cherries abound on garden trees. The bounty is turned into all manner of desserts, such as this baked custard, which pairs tart cherries with nutty almonds.

2 lb (1 kg) sweet cherries such as Bing or Tartarian

4 eggs

¾ cup (6 oz/185 g) granulated sugar

1 tablespoon *vin santo*

1 cup (8 fl oz/250 ml) milk

¾ cup (4 oz/125 g) all-purpose (plain) flour

⅓ cup (1½ oz/45 g) slivered blanched almonds

Confectioners' (icing) sugar for dusting

Serves 6

1 Remove the stems and pits from the cherries. Preheat the oven to 375°F (190°C). Lightly butter a 10-inch (25-cm) shallow baking dish or pie pan.

2 In a large bowl, using a whisk, beat together the eggs and granulated sugar until creamy. Add the *vin santo* to the milk, then stir into the egg mixture. Slowly incorporate the flour, stirring constantly. Let the batter rest for 15 minutes.

3 Place the cherries in the bottom of the prepared dish or pan. Pour the batter through a fine-mesh sieve held over the cherries. Sprinkle the almonds evenly over the top.

4 Bake for 10 minutes. Reduce the heat to 350°F (180°C) and continue to bake until golden and glossy, about 30 minutes longer. Transfer the custard to a wire rack and let cool for 10 minutes. Using a sieve, dust the surface of the custard with the confectioners' sugar. Cut into wedges and serve warm.

Venetian Carnival Fritters

Frappe • Veneto • Italy

Every region of Italy has its own variety of fried cookies. In this version, a splash of fiery grappa is used for flavoring. Substitute a favorite brandy or a liqueur, if you prefer.

1 cup (5 oz/155 g) all-purpose (plain) flour

2 tablespoons granulated sugar

½ teaspoon salt

2 tablespoons unsalted butter, at room temperature

1 egg

2 tablespoons grappa

Vegetable oil for deep-frying

Confectioners' (icing) sugar

Makes about 3 dozen

1 In a small bowl, stir together the flour, sugar, and salt. In a large bowl, combine the butter, egg, and grappa. Add the dry ingredients and stir until the dough becomes stiff. Transfer to a floured work surface and knead until smooth, about 1 minute. Cover with an inverted bowl and let rest for 30 minutes.

2 Divide the dough in half. Roll out each half as thinly as possible, lifting and turning often to avoid sticking. With a fluted pastry cutter or a small, sharp knife, cut into 4-by-1½-inch (10-by-4-cm) strips.

3 In a deep, heavy saucepan, pour in oil to fill the pan one-third full. Heat the oil to 350°F (180°C) on a deep-frying thermometer. Shake the dough strips to remove any excess flour. Working in batches, slip the strips, a few at a time, into the oil and fry until puffed and golden, about 3 minutes. Using a slotted spoon, transfer to paper towels to drain. Fry the remaining dough strips in the same manner.

4 When completely cool, place confectioners' sugar in a small sieve and dust the cookies generously. Toss them gently to coat evenly. Store in an airtight container at room temperature for up to 1 week.

GRAPPA

Renowned grappa maker Romano Levi drops a tiny vial, no bigger than a thimble, tied with a long string down into a wooden barrel. It fills with clear liquid and then he draws it out, pouring a drop into his palms and rubbing vigorously. Opening his hands, he takes a long, deep sniff of the essence: warm, woody, and inviting. "Ah, grappa!" he proclaims.

Distilled in many different regions of northern Italy, grappa was traditionally a peasant's liquor, a raw, rough potion, often poured into cups of hot coffee to warm farmers and hunters on cold mornings. Made today with modern techniques and equipment, grappa is a sophisticated and expensive after-dinner drink. Some producers, like the Veneto's Jacopo Poli,

present their grappa in elegant blown-glass bottles. In Friuli–Venezia Giulia, the Nonino family is famous for their *grappa monovitigno*, made from single grape varieties, and *acquavite,* a beverage made from whole fruits like apricots, cherries, or peaches.

Grappa is usually sipped straight up after meals, although it is occasionally added to desserts. One typical use in Friuli is to pour a glassful over portions of *gubana,* a delicious fruit- and nut-filled cake. In the Alto Adige, a mixture of hot coffee, grappa, lemon, and sugar is passed around after meals in what is called the *coppa dell'amicizia,* or "friendship cups," a special carved wooden bowl with several spigots. According to legend, it is bad luck to leave the table until all of the beverage has been consumed.

Christmas Fig Ring

Buccellato · Sicily · Italy

Pastries filled with ground figs, nuts, and spices are traditional Christmas sweets found all over Sicily. Sometimes they are formed into ring-shaped cakes, and other times they are made into individual pastries or smaller cookies. During the holiday season, Sicilian women get together to bake, sharing the work and vying to see who can make the most elaborate-looking desserts, forming them into flowers, birds, or other fanciful creations.

PASTRY

3 cups (15 oz/470 g) unbleached all-purpose (plain) flour

½ cup (4 oz/125 g) sugar

2½ teaspoons baking powder

½ teaspoon salt

6 tablespoons (3 oz/90 g) unsalted butter, at room temperature, cut into small pieces

2 eggs

¼ cup (2 fl oz/60 ml) milk

1 teaspoon vanilla extract (essence)

FILLING

2 cups (1 lb/500 g) dried figs, stemmed

½ cup (2 oz/60 g) walnuts, lightly toasted (page 224)

⅓ cup (4 oz/125 g) honey

¼ cup (2 fl oz/60 ml) fresh orange juice

1 teaspoon grated orange zest

1 teaspoon ground cinnamon

⅛ teaspoon ground cloves

DECORATION

1 egg white, beaten

Colored candy sprinkles (optional)

Serves 16

1 To make the pastry, in the bowl of a stand mixer, stir together the flour, sugar, baking powder, and salt. With the mixer set on medium speed, beat in the butter. In another bowl, whisk together the eggs, milk, and vanilla until blended. Pour it over the flour mixture and mix until blended. Gather the dough into a ball. Place on a sheet of plastic wrap and flatten into a disk. Wrap well and refrigerate for at least 3 hours or for as long as overnight.

2 To make the filling, in a food processor, combine the figs and walnuts. Pulse to chop coarsely. Add the honey, the orange juice and zest, the cinnamon, and the cloves. Process until blended.

3 Preheat the oven to 375°F (190°C). Butter a large baking sheet.

4 On a lightly floured work surface, shape the dough with your hands into a thick rectangle. Roll out into an 18-by-9-inch (45-by-23-cm) rectangle. Using a sharp paring knife or a pastry wheel, trim the edges so they are straight, reserving the scraps. Spoon the filling into an even strip 2 inches (5 cm) wide lengthwise down the center of the rectangle. Lift one long side of the dough over the filling, then fold the other side over the top. Press to seal. Carefully slide the log onto the prepared baking sheet, placing it seam side down. Bring the ends together to form a ring and pinch together to seal.

5 Reroll the scraps. With a paring knife or cookie cutters, cut out flowers, vines, and leaves. Brush the top and sides of the ring with some of the egg white. Arrange the decorations on top of the ring. Brush the ring and decorations with egg white. Sprinkle with the candy sprinkles, if using.

6 Bake until golden brown, about 40 minutes. Transfer to a rack and let cool on the baking sheet for 10 minutes. Slide the cake onto the rack and let cool completely.

7 Serve at room temperature, cut into thin slices. To store, wrap tightly and keep at room temperature for up to 3 days.

Almond Biscotti

Cantuccini • Tuscany • Italy

Although delicious right out of the oven, traditionally *cantuccini* are left to harden for three days, turning them into the perfect crunchy cookie for dipping into a glass of *vin santo*.

2 whole eggs, plus 1 egg yolk

¾ cup (6 oz/185 g) sugar

2½ cups (10 oz/315 g) cake (soft-wheat) flour

1 teaspoon baking powder

1 teaspoon salt

1½ teaspoons grated lemon zest

1 cup (5½ oz/170 g) almonds, toasted (page 224) and coarsely chopped

2 tablespoons milk

Makes 24–30 cookies

1 In a bowl, using a fork, beat together the whole eggs, egg yolk, and sugar until light and creamy. Pour the flour into a mound on a work surface. Add the baking powder, salt, and lemon zest and stir briefly. Make a well in the center of the mound and add the egg mixture. Using the fork, swirl the mixture, slowly incorporating the flour from the sides of the well. Add the almonds and knead to distribute evenly. The dough will be sticky. Spoon into a large, heavy-duty plastic bag and refrigerate for 1 hour.

2 Preheat the oven to 375°F (190°C). Line a baking sheet with parchment (baking) paper.

3 Snip a large corner off the bag containing the dough. Squeeze the dough onto the lined baking sheet, making 2 logs each about 2 inches (5 cm) wide and 12 inches (30 cm) long. (Alternatively, roll the dough into 2 logs on a floured work surface.) Space them far apart, as they will expand in the oven. Brush the top of each log with the milk. Bake the logs until light gold, about 25 minutes. Remove from the oven and reduce the temperature to 275°F (135°C). Let the baked dough cool for 5 minutes.

4 Transfer the logs to a cutting board and, using a long serrated knife, cut crosswise into slices ¾ inch (2 cm) wide. Place the slices cut side down on the baking sheet and bake until golden, about 30 minutes longer. They will be quite dry. The biscotti can be stored in an airtight container for up to 1 week.

VIN SANTO

The ritual is almost always the same: dinner plates are cleared from the table and replaced by a bowl of almond biscotti and a tray bearing tiny glasses of *vin santo*.

This so-called "holy wine" is an amber dessert wine with a slightly caramel flavor laced with hints of almond and fig. A bottle of good-quality *vin santo* (the only kind worth drinking) will bear a vintage date on its label and a rather high price tag that is justified by the tremendous amount of time and effort that goes into making the wine.

In the fall, the best white wine grapes, usually Malvasia and Trebbiano, are hung or laid on rush mats to dry in large, airy rooms or barns. Powdered sulfur set out in small dishes near the grapes is burned to keep them from molding as they dry. In late winter, the semidry grapes are pressed and then allowed to ferment in small oak or chestnut barrels called *caratelli*. The barrels are sent to the *vinsantaia,* an attic or other place where the wine will be exposed to the great fluctuations in temperature necessary for making fine *vin santo*. The sweet wine is left to age three to four years, and occasionally longer, before being bottled.

Spiced Fruit Cake

Panforte · Tuscany · Italy

Panforte is rarely made at home, since the bakers in Siena make it so well, but this simple recipe is worth trying for the dense, rich cake it produces.

1 cup (8 oz/250 g) granulated sugar

½ cup (6 oz/185 g) honey

1 lb (500 g) assorted chopped candied fruits such as pear, apricot, and citron but no apple

¼ cup (1½ oz/45 g) candied orange peel, chopped

1 cup (5½ oz/170 g) blanched almonds, coarsely chopped

½ cup (2 oz/60 g) cake (soft-wheat) flour

½ teaspoon *each* salt, crushed coriander seed, and ground cinnamon

¼ teaspoon ground mace

Confectioners' (icing) sugar for dusting

Serves 12

1 Preheat the oven to 375°F (190°C). Lightly butter a 10-inch (25-cm) springform pan, then dust with flour, tapping out the excess.

2 In a large saucepan over medium heat, combine the granulated sugar, honey, and 2 tablespoons water and bring to a simmer, stirring to dissolve the sugar. Simmer until a thick syrup forms, 5–10 minutes. Do not allow the syrup to caramelize. Remove from the heat.

3 Immediately stir in the candied fruits and orange peel and the nuts until blended. Sift in the flour and add the salt, coriander, cinnamon, and mace. After the mixture has cooled, moisten your hands with water and use them to combine the ingredients well. The dough will be stiff and sticky. Transfer to the prepared pan, patting down with your fingers.

4 Bake until dark golden, about 40 minutes. Transfer to a wire rack and let cool completely. Remove the pan sides and slide the cake onto a serving plate.

5 Just before serving, using a fine-mesh sieve, dust the top of the cake with confectioners' sugar. To serve, cut into wedges with a very sharp knife.

Cannoli Cream with Fresh Fruit

Crema di Ricotta alla Frutta Fresca · Sicily · Italy

The cream used to fill cannoli is also a nice accompaniment to fresh fruit; tangy fresh Sicilian ricotta is especially delicious. Vary the mixture of fruits according to the season.

2 cups (1 lb/500 g) whole-milk ricotta cheese

¼ cup (1 oz/30 g) confectioners' (icing) sugar

1 teaspoon vanilla extract (essence)

½ teaspoon grated lemon zest

Pinch of ground cinnamon

6 apricots, pitted and sliced

4 kiwifruits, peeled and sliced

2 tablespoons sugar

2 tablespoons orange- or cherry-flavored liqueur

½ pint (4 oz/125 g) raspberries

3 tablespoons chopped semisweet (plain) chocolate

Serves 8

1 In a bowl, using a whisk or wooden spoon, beat the ricotta cheese until smooth and creamy. Beat in the confectioners' sugar, vanilla, lemon zest, and cinnamon until blended.

2 In a small bowl, combine the apricots, kiwifruits, sugar, and liqueur. Using spoons, toss well, being careful not to bruise the fruit. Scatter the raspberries over the top.

3 Spoon the fruits into goblets or other attractive serving vessels. Top each serving with an equal amount of the ricotta mixture. Sprinkle with the chocolate and serve at once.

Hazelnut Cake

Torta di Nocciola • Piedmont • Italy

This cake, which is traditional in the Piedmont region, is made with only egg whites and contains no butter, so the pure flavor of the hazelnuts comes through.

2 cups (10 oz/315 g) hazelnuts (filberts)

1¼ cups (10 oz/310 g) sugar

⅓ cup (2 oz/60 g) all-purpose (plain) flour

8 egg whites, at room temperature

½ teaspoon salt

1 teaspoon vanilla extract (essence)

Serves 8

1 Preheat the oven to 350°F (180°C). Butter a 9-inch (23-cm) springform pan with 3-inch (7.5-cm) sides. Dust the pan with flour and tap out the excess.

2 In a food processor, combine the nuts with ½ cup (4 oz/125 g) of the sugar and process to chop finely. Add the flour and pulse to blend. Transfer to a large bowl and set aside.

3 In another bowl, using an electric mixer set on low speed, beat together the egg whites and salt until foamy. Increase the speed to high and gradually beat in the remaining ¾ cup (6 oz/185 g) sugar until the whites form soft peaks. Add the vanilla and beat until stiff, about 2 minutes longer. Using a rubber spatula, fold about one-third of the egg whites into the ground nut mixture to lighten it. Gradually fold in the remaining whites just until no white streaks remain. Spoon the mixture into the prepared pan, spreading it evenly.

4 Bake until a wooden toothpick inserted into the center comes out clean, about 55 minutes. Transfer to a wire rack and let cool in the pan for 10 minutes. Release the pan sides and slide the cake off the base onto the rack. Let cool completely before serving.

Marinated Oranges

Arance Marinate • Sicily • Italy

Sicilian blood oranges, known as *sanguinelli,* with their deep red color, are an especially attractive addition to this light dessert. Serve after a rich dinner or one that features fish.

4 navel oranges

2 blood oranges

10 cups (80 fl oz/2.5 l) water

¾ cup (6 oz/185 g) sugar

Serves 4

1 Using a serrated knife, remove the zest in wide strips from 2 of the navel oranges and both blood oranges; avoid the white pith as much as possible. Set the oranges aside. Scrape away any pith from the zest. Stack the zest pieces and cut into narrow strips.

2 In a small saucepan, bring 3 cups (24 fl oz/750 ml) of the water to a boil. Add the orange zest, blanch for 1 minute, then drain and rinse under cool water. Repeat two more times, using 3 cups (24 fl oz/750 ml) fresh water each time, to eliminate any bitterness in the zest. In the same saucepan over medium heat, combine ½ cup (4 oz/125 g) of the sugar and the remaining 1 cup (8 fl oz/250 ml) water. Bring to a boil, stirring to dissolve the sugar. Add the zest and cook, uncovered, until the syrup thickens slightly, 5–10 minutes. Remove from the heat, let cool completely, cover, and refrigerate until serving.

3 Using the serrated knife, trim away the white pith from the 4 oranges from which the zest has been removed. Cut the oranges crosswise into slices ¼ inch (6 mm) thick and place in a bowl. Halve the remaining 2 navel oranges and squeeze their juice into the bowl. Stir in the remaining ¼ cup (2 oz/60 g) sugar. Cover and refrigerate for 1 hour.

4 To serve, spoon the orange slices into bowls or glasses. Top each with zest and syrup.

SNACKS

The traditional system of Tuscan meals—*colazione* (breakfast), *pranzo* (lunch), and *cena* (dinner)—is punctuated by two additional appointments, one in the morning at around 10:30 and the second in the afternoon, usually around 4:00. These little gastronomic breaks in the day are known as *merende,* which, roughly translated, means "snacks"—though in truth they have none of the casual randomness often associated with eating between meals.

The morning *merenda* is the only chance a school-age child has to bring something to eat from home, since school lunches are full-scale meals complete with first course, meat, vegetable, and fruit. Kids might bring a piece of *schiacciata* fresh from the bakery or a small sandwich of bread and Nutella (a much-beloved chocolate-hazelnut spread—the Italian response to peanut butter) and sometimes seasonal fruit, such as a couple of tangerines or plums, a handful of cherries or grapes, or whatever travels well in their backpacks.

The afternoon *merenda* is almost always at home, or it might be a stop at the neighborhood bar for a gelato, a slice of Florentine carnival cake, or a wedge of blackberry jam torte, depending on the weather and the season. The reigning *merenda* of choice is the same as it has been in Tuscan homes for centuries, *pane e olio* (bread and olive oil). The simple presentation includes bread (usually toasted), plates, a tiny saucer of salt, and a bottle of fruity green olive oil. Packaged sweet snacks have all but replaced another favorite Tuscan *merenda*—sliced country bread dipped in wine and sprinkled with sugar.

Generally speaking, it is children who have *merenda.* Adults treat themselves to a *spuntino,* a term that means roughly the same thing, though it is more likely to include a wedge of cheese, a handful of olives, or a few slices of cured meat. This adult snack is usually accompanied by an appropriately grown-up beverage—an espresso, a cup of tea, or a glass of wine.

Chestnut Flour Cake

Castagnaccio • Tuscany • Italy

It is said that the recipe for *castagnaccio* is as old as the Tuscan mountains upon which the chestnut trees grow. Some say this earthy cake originated in Siena.

¾ cup (4½ oz/140 g) dried currants or raisins

2½ cups (10 oz/315 g) chestnut flour

¼ teaspoon salt

1½ cups (12 fl oz/375 ml) water

5 tablespoons (2½ fl oz/75 ml) extra-virgin olive oil

Leaves from 2 fresh rosemary sprigs

12 walnut halves, broken into pieces

⅓ cup (2 oz/60 g) pine nuts

Serves 6

1 In a small bowl, combine the currants or raisins with warm water to cover. Let soak for 20 minutes. Preheat the oven to 400°F (200°C). Butter a 9-by-13-by-2-inch (23-by-33-by-5-cm) baking pan.

2 In a large bowl, stir together the flour and salt. Add the water in a steady stream, stirring constantly with a wooden spoon to prevent any lumps from forming. Stir in 2 tablespoons of the olive oil and then allow the batter to rest in the bowl for at least 15 minutes or up to 25 minutes. It will be very thin and aromatic.

3 In a small frying pan over medium heat, warm the remaining 3 tablespoons olive oil. Add the rosemary leaves and heat until they are fragrant but not brown, about 1 minute. Remove from the heat, then lift out the rosemary with a spoon. Reserve the rosemary and the oil separately.

4 Drain the currants or raisins and stir them into the batter. Pour the batter into the prepared pan. Sprinkle the sautéed rosemary and the nuts evenly over the surface. Using a pastry brush, spread the reserved oil evenly over the surface.

5 Bake until the crust is dark but not burned and a wooden skewer inserted into the center of the cake comes out clean, 30–45 minutes. Transfer the pan to a wire rack and let cool completely. Cut the cake into slices and serve directly from the pan.

Lemon Cream Puffs

Bignè al Limone • Campania • Italy

At a restaurant high along the Amalfi coast, the high point of lunch is not the view of the Bay of Naples, but this dessert, cream puffs served with lemon custard and lemon cream.

CREAM PUFFS

½ cup (4 oz/125 g) unsalted butter

1 cup (8 fl oz/250 ml) water

½ teaspoon salt

1 cup (5 oz/155 g) all-purpose (plain) flour

4 eggs

FILLING AND TOPPING

2 cups (16 fl oz/500 ml) milk

⅔ cup (5 oz/155 g) sugar

3 egg yolks

2 tablespoons all-purpose (plain) flour

1 teaspoon vanilla extract (essence)

1 teaspoon grated lemon zest

1 cup (8 fl oz/250 ml) heavy (double) cream

Tiny strawberries or raspberries (optional)

Serves 6–8

1 Preheat the oven to 400°F (200°C). Butter a large baking sheet. Dust the baking sheet with flour and tap out the excess.

2 To make the cream puffs, in a saucepan over medium-low heat, warm the butter, water, and salt until the butter melts and the mixture reaches a boil. Remove from the heat. Add the flour all at once and stir with a wooden spoon until completely incorporated.

3 Return the saucepan to the stove over medium heat. Cook, stirring constantly and turning the dough often, until the dough begins to leave a thin film on the bottom of the saucepan, about 3 minutes. (This step dries out the dough to ensure crisp puffs.) Transfer the dough to a large bowl. Add the eggs, one at a time, beating thoroughly after each addition. Continue to beat until the mixture is smooth and shiny.

4 Drop the dough by rounded spoonfuls onto the prepared baking sheet, forming 12 mounds spaced about 3 inches (7.5 cm) apart. Pat the tops to give them a round shape.

5 Bake until golden brown, 40–45 minutes. Turn off the oven and remove the puffs. With a small knife, make a hole in the side of each puff to allow steam to escape. Return the puffs to the oven for 10 minutes to dry.

6 Using a serrated knife, cut the puffs part way through in half horizontally. Do not cut into 2 separate pieces. Open like a book and scoop out and discard the soft dough inside. Transfer to a wire rack and let cool completely. (The cream puffs can be made ahead and frozen in a plastic bag for up to 2 weeks. Crisp the frozen puffs in a 350°F/180°C oven for 5–10 minutes before proceeding.)

7 To make the topping and filling, in a saucepan over low heat, stir together the milk and sugar until the sugar dissolves and the milk is steaming, 5 minutes. Remove from the heat.

8 In a large bowl, whisk together the egg yolks and flour until pale yellow. Slowly add the warm milk mixture in a thin stream, whisking constantly. Pour the mixture back into the saucepan and place over low heat. Cook, stirring constantly with a wooden spoon, until the mixture comes to a boil and begins to thicken, about 2 minutes. Then cook for 1 minute, remove from the heat, and strain through a fine-mesh sieve into a bowl. Let cool slightly. Stir in the vanilla and lemon zest. Cover with plastic wrap, pressing it against the surface to prevent a skin from forming, and chill well.

9 In a chilled bowl, using chilled beaters, whip the cream until soft peaks form. Cover with plastic wrap and chill until needed.

10 Just before serving, using about half of the custard in all, place a spoonful inside each cream puff. Arrange the puffs in a mound on a large serving platter. Using a rubber spatula, fold the whipped cream into the remaining lemon custard just until no white streaks remain. Spoon the mixture over the cream puffs. Scatter the berries, if using, over the top. Serve immediately.

PINE NUTS

Scattered throughout the Tuscan countryside, especially in the untamed woods near the sea in the Maremma, are Mediterranean pine trees. Unlike their rigidly angular alpine cousins, these trees have thick trunks, gnarled sprawling limbs, and great wide tops, which together make them look a bit like giant green mushrooms leaning into the elements. Not only are they graciously beautiful, but nestled among their scented needles are dusky brown pinecones loaded with ivory-hued nuts.

Pine nuts find their way into both sweet and savory Tuscan recipes. They are used with fresh basil and olive oil in making pesto, a Ligurian specialty, and are sprinkled into pasta or meat sauces. The nuts are also scattered atop the fragrant chestnut-flour batter used to make *castagnaccio* and are incorporated into many tortes and cakes.

A favorite pastime of grade-school children is to hand-harvest pine nuts. They pry open the petals of the pinecones, pull out the *pinoli* still in their pale brown shells, and then use small stones to crack open the shells gently without damaging the sweet nutmeats inside.

Ricotta Tart

Torta di Ricotta • Tuscany • Italy

In Tuscany, ricotta is fashioned from the whey left over from making the region's famous pecorino, or sheep's milk cheeses. When very fresh, it is eaten plain or lightly seasoned with olive oil. *Pasta frolla* is the typical pastry dough used throughout Italy. It is slightly sweeter than pie dough—almost like a sugar cookie—and the sugar in the dough makes it somewhat sticky and difficult to handle. Chilling the dough eases rolling it out and lifting it to line the pan. This tart is lovely paired with a fruit compote and a glass of *vin santo*.

PASTRY

1½ cups (6 oz/185 g) cake (soft-wheat) flour

⅓ cup (3 oz/90 g) sugar

6 tablespoons (3 oz/90 g) unsalted butter, melted and cooled

½ teaspoon grated lemon zest

⅛ teaspoon salt

1 whole egg, plus 1 egg yolk

FILLING

⅓ cup (2 oz/60 g) raisins

1¼ cups (10 oz/315 g) ricotta cheese

2 eggs

⅓ cup (3 oz/90 g) plus 1 tablespoon sugar

1 tablespoon cake (soft-wheat) flour

1 teaspoon grated lemon zest

1 teaspoon vanilla extract (essence)

Serves 6

1 To make the pastry, in a large bowl, mound the flour and make a well in the center. Add the sugar, butter, lemon zest, and salt to the well. In a small bowl, using a fork, beat the whole egg and egg yolk, and then pour into the well. Lightly beat the mixture in the well with the fork, then slowly incorporate the flour in a circular motion until well mixed and a rough dough has formed. Dust your hands with flour and knead the dough briefly in the bowl until it forms a large ball.

2 Flatten the ball into a thick disk, place in a heavy-duty lock-top plastic bag, and refrigerate for 1 hour.

3 Preheat the oven to 375°F (190°C). Lightly butter a 9-inch (23-cm) springform pan, then dust with flour, tapping out the excess.

4 Begin to make the filling by placing the raisins in a small bowl with warm water to cover. Let soak for 20 minutes, then drain.

5 In a bowl, using an electric mixer, beat together the ricotta, eggs, and sugar until the mixture is evenly blended.

6 Sift the flour into the bowl. Add the drained raisins, lemon zest, and vanilla to the bowl. Stir to mix well. Set the filling aside.

7 On a floured work surface, roll out the dough into an 11-inch (28-cm) round about ⅛ inch (3 mm) thick. Drape the round over the rolling pin and carefully ease it into the prepared pan, pressing it into the bottom and sides. (Alternatively, roll out the dough between 2 sheets of plastic wrap, peel off the top sheet, and use the other sheet for transferring the pastry round to the pan.)

8 Pour the ricotta mixture into the lined pan. Trim the edges of the dough, then crimp lightly to form an attractive rim around the filling.

9 Bake until the top is a soft yellow and not quite set in the center, 30–45 minutes. Transfer the pan to a wire rack and let cool for 15 minutes.

10 Release the sides of the pan and use a long metal spatula to transfer the tart to a serving plate. Serve at room temperature.

Almond Semifreddo

Semifreddo alle Mandorle • Emilia-Romagna • Italy

Bologna has always been a prosperous city, and its residents have the reputation of enjoying the good life. Dining there is considered a special treat, as the cooking is often cited as the best in Italy. This *semifreddo* is a classic Bolognese dessert. Lighter than gelato, it is more like a frozen mousse. Because of its airy texture, it never seems as icy cold as ice cream. It can be made with a variety of flavorings, from coffee or rum to praline or fruit.

1 Line a 6-cup (48–fl oz/1.5-l) loaf pan with plastic wrap and place in the freezer.

2 In a large chilled bowl, using chilled beaters, whip the cream on medium speed until stiff peaks form. Cover and refrigerate.

3 Place the egg whites in the large clean bowl of a stand mixer fitted with clean beaters.

4 In a small, heavy saucepan, combine the water and the ½ cup (4 oz/125 g) sugar. Bring to a simmer over low heat, stirring until the sugar dissolves, then stop stirring. Raise the heat to medium-high and heat, washing down the sugar crystals that form on the sides of the pan with a small brush dipped in cool water, until the liquid reaches 210°F (99°C) on a candy thermometer. Begin beating the egg whites as the syrup continues to boil.

5 Beat the egg whites on medium speed until frothy. Add 1 teaspoon of the remaining sugar and beat until soft peaks form. Gradually beat in the remaining 5 teaspoons sugar.

6 When the sugar syrup reaches 238°F (114°C) on the thermometer, turn off the heat. The temperature will continue to rise slightly. As soon as the whites are thick and form soft peaks, begin adding the sugar syrup in a thin stream, beating continuously and pouring it into the whites and not onto the beaters. After adding the syrup, the whites will look glossy and white and triple in volume. Continue to beat them together for several minutes longer until they are at room temperature. They will be very thick and shiny. Beat in the vanilla.

7 Using a rubber spatula, fold about one-third of the whipped cream into the whites. Gradually fold in the remaining whipped cream until the mixture is smooth. Fold in the amaretti and the chopped almonds.

8 Scrape the mixture into the prepared pan, smoothing the top. Cover with plastic wrap and freeze for several hours or for as long as overnight.

9 To unmold, remove the plastic wrap from the surface. Invert a plate over the pan and invert the pan and plate together. Remove the pan and peel off the plastic wrap. Smooth the surface with a rubber spatula, if necessary. Cut into slices, sprinkle with the sliced almonds, and serve.

1 cup (8 fl oz/250 ml) heavy (double) cream

3 egg whites, at room temperature

¼ cup (2 fl oz/60 ml) water

½ cup (4 oz/125 g) plus 6 teaspoons sugar

1 teaspoon vanilla extract (essence)

⅓ cup (1 oz/30 g) crushed amaretti (about 6)

2 tablespoons chopped toasted almonds (page 224)

2 tablespoons sliced (flaked) almonds, lightly toasted (page 224)

Serves 8

Drunken Chestnuts

Bruciate Ubriache · Tuscany · Italy

Pairing chestnuts with fennel dates back to medieval times, when a handful of wild fennel seed was thrown into the water in which chestnuts were boiling, infusing the nuts with a mild anise flavor and the house with an enticing fragrance. This recipe from the mountains of the Garfagnana calls for another famous cold-weather staple, grappa, a fiery, translucent, uniquely Italian spirit made from distilled *vinacce*, the grape skins and seeds left over from the wine-making process. Serve with small glasses of grappa, if desired.

2½ lb (1.25 kg) chestnuts in the shell

2 teaspoons fennel seed, crushed

2 cups (16 fl oz/500 ml) grappa

¼ cup (2 oz/60 g) superfine (caster) sugar

Serves 6

1 Preheat the oven to 375°F (190°C).

2 Cut a small X into the curved side of each chestnut shell (this keeps them from bursting as they roast). Spread the chestnuts in a baking pan and sprinkle with the fennel seed.

3 Roast until dark and puffed out, about 30 minutes. Remove from the oven. When the chestnuts are cool enough to handle, using a sharp paring knife and starting at the X, peel away the hard outer shell and the slightly fuzzy inner skin from each nut.

4 In a saucepan, combine the shelled chestnuts and the grappa and set aside for 1 hour.

5 Cover the saucepan and place over low heat. Warm the alcohol but do not allow it to boil. Remove from the heat and transfer the chestnuts and grappa to a heatproof serving bowl. Using a long kitchen match and extreme caution, ignite the liquid. The alcohol will burn off quickly and the flames will die out. Sprinkle the sugar evenly over the chestnuts.

6 Divide the chestnuts among goblets or small dessert bowls and serve at once.

Watermelon and Mint Sorbet

Sorbetto di Cocomero alla Menta • Tuscany • Italy

Two Tuscan summertime favorites—*sorbetto* and *cocomero*—are combined in this refreshing dessert. During July and August in Tuscany, watermelon stands crop up everywhere—in city squares, along boulevards leading out of town, at the sea, in the countryside. You can buy a whole melon from one of the vendors to take home, but the main reason for stopping is to stand at the counter and eat an ice-cold slice right on the spot. Children eat the melon out of hand; adults use knives to cut it into bite-sized pieces.

3½-lb (1.75-kg) piece watermelon

1 cup (8 fl oz/250 ml) water

½ cup (4 oz/125 g) sugar

20 fresh mint leaves

Makes 2 qt (2 l); Serves 8

1 Cut away the rind and remove any seeds from the watermelon. Cut the melon flesh into chunks. In a food processor or blender, working in batches, purée the flesh. You should have 5 cups (40 fl oz/1.1 l). Transfer the watermelon purée to a bowl, cover, and refrigerate to chill well.

2 In a small saucepan over high heat, combine the water and the sugar and bring to a boil, stirring to dissolve the sugar. Reduce the heat to low and simmer, stirring occasionally, until the sugar has dissolved and a syrup has formed, about 4 minutes. Remove the pan from the heat, add the mint leaves, and let cool completely.

3 Scoop out and discard the mint leaves. Stir the syrup into the chilled watermelon purée.

4 Return the bowl to the refrigerator for 1 hour. Freeze the mixture in an ice-cream maker according to the manufacturer's instructions.

GELATO

What could be better than a gelato on a sweltering Mediterranean summer day, except perhaps a thick wedge of cold watermelon? Tuscany is home to many famous *gelaterie,* but the gelato that typifies all that is wonderful about Italian ice cream comes from Bar Italia in the town of Impruneta.

In the window of the bar is a placard stating *produzione propria,* or "made on the premises," a sign to look for if you want to enjoy the real thing. What truly makes a good gelato is that every flavor tastes exactly like what it is—*gelato di fragola* should taste more like strawberries than ice cream.

Bar Italia offers an ever-changing variety of flavors, ranging from a heavenly *cioccolate* scattered with bits of dark chocolate to a mouth-puckeringly tart lemon *sorbetto.* An order of one "scoop" can be made of up to three flavors, so a customer's curiosities can be satisfied without gorging. There are many irresistible combinations. Try mixing the rich, cream-based *gelati* like *gianduia* (chocolate with hazelnut) or *cocco* (coconut) with a light, refreshing sorbet such as *frutti di bosco* (wild berries).

Mascarpone and Peaches

Coppa di Mascarpone alle Pesche • Lombardy • Italy

Although not a cheese in the true sense of the word (as it is made without a starter), mascarpone is often consumed like one. Sweet white or yellow peaches bathed in liqueur and layered with clouds of rich, velvety mascarpone are the perfect summer dessert.

4 large, ripe peaches

⅓ cup (3 fl oz/80 ml) amaretto or orange-flavored liqueur

1 tablespoon fresh lemon juice

½ lb (250 g) mascarpone

¼ cup (2 oz/60 g) sugar

1 cup (8 fl oz/250 ml) heavy (double) cream

½ cup (1½ oz/45 g) finely crushed amaretti (about 8)

2 tablespoons sliced (flaked) almonds, lightly toasted (page 224)

Serves 6

1 Bring a saucepan three-fourths full of water to a boil. Using a slotted spoon and working with 1 peach at a time, slip a peach into the water and blanch for 30 seconds. Lift it out and drop it into a bowl of cold water. Repeat with the remaining peaches. Using a small knife, lightly score the peaches lengthwise and pull off the skins. Halve, pit, and then cut into thin wedges. Place in a bowl, add the liqueur and lemon juice, and toss to coat.

2 In a large bowl, whisk together the mascarpone and sugar until well blended and fluffy. In a chilled bowl, using chilled beaters, whip the cream until stiff peaks form. Using a rubber spatula or whisk, fold the cream into the mascarpone just until combined. Spoon half of the cream mixture into parfait glasses, dividing evenly. Top with the peaches and then amaretti, again dividing evenly. Spoon on the remaining cream mixture. Cover the glasses and chill well.

3 Sprinkle with the almonds just before serving.

Buttery Apple Cake

Torta di Mele al Burro • Friuli–Venezia Giulia • Italy

This delicious *torta* made of tender apple slices bound together with a small amount of buttery cake is also good made with pears instead of apples.

½ cup (4 oz/125 g) plus 1 tablespoon unsalted butter

3 Renette or Golden Delicious apples, peeled, cored, and cut into slices ¼ inch (6 mm) thick

⅔ cup (3½ oz/105 g) all-purpose (plain) flour

½ teaspoon baking powder

½ teaspoon salt

2 whole eggs, plus 1 egg yolk

1 teaspoon vanilla extract (essence)

1 cup (8 oz/250 g) granulated sugar

½ teaspoon grated lemon zest

Confectioners' (icing) sugar

Serves 8

1 Preheat the oven to 375°F (190°C). Generously butter a 9-inch (23-cm) round cake pan with 2-inch (5-cm) sides.

2 In a large frying pan over low heat, melt the butter. Pour 6 tablespoons (3 fl oz/90 ml) of it into a small bowl or cup and set aside. Add the apple slices to the butter remaining in the frying pan and cook, stirring occasionally, until the apples are tender, about 10 minutes. Remove from the heat.

3 In a small bowl, stir together the flour, baking powder, and salt. In a large bowl, beat the whole eggs and egg yolk until blended. Add the 6 tablespoons (3 fl oz/90 ml) melted butter, the vanilla, the granulated sugar, and the lemon zest. Stir in the flour mixture and the apples. Spoon into the prepared pan, smoothing the top.

4 Bake until the cake is browned, 30–35 minutes. Transfer to a wire rack and let cool in the pan for 5 minutes. Invert the cake onto a plate and lift off the pan, then invert the cake again onto the rack and let cool completely.

5 Just before serving, dust the top of the cake with confectioners' sugar.

COFFEE BARS

The Italian bar-caffè is driven by ritual. From early until midmorning, businessmen and barbers, movie actors and car mechanics alike stream in, newspapers tucked under their arms. They stop first at the *cassa* (cashier) to secure a receipt for their breakfast. Then they place the receipt, anchored with a 100-lire-coin tip, on the counter, and, catching the eye of the white-jacketed barista, call out their order. They drink, eat, scan the newspaper, and are out the door again.

By late morning, many of these same customers have returned for *panini* (sandwiches) of prosciutto or *pomodoro e mozzarella* to quell pre-lunch hunger pangs, or for the energy boost guaranteed by a short, inky espresso. In the late afternoon, another coffee and perhaps a slice of *torta di cioccolata* or a couple of biscotti are in order. After the initial cup of the day, however, the Italian never takes coffee in the form of a milk-rich cappuccino, relying instead on the wealth of nuances offered by the espresso: *lungo*, made with more water; *ristretto*, with less water; *corretto*, with a shot of grappa or other liquor; *macchiato*, "stained" with a streak of steamed milk; or Hag, made with decaffeinated beans. Of course, an *aperitivo* (Cinzano, Campari, Cynar), a *spremuta d'arancia* (fresh orange juice), or a *birra alla spina* (draft beer) can also be taken standing up at the counter or sitting down at one of the small tables.

At a favorite coffee bar in Rome, the Tazza d'Oro, near the Pantheon, the automatic doors slide open as customers approach, and a gust of coffee aroma swirls out and pulls them in over the threshold. Inside, amid the continually hissing and rising steam of the shiny four-piston espresso machine, customers pause briefly at the counter to down a powerful espresso in no more than two quick gulps.

During the hot Italian summer months, Tazza d'Oro's *granita di caffè*, a grainy coffee ice, both cools and refreshes as the crystals melt in the mouth. If ordered *con panna*, it comes topped with a cloud of softly whipped cream. It melts slowly into the icy mass and the granita seems to last forever, giving the diner time to watch the *baristi* flirt with the young girls, gossip with one another, and argue loudly and endlessly about their beloved *calcio* (soccer).

Chocolate Amaretti Cake

Torta di Cioccolata alle Mandorle • Lombardy • Italy

Amaretti are combined with almonds and fine chocolate in this delicious Lombardian cake. Be sure to use crisp, crunchy amaretti. The cake keeps very well for a few days in the refrigerator, or it can be wrapped airtight and frozen for up to a month. Serve it plain or accompanied by ripe seasonal berries topped with whipped cream.

6 oz (185 g) semisweet (plain) chocolate such as Perugina or Callebaut, broken up into small pieces

1 cup (5½ oz/170 g) almonds

1 cup (3 oz/90 g) crumbled amaretti (about 16)

½ cup (4 oz/125 g) unsalted butter, at room temperature

⅔ cup (5 oz/155 g) sugar

4 eggs

Cocoa powder

Serves 10–12

1 Preheat the oven to 350°F (180°C). Butter a 9-inch (23-cm) round cake pan with 2-inch (5-cm) sides. Line the bottom of the pan with parchment (baking) or waxed paper. Butter the paper. Dust the pan with flour and tap out the excess.

2 Place the chocolate in a heatproof bowl placed over (not touching) simmering water in a saucepan. Heat until softened, then remove the bowl from over the water and stir the chocolate until smooth.

3 In a food processor, process the almonds and cookie crumbs until finely ground. Transfer to a bowl. Process the butter and sugar until smooth. With the motor running, add the eggs, one at a time, and blend well, stopping occasionally to scrape down the sides of the bowl. Add the nut mixture and the melted chocolate. Pulse to blend. Pour the batter into the prepared pan.

4 Bake until the center is slightly puffed, about 30 minutes. Let cool in the pan on a wire rack for 15 minutes. Invert onto a serving plate. Lift off the pan, then peel off the paper. Let cool completely.

5 Just before serving, place cocoa powder in a small sieve and dust the top of the cake.

SPAIN AND PORTUGAL

*G**olden, extravagantly rich, eggy sweets are the pinnacle of the pastrymaker's art in Spain and Portugal. Of course, far simpler fare—apple fritters, honey-drizzled cheeses, figs stuffed with chocolate and almonds, sweet peaches steeped in a local red wine—is served in these two nations of sweet lovers as well. But it is in the realm of baking and confectionery that Iberian cooks distinguish themselves from their French and Italian neighbors.*

The Spanish sweet tooth has a long history. The Moors who arrived in the eighth century brought with them a love of intensely flavored confections based on eggs, honey, nuts (especially almonds), citrus, quinces, and dried fruit—the same ingredients that can be found in desserts throughout the Near East and the Mediterranean today. With the Spanish reconquest in the mid-thirteenth century came the flourishing of Christianity and a rapid spread of convents and monasteries throughout the country. Nuns in the new orders preserved the old recipes, baking traditional sweets as gifts for the many patrons who funded the religious houses with generous donations. By the nineteenth century, the nuns began selling their confections, and to this day, many convents continue to offer exquisite pastries to locals and visitors alike.

The preponderance of egg-based sweetmeats in Spain and Portugal has another, much more practical basis: a surplus of egg yolks. Spanish and Portuguese vintners used egg white for clarifying their sherry and port, to remove any particles that might cloud the final product. Large numbers of leftover yolks were the result, and thrifty cooks put them to good use. Egg whites are now used for clarifying only the finest wines, but recipes that call for lavish quantities of egg yolks remain firmly established in the Iberian culinary canon.

Among the most famous Portuguese egg sweets are *papos de anjo,* or "angel's cheeks," small eggy cakes doused in a vanilla-scented syrup; *pudim flan,* a port-scented custard; golden soup, a bread pudding built from sponge cake and flooded with custard; and *ovos moles,* or "soft eggs," a stunningly rich

confection made from egg yolks and thickened sugar syrup that is a specialty of the convents around Aveiro, in Beira Litoral. Often sold packed in small wooden casks in local pastry shops, these soft egg creams are commonly sandwiched between airy meringues or used to fill thin pastry layers. The origin of *toucinho-do-céu*, or "heavenly bacon," a baked egg-yolk custard enriched with almonds and cinnamon, is a source of debate. Several places claim it as their own, including the Convento de Odivelas, near Lisbon; the small town of Murça, in Trás-os-Montes; and even Jérez in Spain, where it is called *tocino de cielo* and has been given an apocryphal nun's story to prove its claim.

Spain has its own versions of these rich sweets. Burnt cream is like *pudim flan* in reverse, with the caramel forming a crackling burnt-sugar top rather than a thin, syrupy sauce. The double-rich, vividly named "gypsy's arm" has a chocolate-custard filling swirled inside a roll of sponge cake (*pão-de-ló* in Portuguese, *bizcocho* in Spain).

The legacy of the Arab fondness for sweets is also evident in the abundance of dried-fruit and nut confections in the Iberian repertoire. Accompanied by a glass of port or Madeira, they make wonderful afternoon snacks or sweet endings to a meal. Similar to the *panforte* of Italy, *pan de higos,* a chewy sweetmeat made from dried figs, almonds, and chocolate, is a Christmastime favorite. Marzipan, the paste of ground almonds and sugar that is known as *maçapão* or *massapão* in Portuguese and *mazapán* in Spanish, is equally popular. Some believe its name comes from the Arabic *mautaban,* from *uataba,* meaning "white," and that it was brought by the Moors. Others place its beginnings in ancient Rome. Still others claim it was first made in Toledo in the early thirteenth century by nuns in the Convent of San Clemente. Today, antique marzipan molds can still be seen in the convent, and many shops on Plaza de Zocodover, in the heart of Toledo's Old Quarter, sell marzipan shaped into whimsical forms: detailed pineapples and pomegranates, tiny piglets, even roosters topped with red-dyed cockscombs.

The orchards of the Algarve, Asturias, and Levante—whose oranges, apples, quinces, and almonds are prized in both countries—inspire sweet dishes, such as marzipan, lemony almond sponge cakes, crepes with sautéed apples, and *membrillo,* a quince preserve traditionally paired with Manchego cheese. Almonds also feature prominently in Basque cuisine, notably in *panchineta,* a tart with custard filling steeped in almonds. The opening of spice routes to Africa, India, the Caribbean, and the Far East—followed by the establishment of Spanish and Portuguese colonies in the New World—added exotic ingredients like cloves, nutmeg, cinnamon, chocolate, vanilla, and pepper to the Iberian larder. They remain a flavorful legacy of a multilayered history.

Left: Spanish markets, with their plump figs, tart kumquats, and clusters of juicy grapes, are a fruit lover's paradise. **Above, left:** The perfect end to any Spanish meal is a *café solo,* with sugar or without. **Above, right:** An eye-catching statue of a proud matador, his cape extended, stands at the front of the Plaza de Toros in Ronda, Spain.

Orange Cake

Delícia de Laranja • Douro • Portugal

Portugal's orange groves are mainly in the Algarve and around Setúbal. Algarve oranges are large, seedless navels, the consummate eating orange, while those from Setúbal are smaller and primarily used for preserves. While a cut orange is the dessert of choice for most Portuguese, this cake makes a more festive ending to a meal.

1¼ cups (6½ oz/200 g) all-purpose (plain) flour

½ teaspoon baking powder

3 eggs, separated

½ cup (4 oz/125 g) plus 2 tablespoons unsalted butter

⅔ cup (5 oz/155 g) granulated sugar

Grated zest of 1 orange

½ cup (4 fl oz/120 ml) fresh orange juice

¼ cup (1 oz/30 g) confectioners' (icing) sugar

Orange sections (optional)

Serves 6–8

1 Preheat the oven to 350°F (180°C). Butter and flour an 8-inch (20-cm) round cake pan.

2 In a small bowl, sift together the flour and baking powder. In a medium bowl, using an electric mixer, beat the egg whites until soft peaks form.

3 In a large bowl, using the electric mixer set on high speed, beat together the butter and the granulated sugar until light and fluffy. Beat in the egg yolks, one at a time. Reduce the speed to low and slowly beat in the flour mixture, the orange zest, and ¼ cup (2 fl oz/ 60 ml) of the orange juice. Fold the beaten egg whites into the yolk mixture just until combined. Spoon the batter into the prepared pan.

4 Bake until a skewer inserted into the center emerges clean, 30–40 minutes. Remove from the oven and let cool in the pan on a rack for 10 minutes. Then turn out onto the rack and let cool to lukewarm. Transfer the cake to a platter.

5 In a small bowl, stir together the remaining ¼ cup (2 fl oz/60 ml) orange juice and the confectioners' sugar until the sugar dissolves and pour evenly over the cake. Garnish with orange sections, if desired.

MADEIRA

In 1419, Portuguese explorers discovered a small, heavily forested volcanic island about five hundred miles (800 km) off the mainland and named it Madeira. By the beginning of the sixteenth century, vineyards had been planted, and wine was being made, but only enough to sell to the island's residents and to arriving sailors, who believed the rustic product was a protection against scurvy. It would be another two hundred years before Madeira would become the drink of kings and czars and of the colonists of America.

Today, much of the fertile land of this sun-drenched, mountainous island is blanketed with tall, grapevine-covered pergolas. Throughout the month of September, farmers pick the fat, sugar-laden grapes, beginning with the vineyards at the sea and slowly working their way up the towering peaks where cooler weather dictates a later harvest.

The ripe grapes are crushed, fermented, and then put in *estufas,* or "hothouses," a system unique to Madeira production in which the wine is "cooked" for several months. It is then fortified with brandy and aged, resulting in four distinct types: dry, straw-gold Sercial and semidry, golden Verdelho, both fine aperitif wines; and semisweet Bual and sweet Malmsey, rich red dessert wines.

Almond Custard Tart

Panchineta • Basque Country • Spain

Steeping almonds in milk intensifies the almond flavor of this simple Basque tart. It is an ideal dessert for entertaining, as the crust can be baked ahead of time and the custard fully prepared and chilled. Just before serving, assemble the tart and bake according to the recipe. You can use a rich tart pastry in place of the prebaked puff-pastry, if you prefer.

1 sheet frozen puff pastry, about 12 by 14 inches (30 by 35 cm) and ¼ inch (6 mm) thick, thawed in the refrigerator

1¾ cups (14 fl oz/430 ml) milk

⅓ cup (3 oz/90 g) sugar

1 cup (5½ oz/170 g) almonds, toasted (page 224)

2 whole eggs plus 3 egg yolks

¼ cup (1½ oz/45 g) all-purpose (plain) flour

¼ teaspoon salt

2 tablespoons unsalted butter, at room temperature

1 teaspoon vanilla extract (essence)

1 teaspoon almond extract (essence)

⅔ cup (2½ oz/75 g) sliced (flaked) almonds, lightly toasted

Serves 8

1 To prepare the puff pastry shell, unfold the sheet of puff pastry and, using a sharp knife, cut into a 9-inch (23-cm) round. Using a fork, prick all over the center of the round, leaving a 1-inch (2.5-cm) border. (This will allow the edges to puff up when baked.) Wrap in plastic wrap and freeze for 1 hour or as long as 12 hours before baking.

2 Preheat the oven to 400°F (200°C). Lightly butter a baking sheet.

3 Transfer the round to the prepared baking sheet. Bake for 10–12 minutes, remove from the oven, and prick again with a fork. Reduce the oven temperature to 350°F (180°C), return to the oven, and bake until crisp and pale golden brown, about 10 minutes longer. Remove from the oven and let cool.

4 To make the custard, combine the milk and sugar in a saucepan and place over medium heat. Heat, stirring to dissolve the sugar, until small bubbles appear along the edges of the pan. Remove from the heat, add the 1 cup (5½ oz/170 g) toasted almonds, and let steep for 1 hour. Strain and discard the almonds.

5 Pour the almond milk into a clean saucepan and bring to a boil over medium heat. In a bowl, whisk together the whole eggs, egg yolks, flour, and salt until blended. Gradually add about ½ cup (4 fl oz/125 ml) of the hot milk to the egg mixture, whisking until well blended. Then return the mixture to the saucepan. Place over medium heat and cook, whisking constantly, until the mixture comes to a boil. Continue to whisk for 2–3 minutes to remove the raw flour taste. Remove from the heat and pour the custard into a bowl nested in a bowlful of ice. Stir in the butter and the vanilla and almond extracts until the butter melts. Cover with plastic wrap, pressing it directly onto the surface of the custard, and refrigerate until cold.

6 Preheat the oven to 325°F (165°C). Pour the custard evenly into the prebaked puff pastry shell. Strew the toasted sliced almonds over the top. Bake until lightly browned and warmed through, 5–10 minutes. Remove from the heat and serve warm.

"Burnt" Cream

Crema Quemada · Catalonia · Spain

Sometimes called *crema de San José,* as it is traditionally served on Saint Joseph's Day, this classic caramelized custard is on the menu of nearly every Barcelona restaurant. Unlike *pudim flan* (page 216), which is poured into a caramelized mold, this custard is chilled and then caramelized, or "burnt," on top just before serving, like a French crème brûlée.

2 tablespoons cornstarch (cornflour)

1 cup (8 fl oz/250 ml) milk

1 cup (8 fl oz/250 ml) half-and-half (half cream) or heavy (double) cream

3 lemon zest strips, each 2 inches (5 cm) long

1 cinnamon stick

6 egg yolks

½ cup (4 oz/125 g) granulated sugar

6 tablespoons (3 oz/90 g) firmly packed brown sugar or granulated sugar

Serves 6

1 In a small bowl, dissolve the cornstarch in a few tablespoons of the milk. Set aside. Pour the remaining milk and the cream into a saucepan and add the lemon zest and cinnamon stick. Place over medium-high heat and heat until small bubbles appear along the edges of the pan. Remove from the heat and discard the lemon zest and cinnamon stick.

2 In a bowl, using an electric mixer set on high speed, beat together the egg yolks and the ½ cup (4 oz/125 g) granulated sugar until thick and pale. Gradually whisk in about ½ cup (4 fl oz/125 ml) of the hot milk-cream mixture. Return the mixture to the pan, whisk in the cornstarch-milk mixture, and place over low heat. Simmer, stirring, until the custard thickens enough to coat a spoon, about 10 minutes. Pour through a fine-mesh sieve placed over a pitcher. Then pour it into six ½-cup (4–fl oz/125-ml) flameproof custard cups or ramekins, dividing evenly. Let cool, cover, and chill well.

3 Preheat a broiler (grill). Place the molds on a baking sheet. Sprinkle 1 tablespoon brown or granulated sugar over the top of each chilled custard and slip under the broiler. Broil (grill) until the sugar is melted and bubbling. Serve at once.

Caramelized Apple Crepes

Filloas • Galicia • Spain

Crisp apples become perfectly tender when caramelized. If you like, garnish these leaf-thin crepes with whipped cream flavored with Calvados or apple brandy.

CREPES

3 eggs

1 cup (8 fl oz/250 ml) milk

¾ cup (6 fl oz/180 ml) water

1 ½ cups (7 ½ oz/235 g) all-purpose (plain) flour

Pinch of salt

2 tablespoons unsalted butter, melted, plus extra melted butter for frying

FILLING

3 tablespoons unsalted butter

1 lb (500 g) Golden Delicious apples, peeled, halved, cored, and sliced lengthwise ½ inch (12 mm) thick

3 tablespoons sugar

½ teaspoon ground cinnamon (optional)

Serves 4–6

1 To make the crepes, in a bowl, whisk together the eggs, milk, water, flour, salt, and the 2 tablespoons melted butter. Let the batter rest for 30 minutes.

2 Meanwhile, make the filling: In a frying pan over medium heat, melt the butter. Add the apples and sauté until softened, about 10 minutes. Sprinkle with the sugar, raise the heat to medium-high, and sauté until the apples begin to caramelize, 10–15 minutes longer. Sprinkle with cinnamon, if using, and keep warm.

3 Lightly brush a 7- to 7½-inch (18- to 19-cm) crepe pan with melted butter and place over medium heat. When the pan is hot, ladle in about 3 tablespoons of the batter and swirl to coat the bottom. Cook over medium heat until just set, 2–3 minutes. Using your fingers, turn the crepe and cook on the second side until set, about 1 minute longer. Do not allow it to color. Slide the crepe onto a clean kitchen towel, then wrap tightly in aluminum foil to keep warm. Brush the pan again with butter and repeat until all of the batter is used. You should have 12 crepes.

4 Place several spoonfuls of the apples in the middle of each crepe and fold into quarters. Divide among individual plates and serve.

Apple Fritters

Buñuelos de Manzana • Catalonia • Spain

Although most of Spain's apples are grown in Asturias and Levante, Catalans are recognized as the masters of the apple fritter. The batter must be assembled ahead of time, but for the best results, beat the egg whites just before you are ready to fry the apples.

1 lb (500 g) apples such as Golden Delicious, Gala, Fuji, or McIntosh, peeled, halved, cored, and sliced lengthwise ½ inch (12 mm) thick

2 tablespoons granulated sugar

1 tablespoon anise liqueur such as *anís del mono* or brandy

2 eggs, separated

½ cup (4 fl oz/125 ml) milk

1 tablespoon olive oil, plus olive oil or vegetable oil for deep-frying

Pinch of salt

1 cup (5 oz/155 g) plus 1 tablespoon all-purpose (plain) flour

Confectioners' (icing) sugar

Serves 4

1 Place the sliced apples in a shallow bowl, add the granulated sugar and liqueur or brandy, and toss to coat. Let stand for a few hours at room temperature.

2 In a separate bowl, whisk together the egg yolks, milk, the 1 tablespoon olive oil, the salt, and the flour. Cover and refrigerate for 1–2 hours.

3 In a bowl, beat the egg whites until they form stiff peaks, and fold into the batter just until combined.

4 In a deep frying pan, pour in oil to a depth of 2 inches (5 cm) and heat to 350°F (180°C) on a deep-frying thermometer. In batches, dip the apple slices in the batter and then slip them into the hot oil. Fry, turning once, until golden, 3–4 minutes total. Using a slotted spoon, transfer to paper towels to drain.

5 Arrange the fritters on a warmed platter and sift confectioners' sugar over the top. Serve piping hot.

COFFEEHOUSES

In Spain and Portugal, the coffeehouse is a beloved institution, with much of its prominence due to historical circumstance. Both countries included important coffee-growing colonies in their one-time empires—Brazil, East Timor, Mozambique, and Angola in the case of Portugal and most notably Colombia in the case of Spain—which gave the populace a taste for fine coffees. Indeed, in Lisbon and other Portuguese cities, shops selling coffee beans often offer some three dozen different blends and individual coffees.

In Spain, the coffee drinker generally selects from a quintet of choices: *solo,* or black coffee; *cortado,* similar to an Italian espresso with a streak of milk; *café con leche,* coffee with milk; *leche manchada,* milk "stained" with coffee; and *café del tiempo,* coffee with ice and a lemon slice—a hangover cure. The Portuguese boast an equally refined coffee menu: The *bica,* a demitasse of superstrong coffee, is the equivalent of an Italian espresso and a coffeehouse standard. The *café* is a rather powerful brew served in restaurants and homes. People who prefer a lighter beverage choose *carioca,* basically half water and half coffee. A *galão* is hot milk and strong coffee mixed together and served in a glass, similar to an Italian caffè latte. Children in this coffee-loving society drink *garoto,* or "urchin," a tiny cup of warm milk flavored with coffee.

But Iberian coffeehouses are more than just a place to drink a superb coffee. They are busy outposts for everything from family gossip to political debates to storytelling. People head to their regular coffeehouse to read the newspaper, visit with an old friend, talk over a business deal, or hook up for a romantic rendezvous.

Egg Cakes in Syrup

Papos de Anjo • Trás-os-Montes • Portugal

Nearly everyone gives a different answer when asked to translate *papos de anjo*. Some say it means angel's breasts, others angel's cheeks or double chins. The cakes are round, tender, and bathed in a vanilla-scented syrup.

8 egg yolks

2 egg whites

Pinch of salt

2 cups (1 lb/500 g) sugar

1 cup (8 fl oz/250 ml) water

1 teaspoon vanilla extract (essence)

Makes 12 small cakes

1 Preheat the oven to 350°F (180°C). Grease 12 standard muffin cups or ½-cup (4–fl oz/125-ml) custard cups with butter. Place in a baking pan.

2 In a bowl, using an electric mixer set on high speed, beat the egg yolks until they are thick and pale and fall in a wide, slowly dissolving ribbon when the beaters are lifted. In a separate bowl, beat the egg whites with the salt until they form stiff peaks. Fold the whites into the yolks just until combined. Divide the mixture evenly among the prepared muffin cups. Pour hot water into the baking pan to reach halfway up the sides of the molds.

3 Bake until a knife inserted into the center of a cake comes out clean, 15–20 minutes. Remove the baking pan from the oven and let the cakes cool in the pan for 5 minutes. Remove the molds from the water bath and invert them onto a large platter. Prick each cake in a few places with a wooden skewer.

4 In a heavy saucepan over high heat, combine the sugar and water. Bring to a boil, stirring until the sugar dissolves, and then boil until the mixture reaches the thread stage, about 230°F (110°C) on a candy thermometer, or until it is very thick. Remove from the heat and stir in the vanilla.

5 Using a large spoon, dip each cake into the syrup, moving it gently to coat it well, and then return it to the platter. Pour the remaining syrup over the cakes. Cover and chill well before serving.

"Soft Eggs"

Ovos Moles • Beira Litoral • Portugal

Although these rich golden egg creams are quite decadent just as they are, some Portuguese cooks enrich them even further with the addition of ground toasted nuts.

1¼ cups (10 oz/315 g) sugar

⅓ cup (3 fl oz/80 ml) water

8 egg yolks

Serves 4–6

1 In a heavy saucepan over high heat, combine the sugar and water. Bring to a boil, stirring until the sugar dissolves, and then boil until the mixture reaches the soft-ball stage, 234°–238°F (112°–114°C) on a candy thermometer. Remove from the heat.

2 In a bowl, using an electric mixer set on high speed, beat the egg yolks until thick and pale. Very slowly add the hot syrup in a thin stream, beating constantly. Pour the mixture into a clean saucepan, place over low heat, and cook, stirring constantly, until the mixture coats a spoon, 5–8 minutes. Do not allow it to boil. Remove from the heat and let cool completely. The mixture will thicken as it cools.

3 Spoon into small cups or a single large serving bowl. Serve at room temperature.

Bread Fritters

Torrijas • New Castile • Spain

In the region of New Castile, especially in Madrid, desserts tend to be simple and rustic. *Torrijas* are typical in that everyday ingredients—bread, egg, milk, and honey—are turned into a satisfying sweet. These fritters are also called *pan de Santa Teresa*, after the nun, a respected teacher and writer, who reformed the Carmelite order in the sixteenth century.

6–8 thick slices day-old white bread, crusts removed

2 cups (16 fl oz/500 ml) milk, or as needed

Orange or lemon zest strips

1 cinnamon stick

Sweet sherry to cover (optional)

3 eggs

Olive oil for frying

Warmed honey or cinnamon-sugar

Serves 6

1 Cut each bread slice into 2 triangles. Place in a single layer in a shallow baking pan.

2 Pour the 2 cups (16 fl oz/500 ml) milk into a saucepan over medium heat, add the citrus zest and cinnamon stick, and heat until small bubbles appear along the edges of the pan. Remove from the heat and let steep for about 30 minutes. Remove the cinnamon stick and citrus zest from the milk and pour the milk over the bread. If it does not cover the bread, add more milk or add sherry as needed to cover. Let stand for about 10 minutes to absorb the milk.

3 In a shallow bowl, whisk the eggs until blended. In a large frying pan, pour in olive oil to a depth of ¼ inch (6 mm) and warm over medium-high heat.

4 In batches, dip the bread into the beaten eggs and slip into the hot oil. Fry, turning once, until golden on both sides, 6–8 minutes total. Transfer to individual plates and drizzle with warm honey or sprinkle with cinnamon-sugar. Repeat with the remaining bread slices, using more oil as needed. Serve at once.

Almond Sponge Cake

Torta de Santiago • Galicia • Spain

This cake is a specialty of Galicia, where granite walls outline each farmer's plot and granite crosses stand at many rural crossroads. The top of the cake is traditionally decorated with a cross in confectioners' sugar, in honor of Saint James, Spain's patron saint.

1 lb (500 g) blanched almonds (about 3 cups)

2¼ cups (18 oz/560 g) granulated sugar

¾ cup (6 oz/180 g) unsalted butter, at room temperature

7 eggs

⅓ cup (2 oz/60 g) all-purpose (plain) flour

Grated zest and juice of 1 large lemon

Confectioners' (icing) sugar

Serves 8–10

1 Preheat the oven to 350°F (180°C). Butter a 9-inch (23-cm) springform pan.

2 Spread the almonds on a baking sheet and toast briefly just until their aroma is released, 8–10 minutes. Transfer to a plate, let cool, and then place in a blender or food processor with a few tablespoons of the granulated sugar. Process until finely ground.

3 In a bowl, using an electric mixer, beat together the butter and the rest of the granulated sugar until fluffy. Beat in the eggs, one at a time, beating well after each addition. Stir in the flour, ground almonds, and lemon zest. Pour into the prepared pan.

4 Bake until a skewer inserted into the center emerges clean, about 1 hour. Remove from the oven and prick the top of the cake with a fork. Sprinkle with the lemon juice. Release the pan sides and slide the cake from the pan bottom onto a rack to cool.

5 Transfer the cake to a serving plate and dust with confectioners' sugar before serving.

Peaches in Wine

Melocotón al Vino • Aragon • Spain

Most travelers pass up landlocked Aragon. They never see the *jota,* a centuries-old regional dance in which the participants leap high repeatedly at a furious pace, or the bullfighting festivals in early fall that draw locals rather than the tourists who flock to Pamplona. But anyone who pursues good food knows that Aragon is famous for its peaches, and savvy travelers stop at the height of the summer to eat the juicy fruit right off the trees. For the rest of the year, they enjoy jars of the peaches in syrup sold at shops throughout the region.

4 large freestone peaches

2½ cups (20 fl oz/625 ml) dry red wine

½ cup (4 oz/125 g) sugar

Zest of 1 lemon, cut into strips

1 cinnamon stick

⅓ cup (3 fl oz/80 ml) brandy (optional)

Serves 4

1 Bring a saucepan three-fourths full of water to a boil. One at a time, add the peaches and blanch for about 20 seconds to loosen the skin. Using a slotted spoon, transfer the peaches to a bowl of cold water. Slip off the skins, cut the peaches in half through the stem end, and remove the pit. Set the peaches aside in a heatproof bowl.

2 In a saucepan over medium heat, combine the wine, sugar, lemon zest, and cinnamon stick and bring to a boil, stirring to dissolve the sugar. Add the brandy, if using, then remove from the heat and pour over the peaches. Let cool, cover, and let steep in the wine for 2 days in the refrigerator.

3 To serve, spoon the chilled peaches, along with some of the liquid, into glass bowls or goblets. Serve cold.

SANGRIA

In Andalusia, a land of citrus groves and Moorish echoes, locals and visitors alike seek a cool, refreshing antidote to the long, blisteringly hot summers. A tall, iced glass of sangria, a drink that originated here but is now drunk all over the country and in neighboring Portugal, is often the choice.

To make it, a fruity red wine is mixed with sparkling water and then a few orange and lemon slices are added. Sometimes a glass of brandy is splashed into the pitcher to fortify the wine. The result is a wonderfully thirst-quenching drink that bears little resemblance to the tutti-frutti mixture of the same name so often served in bars and restaurants beyond the Iberian Peninsula—mixtures that include everything from bananas and peaches to apples and nectarines.

To make an authentic Spanish sangria for four people, in a pitcher, pour a bottle of fruity, dry red wine over a half dozen ice cubes. Add ¼ cup (2 fl oz/60 ml) brandy; 2 tablespoons sugar; 1 or 2 lemons, sliced paper-thin; 2 oranges, sliced paper-thin and slices quartered; and 3 cups (24 fl oz/750 ml) chilled sparkling water. Stir well, pour into chilled glasses, and sip slowly to beat the heat of a summer afternoon.

Quince Preserves

Membrillo · Balearic Islands · Spain

Although you can buy quince preserves in markets that specialize in Iberian or Latin American foods, if you make your own, the texture will be a little softer and more appealing. *Membrillo* is often served with a fresh soft cream cheese, a youngish Manchego, or a mild goat cheese and crackers or toasted bread.

2 lb (1 kg) quinces

4 cups (32 fl oz/1 l) water

3½–4 cups (1¼–2 lb/875 g–1 kg) sugar

1 teaspoon ground cinnamon

Makes about 1 qt (1 l)

1 Wipe the fuzz off the quinces and rinse well. Peel each quince, cut in half, and remove the core and seeds. Reserve the peels, cores, and seeds and place in a square of cheesecloth (muslin). Bring the corners together and tie securely with kitchen string.

2 Slice the quinces and place in a heavy pot, preferably one of enamel-lined cast iron. Add water to cover and the cheesecloth pouch. Bring to a boil over high heat, reduce the heat to low, and cook slowly, uncovered, until very tender, 20–40 minutes; the timing will vary from batch to batch. You may want to stop the cooking a few times, for about an hour or two, to let the quinces rest and redden. Add more water if the mixture begins to dry out. (This process can even be done over 1 or 2 days, without refrigerating between simmerings.)

3 When the quinces are red and very tender, remove the cheesecloth bag and discard. Reserve the cooking water. Purée the quinces in a food processor, or mash them using a potato masher. Combine the pulp and cooking water, 3½ cups (1¼ lb/875 g) of the sugar, and the cinnamon and cook very slowly, stirring often, until thick, about 20 minutes. Taste and add more sugar if the preserves seem too tart.

4 Ladle into hot, sterilized canning jars to within ¼ inch (6 mm) of the top. Wipe each rim clean with a hot, damp kitchen towel, cover with a sterilized canning lid, and seal tightly with a screw band. Process the jars in a hot-water bath for 10 minutes, check the seals, label, and store in a cool pantry for up to 1 year. Jars that do not form a good seal can be refrigerated for up to 1 month.

Golden Soup

Sopa Dourada · Minho · Portugal

The name of this dessert comes from its colorful components: golden Portuguese sponge cake, or *pão-de-ló*, covered either with *ovos moles* (page 200) or with an egg-yolk-loaded custard. In Minho, *sopa dourada* is served during the Christmas holidays, and some cooks give it a more festive air by decorating it with colorful candied fruits or slivered nuts. One variation, *barrigas-de-freira*, or nun's tummies, adds a spoonful of cocoa to the soft egg custard and crumbles the sponge cake.

CUSTARD

4 cups (32 fl oz/1 l) half-and-half (half cream)

2 cups (16 fl oz/500 ml) heavy (double) cream

1 cinnamon stick

1 tablespoon grated lemon zest

7 whole eggs plus 6 egg yolks

1 cup (8 oz/250 g) sugar

¼ teaspoon freshly grated nutmeg

1 teaspoon vanilla extract (essence)

SPONGE CAKE

6 eggs

1 cup (8 fl oz/250 g) sugar

Pinch of salt

½ cup (2 oz/60 g) plus 2 tablespoons sifted all-purpose (plain) flour

6 tablespoons (2 oz/60 g) blanched almonds, toasted (page 224) and finely ground

¼ teaspoon almond extract (essence)

2 teaspoons grated lemon zest

Serves 8

1 To make the custard, pour the half-and-half and cream into a saucepan and place over medium heat until small bubbles appear along the pan edges. Remove from the heat and add the cinnamon stick and lemon zest. Let steep for 2 hours.

2 In a bowl, whisk together the whole eggs and egg yolks, sugar, nutmeg, and vanilla. Pour the steeped milk though a fine-mesh sieve held over the bowl holding the egg mixture. Stir to mix.

3 To make the cake, preheat the oven to 325°F (165°C). Lightly butter a 10½-by-15-inch (26½-by-38-cm) jelly-roll pan. Line the bottom of the pan with parchment (baking) paper and butter the parchment.

4 In a heatproof bowl, whisk together the eggs, sugar, and salt. Place over (but not touching) simmering water in a saucepan and continue to whisk until the mixture is warm and the sugar is dissolved. Remove from over the water and, using an electric mixer set on high speed, beat until the mixture is very thick and falls in a wide, slowly dissolving ribbon when the beaters are lifted.

5 Sift together the flour and ground almonds over the eggs. Using a rubber spatula, gently fold them in along with the almond extract and lemon zest. Pour the batter into the prepared pan and smooth the top.

6 Bake until a skewer inserted into the center of the cake emerges clean and the top is springy to the touch, 10–15 minutes. Remove from the oven and let cool in the pan on a rack for about 5 minutes. Run a knife around the inside edge of the pan to loosen the cake and turn the cake out onto the rack. Peel off the parchment. Let cool completely.

7 Preheat the oven to 350°F (180°C). Lightly butter a 2-qt (2-l) baking dish with 3-inch (7.5-cm) sides.

8 To assemble the pudding, cut the cake into 1-inch (2.5-cm) cubes or thin slices, then distribute evenly in the prepared dish, covering the bottom completely. Pour the custard over the cake, filling the dish. The cake will float to the top. Place the dish in a baking pan. Pour hot water into the pan to reach three-fourths of the way up the sides of the dish.

9 Bake until a small, sharp knife inserted into the center emerges almost clean, about 40 minutes. The pudding will still jiggle slightly when the dish is shaken. Let cool for about 45 minutes before serving.

"Rotten" Cake

Bolo Podre · Alentejo · Spain

A favorite in Alentejo, this delicious honey cake is made with olive oil rather than butter. Despite its unappealing name, its dark, rustic appearance is really quite handsome.

2½ cups (10 oz/315 g) sifted all-purpose (plain) flour or whole wheat (wholemeal) flour

1 tablespoon ground cinnamon

1½ teaspoons baking powder

½ teaspoon ground cloves

6 eggs, separated

½ cup (4 oz/125 g) granulated sugar or ½ cup (3½ oz/105 g) firmly packed brown sugar

Grated zest of 1 orange

1 cup (8 fl oz/250 ml) olive oil or vegetable oil

1 cup (12 oz/375 g) dark honey

¼ cup (2 fl oz/60 ml) brandy

Serves 8–10

1 Preheat the oven to 350°F (180°C). Butter a 10-inch (25-cm) springform pan.

2 In a bowl, sift together the flour, cinnamon, baking powder, and cloves. In another bowl, using an electric mixer set on high speed, beat the egg yolks and sugar until pale and thick. Beat in the orange zest, then drizzle in the oil, beating constantly. Slowly add the honey and brandy, beating until smooth. Reduce the speed to low and add the flour mixture in 3 batches. Beat well after each addition.

3 In a clean bowl, using clean beaters, beat the egg whites until soft peaks form. Fold into the cake batter. Pour into the prepared pan.

4 Bake until a skewer inserted into the center of the cake emerges clean and the edges of the cake begin to shrink from the sides of the pan, 45–50 minutes. Let cool in the pan on a rack for 15 minutes, then run a small knife around the inside edge of the pan to loosen the cake. Release and remove the pan sides and let cool.

5 Transfer the cake to a plate. Cut into very thin slices to serve, as the cake is quite rich.

Fig Loaf

Pan de Higos · Andalusia · Spain

The warm climate of southern Spain produces a bumper crop of figs. Locals consider them among the delights of summer, enjoying them fresh or poached in light sugar syrup. When the population is sated, the balance of the figs is dried and used in cakes or other sweets. This rich, sweet confection is traditionally served during the Christmas holidays.

1½ lb (750 g) dried Mission figs, stems removed and finely chopped

½ cup (3 oz/90 g) almonds, toasted (page 224) and finely chopped

½ cup (2½ oz/75 g) hazelnuts (filberts), toasted and finely chopped

¼ cup (1 oz/30 g) confectioners' (icing) sugar, plus more for sprinkling foil

1 teaspoon ground cinnamon

½ teaspoon ground cloves

1 tablespoon grated lemon zest

2 tablespoons anise liqueur such as *anís del mono* or brandy

2 oz (60 g) semisweet (plain) chocolate, melted

Serves 8–12

1 In a food processor, combine the figs, almonds, hazelnuts, the ¼ cup (1 oz/30 g) confectioners' sugar, cinnamon, cloves, and lemon zest. Pulse until well combined. Stir in the liqueur or brandy and chocolate to moisten the mixture, which will be very stiff.

2 Sprinkle a large square of heavy-duty aluminum foil with confectioners' sugar. Shape the fig mixture into a large loaf and wrap it in the foil. (Alternatively, use 2 foil squares and make 2 small loaves.) Refrigerate for at least 2 days or for as long as 3 months.

3 To serve, dip a very sharp knife in hot water and cut the loaf into slices.

CHOCOLATE

On his fourth voyage to the New World, in 1502, Columbus sent back the first cacao beans to Spain. The recipients, alas, were mystified as to what to do with the bitter seeds, and Columbus provided no insights. Nearly two decades later, however, Hernán Cortés, who had drunk cups of chocolate at Aztec dinner tables, returned to Spain not only with the beans, but also with the knowledge of how to use them.

The Spanish did not at first realize the cacao bean's dessert possibilities, but they did manage to fashion the beans into tablets, which they sweetened with sugar and later flavored with cinnamon and vanilla. They jealously guarded the secrets of chocolate production. The tablets were used to make hot chocolate, a sweet, molten liquid that soon took the country by storm despite early objections from the Catholic Church, who viewed it as potentially sinful.

Today, chocolate is used in sweets, of course, but it also flavors savory dishes in Aragon and Navarre, such as small white onions in a chocolate-flavored sauce. And many Spaniards still enjoy a big cup of thick hot chocolate for breakfast, often served with a *churro*, which is a wonderful loop or finger of deep-fried dough dusted with sugar—a cruller of sorts.

Chocolate and Almond Stuffed Figs

Figos Recheados • Algarve • Portugal

Figs have been grown in the Algarve for centuries. Indeed, dried figs from the Algarve were so highly regarded in the 1600s that they were exported to Levant and Flanders. Almonds, introduced by the Moors, are cultivated in the Algarve as well. Here, they are combined with chocolate, introduced from Mexico, and the mixture is stuffed into moist dried figs for an ideal after-dinner sweet. Pour a glass of port or Madeira for each guest.

¼ cup (1½ oz/45 g) blanched whole almonds, plus 12 extra

2 tablespoons sugar

1 oz (30 g) semisweet (plain) chocolate, finely chopped

12 large dried figs

Serves 6

1 Preheat the oven to 350°F (180°C).

2 Spread all the almonds on a baking sheet and toast them until they take on color and are fragrant, 8–10 minutes. Remove from the oven and let cool.

3 Set aside the 12 almonds. Combine the remaining almonds, the sugar, and the chocolate in a food processor. Pulse until well combined.

4 Cut the stems off the figs. Cut a slit in the top of each fig and stuff with 1–2 teaspoons of the chocolate-nut mixture. Pinch the openings closed. Place the figs, stem ends up, on a baking sheet. Bake for 5 minutes. Then turn the figs over and bake for another 5 minutes to heat through.

5 Remove from the oven and press an almond into the slit in the top of each fig. Serve warm or at room temperature.

"Heavenly Bacon"

Toucinho-do-Céu • Estremadura • Portugal

The birthplace of this centuries-old dessert, which today is prepared all over Portugal, is hotly debated among food scholars, with the Convento de Odivelas, located near Lisbon and known for its exquisite sweets, the leading contender. But the Spanish claim the dessert (*tocino de cielo*), too, citing this story: One day in Jerez an absentminded nun set out to make an egg-and-milk custard. But she forgot to add the milk, producing a rather firm, dark brown dessert that looked remarkably like a slab of bacon, thus the name.

3 tablespoons unsalted butter, softened

2 tablespoons plus 1¼ cups (10 oz/315 g) sugar

7 tablespoons (3½ fl oz/105 ml) water

12 egg yolks

1½ cups (6 oz/185 g) finely ground almonds, plus chopped almonds for garnish (optional)

¼ teaspoon ground cinnamon

Serves 8

1 Preheat the oven to 400°F (200°C). Using the butter, grease an 8-inch (20-cm) springform pan, preferably nonstick. Sprinkle with 1 tablespoon sugar.

2 In a heavy saucepan over high heat, combine the 1¼ cups (10 oz/315 g) sugar and water. Bring to a boil, stirring until the sugar dissolves, and then boil until the mixture reaches the thread stage, about 230°F (110°C) on a candy thermometer, or until very thick. Remove from the heat and let cool.

3 In a bowl, using an electric mixer set on high speed, beat the egg yolks until light and fluffy. Very slowly add the hot syrup in a thin stream, beating constantly. Beat in the ground almonds and cinnamon. Pour into a clean saucepan over low heat and cook, stirring, until thickened, about 5 minutes. Do not allow it to boil. Pour into the pan.

4 Bake until a wooden skewer inserted into the center of the custard emerges clean, about 10 minutes. Let cool for 15 minutes, then run a knife blade around the inside edge of the pan and unmold onto a platter. Sprinkle with the remaining 1 tablespoon sugar and top with the chopped almonds, if using. Cut into wedges to serve.

Gypsy's Arm

Brazo de Gitano • Andalusia • Spain

Andalusia is home to Spain's Gypsies and flamenco, and this custard-filled cake symbolizes an arm raised in the dramatic gesture of the dance. In the recipe, a classic génoise is rolled around a sweet filling of chocolate custard. This is a dessert for a special occasion, but it is not difficult to make, as the custard can be prepared the day before, covered, and stored in the refrigerator, and the finished cake can be assembled up to six hours in advance and refrigerated. Bring to room temperature before serving.

FILLING

2½ cups (20 fl oz/625 ml) milk

1 lemon or orange zest strip

1 cinnamon stick

4 oz (125 g) semisweet (plain) chocolate, chopped

8 egg yolks

¾ cup (6 oz/185 g) granulated sugar

½ cup (2½ oz/75 g) all-purpose (plain) flour

1 tablespoon unsalted butter

SPONGE CAKE

5 eggs

½ cup (4 oz/125 g) granulated sugar

1 teaspoon grated lemon zest

1 cup (4 oz/125 g) sifted all-purpose (plain) flour

¼ cup (2 oz/60 g) clarified unsalted butter, melted and cooled

Confectioners' (icing) sugar

Ground cinnamon

Serves 8

1 To make the filling, pour the milk into a saucepan and add the citrus zest strip and cinnamon stick. Place over medium-high heat, bring almost to a boil, and reduce the heat to low. Simmer for 15 minutes, then remove from the heat and strain, discarding the zest and cinnamon stick.

2 Meanwhile, place the chocolate in a heatproof bowl over (but not touching) simmering water in a saucepan. Heat, stirring occasionally, until melted. Remove from the heat.

3 In a bowl, using an electric mixer set on high speed, beat the egg yolks until thick and pale. Add the granulated sugar and continue to beat until the mixture is very thick and falls in a wide, slowly dissolving ribbon when the beaters are lifted. Stir in the flour, mixing well, and gradually add the hot milk while stirring constantly. Transfer to a large saucepan and cook over medium heat, stirring constantly, until the mixture thickens to the consistency of pudding, about 5 minutes. Remove from the heat, stir in the butter, and then fold in the melted chocolate. Nest the bowl in a larger bowl filled with ice and let cool completely, stirring from time to time.

4 While the custard is cooling, make the sponge cake: Preheat the oven to 375°F (190°C). Butter an 11-by-15-inch (28-by-38-cm) jelly-roll pan. Line the bottom with parchment (baking) paper and butter the parchment.

5 In a heatproof bowl, whisk together the eggs and granulated sugar. Place over (but not touching) simmering water in a saucepan and continue to whisk until the mixture is warm and the sugar is dissolved. Remove from over the water and, using an electric mixer set on high speed, beat until very thick and pale, 8–10 minutes. Beat in the lemon zest, and then fold in the flour. Using a rubber spatula, fold in the butter. Pour the batter into the prepared pan and smooth the top with the spatula.

6 Bake until golden and springy to the touch, about 10 minutes. Meanwhile, sprinkle a kitchen towel slightly larger than the dimensions of the cake with confectioners' sugar. Remove the cake from the oven, invert the pan onto the towel, and lift off the pan. Peel off the parchment paper. Working carefully, roll up the cake and towel together into a cylinder. Keep covered with a kitchen towel until ready to fill.

7 To fill the cake, unroll it on a work surface and remove the towel. Spread the cake with the room-temperature custard and roll it up once again. Carefully transfer to a serving plate. If not serving immediately, cover with plastic wrap and refrigerate.

8 To serve, dust heavily with confectioners' sugar flavored with a little cinnamon, and then cut into slices.

Port-Scented Custard

Pudim Flan · Douro · Portugal

Flan is the most popular dessert in Spain and Portugal. The addition of port here places this version in Oporto, a city celebrated for its distinctive fortified wine.

1 Pour the milk and cream into a saucepan and add the cinnamon stick and orange zest strips. Place over medium-high heat and heat until small bubbles appear along the edges of the pan. Remove from the heat and let steep for 1 hour.

2 Have ready six ½-cup (4–fl oz/125-ml) ramekins or custard cups. In a small, heavy saucepan over high heat, combine ½ cup (4 oz/125 g) of the sugar and the water and heat, stirring until the sugar dissolves and the mixture comes to a boil. Continue to boil, without stirring, until the mixture is golden brown, 6–8 minutes. Be careful not to let it get too dark, or the custard will taste bitter. Remove from the heat and carefully pour the hot syrup into the ramekins or custard cups, dividing it evenly and quickly swirling the cups to coat with the caramel. Place the molds in a large baking pan. Set aside.

3 Preheat the oven to 325°F (165°C).

4 Strain the milk mixture through a fine-mesh sieve, discarding the cinnamon stick and orange zest. Return the liquid to the pan and place over medium-high heat. Heat until small bubbles appear along the edges of the pan. Remove from the heat.

5 In a bowl, using an electric mixer set on high speed, beat together the whole eggs and egg yolks until frothy. Gradually add the remaining ½ cup (4 oz/125 g) sugar, beating until the mixture is pale yellow and thick, about 10 minutes. Add the hot milk mixture, a little at a time, beating constantly. Stir in the port and vanilla. Pour the mixture through a fine-mesh sieve placed over a pitcher. Then pour the strained mixture into the caramel-lined molds, dividing evenly. Pour hot water into the baking pan to reach halfway up the sides of the molds. Cover the pan with aluminum foil and bake until a knife inserted into the center of a custard emerges clean, about 30 minutes. Remove the custards from the water bath, let cool, and refrigerate until chilled.

6 To serve, run a knife around the inside edge of each mold and unmold into shallow dessert bowls, allowing any caramel in the molds to drizzle over the custards.

1 cup (8 fl oz/250 ml) milk

1 cup (8 fl oz/250 ml) heavy (double) cream

1 cinnamon stick

Zest of 1 orange, in long strips

1 cup (8 oz/250 g) sugar

2 tablespoons water

3 whole eggs plus 2 egg yolks

2 tablespoons tawny port

½ teaspoon vanilla extract (essence)

Serves 6

PORT

The Douro River twists and turns for approximately 140 miles (215 km) through the narrow—and beautiful—valley of the same name and then crosses from Portugal into Spain. On either side of the waterway rise steep hills covered with terraced vineyards. However, only the upper portion of the Douro—a land of hot summers, wet winters, and picturesque manor houses near the city of Oporto—is port wine country.

Port is one of world's best fortified wines. Although unquestionably a Portuguese product, it owes its existence to the British, who, during a disagreement with the French in the early eighteenth century, decided to look elsewhere for their refreshment. The British ambassador executed an agreement that put Portuguese wines on London tables for a fraction of the cost of their French rivals.

But the wines that reached Britain were unpleasantly sharp, as their sugars had nearly vanished. Enterprising English merchants, who had settled in Oporto in the sixteenth century, were the first to hit upon the idea of fortifying the wine with brandy before fermentation was finished, thereby wiping out the bitter yeasts and maintaining some of the sugars. With that move, modern-day port was born.

Basically two kinds of port exist, vintage port and wood port. Vintage port is made exclusively of wine pressed from the best vineyards in the same year. These are products of great character, created when the weather and soil cooperate perfectly.

Tawny and ruby ports are the wood ports. The former are blended wines from different years that spend a long time in wood before bottling. They take their name from their pale, or tawny, color, a result of redness lost during prolonged cask storage. The payoff is a memorable, soft finish. Ruby ports, slightly younger blended wines, are named for their distinctive color as well.

Minted Cheese Tart from Ibiza

Flaon • Balearic Islands • Spain

Ibiza is the southernmost island of the Balearic chain and the one closest to the mainland. Pine, almond, and olive trees flourish in its dry climate, as do herbs such as mint, fennel, marjoram, and thyme. Mint is featured in this lovely cheese tart, an ancient recipe that calls for a yeast-leavened pastry dough. For a special occasion, sprinkle the tart with cinnamon and garnish with fresh mint sprigs.

1 To make the pastry shell, in a large bowl, sprinkle the yeast over the warm milk and let sit until frothy, 5–8 minutes.

2 Meanwhile, place the flour and sugar in a food processor and pulse briefly to combine. Add the lard or butter and pulse until the mixture resembles coarse crumbs. Add the milk mixture and the egg and pulse just until the dough comes together. Turn out onto a lightly floured work surface and knead until smooth, about 5 minutes. Cover with a kitchen towel and let rest for 20 minutes.

3 Preheat the oven to 350°F (180°C). Lightly butter a 10-inch (25-cm) tart pan with a removable bottom.

4 Lightly flour the work surface and roll out the dough into an 11-inch (28-cm) round. Transfer the round to the prepared tart pan, pressing it smoothly against the bottom and sides. Trim the edges even with the pan rim. Set aside.

5 To make the filling, in a bowl, using an electric mixer, beat together the cheese, sugar, and eggs until creamy. Add the liqueur and mix well. If desired, chop 2 of the mint leaves and mix them in as well. Beat in the cinnamon, if using.

6 Pour the cheese mixture into the pastry-lined pan. Arrange the mint leaves on top, gently pushing them into the surface.

7 Bake until the top of the tart is pale gold, 25–30 minutes. Transfer to a rack and let cool completely. Remove the pan rim and slide the tart onto a plate. Serve at room temperature.

PASTRY SHELL

1 teaspoon active dry yeast

½ cup (4 fl oz/125 ml) milk, barely warmed

2 cups (10 oz/315 g) all-purpose (plain) flour

1 tablespoon sugar

¼ cup (2 oz/60 g) chilled lard or unsalted butter, or 2 tablespoons of each, cut into small pieces

1 egg

FILLING

1 lb (500 g) whole-milk ricotta or cream cheese

1 cup (8 oz/250 g) sugar

4 eggs

¼ cup (2 fl oz/60 ml) anise liqueur such as *anís del mono* or Pernod

12 fresh mint leaves

Pinch of ground cinnamon (optional)

Serves 8

Snow Pancakes

Farófias • Estremadura • Portugal

This light, not-too-sweet dessert is traditionally served for Carnival and New Year's.

3 eggs, separated, plus 2 egg yolks

Pinch of salt

1 cup (8 oz/250 g) sugar

4 cups (32 fl oz/1 l) milk

1 vanilla bean, split in half lengthwise

Cinnamon-sugar

Serves 6

1 In a bowl, using an electric mixer, beat the egg whites with the salt until foamy. Gradually beat in ½ cup (4 oz/125 g) of the sugar until the mixture forms stiff peaks.

2 Pour the milk into a wide saucepan and add the vanilla bean. Place over low heat and bring to a gentle simmer. Using a large spoon and working in batches, drop in the egg whites by spoonfuls, forming ovals. Simmer for 2–3 minutes. Turn the ovals over and cook gently until set, 2–3 minutes longer. Using a slotted spoon, transfer the ovals to paper towels to drain. You want to make at least 12 snow pancakes, allowing 2 per person. If you make them smaller, they may poach a bit more quickly. Remove the pan from the heat and pour the milk through a fine-mesh sieve placed over a measuring pitcher.

3 To make the custard sauce, beat the egg yolks lightly in a heatproof bowl placed over (but not touching) barely simmering water in a saucepan. Stir in the remaining ½ cup (4 oz/125 g) sugar, then stir in 3 cups (24 fl oz/750 ml) of the strained milk. Continue to cook, stirring constantly, until the mixture thickens and coats a spoon, 5–8 minutes. Pour the custard through the sieve into a serving bowl, cover the bowl with plastic wrap, pressing it directly onto the surface of the custard, and refrigerate until cold.

4 To serve, gently spoon the custard into individual bowls and place the egg-white ovals on top. Sprinkle with cinnamon-sugar.

GLOSSARY

ACITRÓN The name suggests kinship with citrus fruit, but mildly sweet *acitrón* is actually a crystallized form of the biznaga cactus. It is sold in small rectangular bars and can be found in well-stocked Hispanic markets. Acitrón will keep, well wrapped, for several months in a cool, dry place. The most acceptable substitute is candied pineapple.

AMARETTI These small, crisp macaroons, a specialty of the Lombardy region in Italy, get their name from the ground bitter (*amaro*) almonds that are their key ingredient. The leading brand, widely available in Italian delicatessens, is Lazzaroni di Saronno, whose cookies are distinctively packaged in tissue-wrapped pairs piled inside an old-fashioned red tin. Serve amaretti with after-dinner coffee and liqueurs or use them crushed as a dessert ingredient. To crush amaretti, place inside a heavy-duty plastic bag and shatter with a rolling pin.

AMARETTO This pale gold, sweet liqueur, now one of Italy's most popular, has a rich almond flavor derived from both bitter almonds and the tender kernels inside apricot pits. According to legend, it was first concocted by a young widow in the Lombardy town of Saronno in the early sixteenth century. She served it to a disciple of Da Vinci, the painter Bernardino Luini, who had come to Saronno to paint a fresco of the nativity in a local *sanctuario*. So enamored was he of the woman and her liqueur that he immortalized her face as that of the Madonna.

ARMAGNAC Named for the district surrounding Auch, the capital of Gascony in southwestern France, this fine brandy is distilled a single time (unlike its better-known cousin, twice-distilled Cognac) from local white wines, then aged in new casks made from the tight-grained heartwood of local oak trees. The result is a fragrant, earthy spirit that is sipped after meals or used as an ingredient in both savory and sweet dishes.

BOURBON, AGED KENTUCKY Much of America's high-quality bourbon is still produced in Kentucky. The slightly sweet whiskey is made from fermented corn and must be aged for at least two years in new, charred white-oak barrels. Straight bourbon is distilled from a grain mash that includes at least 51 percent corn, though most bourbons are made from 60 to 70 percent corn. By law, blended bourbon must contain at least 51 percent straight bourbon.

BUTTERMILK Originally, buttermilk was the tangy liquid left over after churning butter from fresh milk. Today, it is made commercially by adding a bacterial culture to skim or nonfat milk. Still valued for its slightly tart flavor, buttermilk is also available in a dehydrated form. To make a quick substitute for buttermilk, stir 1 tablespoon fresh lemon juice into 1 cup (8 fl oz/250 ml) lukewarm milk and let stand for 10 minutes until thickened.

CANE SYRUP Workers from the sugarcane plantations of the Caribbean introduced this very sweet, thick, amber-colored syrup to cooks in the American South. Also known as golden syrup or light treacle, cane syrup is available in tins at shops that specialize in Southern, Caribbean, or British ingredients. If unavailable, substitute a mixture of 2 parts light corn syrup and 1 part molasses, or stir together equal parts corn syrup and honey.

CARDAMOM This tall perennial shrub grows profusely on the Malabar coast of southern India. The fruits, or pods, must be harvested by hand, making this the costliest spice in the world after saffron. The pale green, three-sided oval pods are about ½ inch (12 mm) long, each of which contains up to 20 small, black seeds. When ground, the seeds give off an intense camphorlike aroma, although the taste is sweet and mild, with lemony and grassy notes. The loose and ground seeds lose flavor quickly, so it is best to buy whole pods and remove and grind the seeds as they are needed for individual recipes.

CASHEW FENNI The Portuguese introduced the cashew plant to India when they began colonizing Goa in 1510. Today, the ripe fruits are tapped and fermented, producing a strong-tasting and assertive liquor. Purists prefer to sip *fenni* straight, like a Cognac, but the most popular way to enjoy this popular drink is to serve it with lime soda over ice. Cashew fenni is the "secret ingredient" in many Goan seafood marinades. Coconut *fenni* is also available, but it has a milder taste.

CHESTNUT FLOUR This extremely fine flour, milled from sweet, starchy chestnuts, thickens sauces and is used in many traditional desserts. The best *farina di castagne* comes from the Garfagnana area, north of Lucca. Chestnuts from high-altitude forests are dried slowly on straw mats over smoldering wood, lending a smoky flavor to the flour. Store chestnut flour in the refrigerator to prevent it from turning rancid.

CHOCOLATE Although Columbus reputedly encountered chocolate in Nicaragua on his fourth voyage, in 1502, it was Spanish explorer Hernán Cortés who first brought cacao beans back to Spain from Mexico's Aztec court in 1528. Soon, chocolate caught on as a popular breakfast drink, and it is still enjoyed in Spain, whisked into boiling milk. For cooking or eating, seek out semisweet chocolate, a lightly sweetened form made with at least 40 percent—but preferably 50 percent—cocoa solids. Bittersweet chocolate has less sugar and a higher percentage of cocoa solids, sometimes up to 70 or 80 percent. Unsweetened chocolate, also known as bitter or baking chocolate and sold in small blocks, is composed of half cocoa butter and half cocoa solids. It is unpalatable on its own but adds a rich chocolate taste to recipes that also contain a sweetener.

CINNAMON BARK, TRUE *Canela*, the flaky, aromatic bark of a laurel tree native to Sri Lanka, is true cinnamon. The paper-thin inner layer of the bark is laboriously hand-stripped from the trees in many layers that are then rolled into cylinders, known as quills, about ½ inch (12 mm) in diameter. The quills may be up to 3 feet (1 m) in length. The length commonly found in stores and called for in recipes, however, is about 3 inches (7.5 cm). When used in recipes, the quills are more commonly known as cinnamon sticks. Once harvested, the quills are dried; small or broken quills are ground to a powder. Cassia, a close relative of cinnamon, has a coarser texture and comes from the bark of a Southeast Asian variety of laurel tree. Its flavor is similar, but stronger and more astringent. Products that are labeled as "cinnamon" in the United States and Europe are usually cassia, but in many countries, the two ingredients are considered interchangeable.

COCONUT CREAM, COCONUT MILK Coconut cream and coconut milk are both derived from an infusion of grated coconut flesh in water or, less commonly, milk. (They are not to be confused with the clear juice inside the whole nut.) The first infusion yields coconut cream, a thick liquid with a high fat content. If the same batch of coconut is steeped again, the resulting liquid is called coconut milk. A third steeping produces thin coconut milk. Freshly grated coconut gives the best results, but commercially packaged, unsweetened coconut can also be used. Good-quality unsweetened canned coconut milk is a welcome shortcut when time is at a premium. Do not shake the can before opening. Once it is open, first scrape off the thick mass on top, which is the cream. The next layer is opaque white coconut milk, and finally there is a clear liquid, which is thin coconut milk.

COCONUT, SHREDDED The rich, chewy white flesh of the mature fruit of a tropical palm tree is used in sweet and savory recipes. Toasting gives it an even richer, nutlike flavor.

To toast shredded coconut, preheat an oven to 350°F (180°C). Evenly spread the coconut in a thin layer in a baking dish and toast, stirring frequently, until golden brown, 7–10 minutes.

COGNAC Produced in a strictly delineated region in western France surrounding the Charente town of the same name, this world-renowned brandy is twice distilled from white wine made from grapes of the region, and is then aged for as few as 2 years or as many as 50 years in old oak casks that give it a distinctive amber hue and rich aroma and flavor. Many Cognacs are produced by blending older and younger vintages to make products of uniform quality.

CORN SYRUP Derived from the sucrose in cornstarch (cornflour), this thick, liquid sweetener is used primarily in desserts. Baked goods made with corn syrup retain their moisture longer than those containing granulated sugar. Because it does not become grainy when cold, corn syrup is an essential ingredient in many confections, frostings, and dessert sauces. Light corn syrup is almost clear and has a more delicate flavor than dark corn syrup. Difficult to find outside the United States, it can be substituted with an equal amount of golden syrup or honey.

CREAM OF TARTAR This acidic powder is extracted during the wine-making process and is used as an additive to stabilize egg whites and increase their heat tolerance. It is also commonly combined with baking soda to make baking powder.

CREMA Although *crema* translates simply as "cream," in Mexico, it usually refers to a thick, rich, slightly soured variety found commercially in grocery stores. In its place, you can use the more widely available French crème fraîche, which is similar in consistency. An adequate substitute may be made by thinning commercial sour cream slightly with whole milk or half-and-half (half cream).

To make crema, in a small nonaluminum bowl, stir together 1 cup (8 fl oz/250 ml) heavy cream (do not use an ultrapasteurized product) and 1 tablespoon buttermilk or good-quality plain yogurt with active cultures. Cover with plastic wrap, poke a few holes in the plastic, and leave at warm room temperature (about 85°F/30°C) until well thickened, 8–24 hours. Stir, cover with fresh plastic wrap, and refrigerate until firm and well chilled, about 6 hours. If the *crema* becomes too thick, thin with a little whole milk or half-and-half (half cream).

CRÈME FRAÎCHE Thick enough to spread when chilled, but fluid enough to pour at room temperature, this tangy, slightly acidulated fresh cream is popular in France as a topping for fresh fruit and other sweets. Look for it in the dairy case of well-stocked supermarkets or specialty food stores, or follow the recipe for *crema*, above.

CUSTARD POWDER A mixture of cornstarch (cornflour), sugar, and artificial coloring and flavorings, custard powder is added to hot milk to make a custard sauce that may be eaten hot or cold or used as the basis for various puddings. A British product, it is available in stores specializing in British foods or in Indian or Asian grocery stores.

EGGS, SEPARATING To separate an egg, crack the shell in half by tapping it against the side of a bowl and break the shell apart with your fingers. Holding the shell halves over the bowl, gently transfer the yellow yolk back and forth between them, letting the clear white drop away into the bowl. Taking care not to break it, transfer the yolk to another bowl. Alternatively, gently pour the egg from the shell onto the slightly cupped fingers of your clean hand, held over a bowl. Let the whites fall between your fingers into the bowl; the whole yolk will remain in your hand. The same basic function is performed by an egg separator placed over a bowl. The separator holds the yolk intact in its cuplike center and allows the white to drip out into the bowl through slots in its side.

FIGS Fragile and highly perishable, sweet, succulent fresh figs typically ripen in late summer. Popular varieties include the golden Smyrna and the deep purple Mission. Although delicate in flavor, figs are versatile in the kitchen. The fresh fruit is excellent macerated, poached, baked, glazed on tarts, or transformed into jam. Once dried, figs become even sweeter and gain a firm, chewy texture that is perfect for cakes and confections. Figs do not ripen off the tree, so choose fresh fruits that are soft but smooth, with a plump shape and a firm stem. Eat the fresh fruits as soon as possible after purchasing, keeping them at room temperature in a single layer to prevent bruises. When buying dried figs, look for ones that are still moist and flexible. Dried Mission figs have a particularly intense, rich taste. Store dried figs in an airtight container away from light and heat.

FLOUR, WINTER-WHEAT Flour finely milled from pure, soft winter wheat has a lower protein content than flour milled from hard wheat, making it particularly suited to quick breads, biscuits, and cakes. Many cake recipes handed down in American southern families assume the cook is using a presifted, finely textured soft winter-wheat flour such as that sold under the White Lily brand. Self-rising soft-wheat flours incorporate salt and leavening for more convenient cooking.

GHEE Used throughout Indian cooking, *ghee* literally means "fat." There are two types: *usli ghee* (clarified butter) and *vanaspati ghee* (vegetable shortening). A recipe that calls simply for ghee is understood to mean *usli ghee*. Indian clarified butter differs from the European equivalent in having been simmered until all the moisture is removed from the milk solids and the fat is amber colored. This gives *usli ghee* its unique nutty taste. Clarification also increases the butter's storage life. *Vanaspati ghee* is a pale yellow, hydrogenated blend of various vegetable oils that is processed to look, smell, and taste very similar to *usli ghee*. Both types of ghee are readily available; *usli ghee* can also be easily made at home.

To make usli ghee, heat ½ lb (250 g) butter in a pan over medium-low heat, uncovered, until it melts. Increase the heat to medium and simmer the butter, stirring often, until the clear fat separates from the milk solids, about 15 minutes. During this process a layer of foam will rise to the top of the butter and the butter will crackle as its milk solids lose moisture. When the milk solids lose all moisture, the fat as well as the milk residue will turn amber colored. When this occurs, remove the pan from the heat and let the residue settle on the bottom. When cool enough to handle, pour the clear fat, which is the *usli ghee,* into a jar, ensuring that no residue gets in. Alternatively, strain it through two layers of cheesecloth (muslin). Discard the residue. *Usli ghee* may be refrigerated, covered, for up to 6 months or frozen for up to 12 months. Allow to thaw before use. Makes ¾ cup/6 fl oz/180 ml *usli ghee*.

GINGER (FRESH, CRYSTALLIZED, GROUND) The rhizome of the tropical ginger plant, which yields a sweet, strong-flavored spice, fresh ginger is found in the produce section of well-stocked markets. Crystallized ginger, also called candied ginger, is made by first preserving pieces of ginger in sugar syrup and then coating them with granulated sugar. It can be found in the baking or Asian food section. Ground dried ginger, which is often used to add a delightful fragrance and flavor to baked goods, is found in the spice section.

JAGGERY Jaggery—dehydrated sugarcane juice—is a by-product of sugar refining. Golden brown and with a maple-syrup-like flavor, it is used in Indian desserts and candies. Brown sugar, palm sugar, maple syrup, or maple sugar may be substituted, although they don't accurately replicate jaggery's flavor.

KEWRA EXTRACT Kewra extract (essence) comes from male flowers of one of the 500 species of pandanus, or screwpine. It may be yellow or colorless and has an intense fragrance with notes of musk and jasmine. It is used in some meat, poultry, and rice dishes

and in desserts, candies, and cold beverages. If unavailable, omit it or substitute an equal amount of rose or vanilla extract (essence) for a different but still pleasant flavor.

KIRSCH A signature fruit brandy of the French province of Alsace, kirsch is twice distilled from highly acidic wild cherries along with their stones, which contribute a hint of almond flavor to the fruity but dry eau-de-vie. It is most often enjoyed after meals, sipped as a digestif, and is also included as a flavoring in fruit dishes, baked goods, and candies.

LAVENDER Fragrant, highly perfumed lavender blossoms are particularly appreciated by cooks in the south of France, who highlight its floral sweetness in vinegars, sauces, honey, ice cream, and drinks. Be sure to use only chemical-free lavender from an organic garden or flowers packaged specifically for cooking, as those sold for floral arrangements have been treated with chemicals. Look for small, dried flowers in the bulk herb section of health-food stores or the baking aisle of fine grocers. They should retain a vivid violet hue and flowery fragrance.

LOTUS SEED PASTE Mashed, sweetened lotus seed paste is a popular filling for Chinese sweet buns and pastries, and is sold canned or frozen in Asian grocery stores. Unused lotus seed paste can be stored in the refrigerator for several weeks in a covered container.

MANGO Native to India, the mango thrives in tropical climates, and its many varieties are enjoyed as a refreshing breakfast food, dessert, or snack. Canned mango is a popular flavoring for ice creams and other sweets. To avoid any mess when preparing the fresh fruit for use in a recipe, cut and peel it in the following manner.

To prepare a mango, place it horizontally on a cutting board and make a slice that is slightly off-center, cutting off the flesh from one side of the flat pit in a single piece. Repeat on the other side. Hold each slice, cut side up, and score the flesh lengthwise to make slices. Then, if desired, score crosswise in a lattice pattern, creating cubes of the dimension called for in a particular recipe. Do not cut through the peel. Press against the skin side of the peel to invert the slice, then carefully slice the flesh from the peel. Place the fruit in

a nonmetallic bowl. Cut the remaining skin from around the pit, cut away any flesh, and use as directed in the recipe.

MARZIPAN A traditional holiday sweet, marzipan is a fine-textured blend of almond paste, sugar, and frequently egg whites. It is used as a filling or icing for sweet breads and cakes and for making candies in a variety of shapes—including fruits, vegetables, and animals. Marzipan is available in 7-oz (220-g) cylinders in specialty-food shops and many supermarkets. Be sure your marzipan is fresh; it should be soft and pliable in the package.

MASCARPONE This fresh Italian cheese, made from cream, has a very rich, buttery flavor and a smooth texture reminiscent of sour cream.

MEXICAN CHOCOLATE A mixture of cacao beans, almonds, sugar, and often cinnamon and vanilla, Mexican chocolate is formed into disks, or tablets, usually weighing 3 ounces (90 g). It is used predominantly to make hot chocolate. Coarser and grainier than typical cooking chocolate, it is not suitable for use in baking or candymaking.

MOLASSES A full-flavored liquid derived from the syrupy residue left after sugar crystals have been extracted from fresh cane juice, molasses comes in many forms. A light, mild molasses is obtained from the first boiling of the sugar, while the second boiling yields a deep, smoky dark molasses whose slightly bitter edge offsets its sweetness. Iron-rich blackstrap molasses, too strong and bitter for most palates, remains after the third and final boiling. Unsulfured molasses is milder and sweeter than sulfured, which contains sulfur dioxide as a preservative. Dark corn syrup, black treacle, and maple syrup are adequate substitutions for dark molasses.

NUTS When purchasing nuts, seek out only those that are free of cracks, holes, and discoloration. To make sure the nutmeat is not dried out inside, shake the shells.

ALMONDS These oval nuts are the meat found inside the pit of a dried fruit related to the peach—which is why almonds pair so well with peaches and other stone fruit like cherries and plums. Almonds are delicate and fragrant and have a smooth texture. They are sold unblanched, with their natural brown skins intact, and blanched, with the skins removed to reveal their light ivory color. To blanch and peel almonds yourself, put the shelled nuts in a heatproof bowl and pour boiling water over them. Let stand for about 1 minute, then drain the nuts in a colander and rinse with cold running water to cool. Pinch each almond to slip off its bitter skin.

CASHEWS Cashew trees measure up to 40 feet (12 m) in height and produce fruits called cashew apples (though actually pear shaped), inside of which the nut develops. When the fruits ripen, the nuts protrude from the end of them. The shells of the nuts contain an acidic, oily substance that can burn and blister the skin but which is neutralized by heating.

HAZELNUTS Also known as filberts, grape-sized hazelnuts have very hard shells that come to a point and resemble an acorn, cream-colored flesh, and a sweet, rich, buttery flavor. They can be difficult to crack, so they are usually sold already shelled.

PEANUTS Not really a nut at all, but rather a type of legume that grows underground, peanuts are seeds nestled inside waffle-veined pods that become thin and brittle when dried.

PECANS Native to North America, the pecan has two deeply crinkled lobes of nutmeat, much like its relative the walnut. The nuts have smooth, brown, oval shells that break easily. Their flavor is sweeter and more delicate than that of walnuts.

PISTACHIOS Pistachios have thin, very hard, rounded outer shells that are naturally creamy tan in color but are sometimes dyed bright red. As the nuts ripen, their shells crack to reveal light green kernels.

WALNUTS The furrowed, double-lobed nutmeat of the walnut has an assertive, rich flavor. The most common variety is the English walnut, also known as the Persian walnut, which has a light brown shell that cracks easily. Black walnuts have a stronger flavor and tougher shells but can be hard find.

To toast nuts, spread them on a baking sheet and toast in a 325°F (165°C) oven until they are fragrant and take on a golden color, 10–20 minutes; the timing depends on the type of nut and the size of the nut or nut pieces. Stir once or twice to ensure even cooking. Remove from the oven and immediately pour onto a plate, as they will continue to darken if left on the hot pan. Toast small amounts of nuts in a frying pan over medium-low heat, stirring frequently, until fragrant and golden.

To remove the skin from hazelnuts, while they are still warm from toasting, transfer the nuts to a thick, clean kitchen towel. Wrap the towel around them and rub them briskly to remove their skin. Gather the hazelnuts up carefully with your hands, leaving behind as much of the loose skin as you can.

ORANGE FLOWER WATER Distilled from the blossoms of bitter oranges, this perfumed liquor is used to flavor many sweet dishes and desserts and is also often added to a wide variety of cocktails. It can be found in most well-stocked liquor stores.

PALM SUGAR Derived from the sap of the coconut or other palms, and sometimes called coconut sugar, palm sugar is prized in Indonesia, Malaysia, and Thailand for its fragrant caramel-like flavor and dark brown color. Vietnamese cooks use a lighter, milder version. The sugar is often sold formed into dark, hard disks or cylinders, which may be grated or shaved for use. Very hard palm sugar can be softened by heating it briefly in a microwave oven. Light or dark brown sugar, depending upon the color desired, can be substituted, although the flavor will not be the same.

PANDANUS LEAVES, PANDANUS EXTRACT With a taste reminiscent of butterscotch or vanilla, the pandanus leaf, which resembles a small green whisk-broom, is plucked from the screw pine tree. It adds flavor and green color to sweet dishes in Malaysian and Indonesian kitchens. Dried or frozen leaves, as well as a powerful extract (essence), are more readily found in markets. If fresh leaves are not available, use frozen.

PEACHES, PEELING Cut out the stem and score a shallow X in the blossom end of the fruit. Plunge the fruit into a pot of boiling water for 20–60 seconds; it is ready when the skin starts to wrinkle. Using a fork or tongs, carefully transfer the fruit to a bowl of very cold water. When it has cooled, peel away the skin using your fingers or a sharp knife.

PLANTAIN Closely related to the banana, the large plantain, or *plátano,* is starchier and firmer. It is always cooked before eating. For sweet dishes, use fully ripe, black-skinned plantains that yield to gentle finger pressure.

PUFF PASTRY Dishes made with puff pastry look very grand, but making the pastry appears far more difficult than it actually is. The pastry can also be purchased fresh or frozen from a good French bakery or specialty shop. For the best quality, check the ingredients list to make sure the pastry uses butter, not margarine.

QUINCES Popular throughout the Mediterranean and Near and Middle East, these fragrant autumn fruits resemble large, lumpy, yellow-green apples. Unlike apples, they are inedible when raw, with an unpleasantly astringent taste and rock-hard texture. Cooked with sugar, however, they turn deep pink and develop a wonderfully aromatic, almost spicy flavor and tender consistency. Quinces may be included in baked desserts or even some savory dishes, but most often they are featured in jams, jellies, and confections. Quinces were prized by early American settlers, but were later supplanted by apples and pears.

RICE, GLUTINOUS Also known as sticky rice or sweet rice, this starch-rich white rice is the daily grain of people living in the Golden Triangle and throughout Laos. It cooks up into a sticky mass, and traditional diners, eating with their hands, roll the rice into small balls, which they dip into sauces and curries. Elsewhere, the rice is used primarily to make sweets. Both short-grain and long-grain varieties are available, as is black glutinous rice. Glutinous rice flour, sometimes labeled "sweet rice flour," is used for making cakes and other sweets.

RICE FLOUR Raw long-grain rice is ground to produce a flour that is used for making rice noodles and rice paper and also as an ingredient in batters for crêpes, fritters, and steamed cakes. This type of rice flour should not be confused with glutinous rice flour, which is made from short-grain glutinous rice and is used for making dumplings and desserts with a chewy consistency.

ROSE ESSENCE AND ROSE WATER Many classic Mogul dishes feature rose essence, which is extracted from small, intensely perfumed, deep-red roses grown for this purpose only. Rose essence may be used in its concentrated form or diluted to make rose water. Both preparations are used in Indian candies, desserts, and cold beverages.

SAFFRON The world's most costly spice by weight, saffron comes from the perennial *Crocus sativus*. The crocus blossoms are hand-harvested, then the three stigmas from each flower are delicately removed, also by hand, and dried. Only when they are dried do they develop their intense, semisweet, woody aroma and pungent, earthy, slightly bitter flavor. Even more than for its flavor and aroma, however, saffron is valued for its brilliant orange-yellow color. (A natural dye in the stigmas is activated by water, which is why saffron is often infused in water, stock, or milk before being added to other ingredients.) Saffron should be used sparingly not only because of its cost, but also because increasing the quantity will not increase the aroma or flavor that it imparts.

SAGO PEARLS Sago is a starch extracted from the sago palm. The pearls, extruded tiny pellets made by pressing the wet starch through a sieve, are sold dried. When cooked, usually in a pudding, they become translucent, much like tapioca pearls. In general, sago and tapioca pearls can be used interchangeably in recipes.

SALT Some cooks contend that the fine grains of table salt lack the texture and depth of flavor of sea salt or kosher salt. Sea salt, gathered from evaporated seawater, retains small amounts of naturally occurring minerals, and it often carries a slight tint of gray or pink from these minerals. Available in both fine and coarse crystals, sea salt is excellent used in cooking. Kosher salt was originally developed for the preparation of kosher meats, but its flat, coarse grains dissolve quickly, an often-desirable quality.

SEMOLINA Milled from the center of the durum (hard) wheat berry, this flour provides the ideal properties for making dried pasta and is also frequently used for bread making. Some of Italy's best wheat is said to grow along the Po River in Emilia-Romagna.

SESAME SEEDS Tiny sesame seeds, white or black, are used as garnishes and textural elements or to add a warm. nutty taste to many sweet dishes. Because of their high oil content, they should be stored in the refrigerator. To toast sesame seeds, cook them gently in a dry frying pan. Watch them closely to ensure that they do not burn.

STAR ANISE Named for their resemblance to eight-pointed stars, these small, brown, hard seedpods have a sweet licorice flavor and are used frequently in Vietnamese and Chinese dishes. The whole pods or individual points broken from them may be added to long-simmering dishes. Pulverized star anise is one of the key elements in five-spice powder.

SUGAR, CRYSTAL Also known as sanding sugar or coarse sugar, crystal sugar is white granulated sugar that has been processed into large, oblong grains. Sprinkled over cookies, pies, and other baked goods, it adds an attractive sparkle and a pleasant crunch. Look for it in baking-supply stores

TAPIOCA PEARLS, TAPIOCA FLOUR Made from the tubers of the cassava plant, pearl-shaped particles of tapioca contribute a mild, soothing flavor and thick, slightly gelatinous consistency to a wide variety of Southeast Asian sweets. Finely ground tapioca flour, also called tapioca starch, is used to thicken sauces, to coat steamed dumplings, and as an ingredient in batters for fried foods.

TEQUILA Made near the town of the same name, tequila is a spirit distilled from the sap of the blue agave, a large succulent indigenous to the arid highlands of central Mexico. Young, clear blanco tequila has a distinct agave flavor and a less refined edge than more aged tequilas. Sharper, peppery *reposado* tequila is aged in wood for 2 to 12 months, while a smooth, subtle *añejo* tequila may have been aged for up to 5 years. For high-quality tequila, check that the label indicates the spirit is 100 percent blue agave or *agave azul* and was bottled in Mexico. Less expensive *mixto* versions may be fermented with sugar and mixed with up to 40 percent grain alcohol and other additives.

VANILLA BEANS, SCRAPING To scrape the seeds from a vanilla bean, first soak the bean in water and cut it in half lengthwise, as directed in the recipe. Use a small, sharp paring knife to scrape the seeds from the interior of the pod, and add both the seeds and the pod as instructed. Be sure to remove the pod from the mixture before serving. Vanilla beans should be stored in an airtight container and will keep for up to 6 months if stored in a cool, dark place.

WHIPPED CREAM One of the most popular ways to serve heavy (double) cream is as a whipped topping for pies, ice cream sundaes, and fruit desserts.

To make sweetened whipped cream, in a chilled bowl, combine 1½ cups (12 fl oz/375 ml) chilled heavy (double) cream, 3 tablespoons sugar, and ½ teaspoon vanilla extract (essence). Using an electric mixer set on medium-high speed, beat until medium-firm peaks form, about 3 minutes. Cover and refrigerate until ready to serve or for up to 2 hours. Makes 3 cups (24 fl oz/750 ml) whipped cream.

ZESTING CITRUS Zest is the thin, brightly colored, outermost layer of a citrus fruit's peel, containing most of its aromatic essential oils, and is a lively source of flavor. When zesting fruit, try to buy organic varieties or be sure to scrub the fruit well in order to remove any wax or chemicals on the surface. A variety of tools are available for removing zest. They include old-fashioned handheld graters with fine rasps, Microplane graters with razor-edged holes, zesters that remove fine strips in a single stroke, and paring knives or vegetable peelers for cutting away zest in long strips.

INDEX

ACKNOWLEDGMENTS

Weldon Owen wishes to thank the following people for their generous support in producing this book: Ken DellaPenta, Arin Hailey, Carolyn Keating, Andrew William Reccius, Shadin Saah, and Sharron Wood.

CREDITS

Recipe photography by Noel Barnhurst, except for the following by Andre Martin: Pages 69, 70, 71, 72, 76, 79, 80, 82, 83, 86, 88, 89.

Travel photography by Lou Dematteis: ©Page 63; Michael Freeman: Pages 5 (left), 8, ©60–61, 64, ©65, 226; Stuart Isett: ©Page 62 (bottom); Jason Lowe: Pages 6 (top and bottom), 7, 62 (top), 65 (left), 90–91, 92 (top), 93, 94, 140–141, 142 (bottom), 143, 145 (right), 230; Michael Melford: ©Page 14; Erik Rank: ©Page 13; Steven Rothfeld: Pages 4 (right), 9 (top and bottom), 92 (bottom), 95 (left and right), 142 (top), 145 (left), 186–187, 188 (top and bottom), 191 (left and right); Ignacio Urquiza: Pages 12 (top and bottom), 15 (left and right), 220; George White Jr.: ©Pages 10–11.

Recipes and sidebars by Georgeanne Brennan: Pages 98, 100, 105, 106, 107, 108, 109, 112, 115, 117, 121, 122, 125, 127, 134, 136, 137, 138; Kerri Conan: Pages 17, 20, 21; Lori de Mori: Pages 148, 150, 154, 156, 157, 160, 161, 167, 168, 172, 173, 176, 177, 179, 181; Abigail Johnson Dodge: Pages 35, 42, 44, 56, 57, 59; Janet Fletcher: Pages 28, 29, 32, 39, 41; Joyce Goldstein: Pages 193, 194, 195, 196, 198, 199, 201, 202, 203, 204, 207, 208, 209, 211, 212, 213, 214, 216, 217, 218, 219; Diane Holuigue: Pages 97, 99, 102, 103, 110, 113, 116, 118, 124, 128, 130, 131, 133; Joyce Jue: Pages 67, 74, 78, 84, 85; Cynthia Nims: Pages 25, 53; Ray Overton: Pages 18, 24, 47, 50, 51; Jacki Passmore: Pages 71, 76, 77, 81, 82, 83, 88; Julie Sahni: Pages 68, 70, 73, 79, 87, 89; Michele Scicolone: Pages 147, 151, 152, 153, 159, 163, 164, 169, 171, 174, 178, 183, 184, 185; Marilyn Tausend: Pages 19, 22, 27, 30, 33, 36, 37, 38, 45, 48, 54, 55, 58.

OXMOOR HOUSE INC.

Oxmoor House books are distributed by Sunset Books
80 Willow Road, Menlo Park, CA 94025
Telephone: 650-321-3600 Fax: 650-324-1532
Vice President/General Manager Rich Smeby
National Accounts Manager/Special Sales Brad Moses
Oxmoor House and Sunset Books are divisions of
Southern Progress Corporation

WILLIAMS-SONOMA

Founder and Vice-Chairman Chuck Williams

THE SAVORING SERIES

Conceived and produced by Weldon Owen Inc.
814 Montgomery Street, San Francisco, CA 94133
Telephone: 415 291 0100 Fax: 415 291 8841

In collaboration with Williams-Sonoma, Inc.
3250 Van Ness Avenue, San Francisco, CA 94109

A WELDON OWEN PRODUCTION

Set in Minion and Myriad.
Color separations by Bright Arts in Singapore.
Printed and bound by Tien Wah Press in Singapore.

First printed in 2005.
10 9 8 7 6 5 4 3 2 1

Library of Congress Cataloging-in-Publication data is available.
ISBN: 0-8487-3125-5

First published in the USA by Time-Life Custom Publishing
Originally published as Williams-Sonoma Savoring:
Savoring France (© 1999 Weldon Owen Inc.)
Savoring Italy (© 1999 Weldon Owen Inc.)
Savoring Southeast Asia (© 2000 Weldon Owen Inc.)
Savoring Spain & Portugal (© 2000 Weldon Owen Inc.)
Savoring India (© 2001 Weldon Owen Inc.)
Savoring Mexico (© 2001 Weldon Owen Inc.)
Savoring Tuscany (© 2001 Weldon Owen Inc.)
Savoring America (© 2002 Weldon Owen Inc.)
Savoring Provence (© 2002 Weldon Owen Inc.)
Savoring China (© 2003 Weldon Owen Inc.)

WELDON OWEN INC.

Chief Executive Officer John Owen
President and Chief Operating Officer Terry Newell
Chief Financial Officer Christine E. Munson
Vice President International Sales Stuart Laurence
Creative Director Gaye Allen
Publisher Hannah Rahill

Senior Editor Kim Goodfriend
Assistant Editor Juli Vendzules

Designer Rachel Lopez

Production Director Chris Hemesath
Color Manager Teri Bell
Production and Reprint Coordinator Todd Rechner

Food Stylists George Dolese, Sally Parker
Illustrations Marlene McLoughlin
Text Stephanie Rosenbaum

A NOTE ON WEIGHTS AND MEASURES

All recipes include customary U.S. and metric measurements. Metric
conversions are based on a standard developed for these books and
have been rounded off. Actual weights may vary.